Music After Modernism

MUSIC
AFTER
MODERNISM

SAMUEL LIPMAN

Basic Books, Inc., Publishers / New York

Chapters 9, 13, 15, 16, and 17 originally appeared in the *Times Literary Supplement*. Reprinted by permission.

Chapter 18 originally appeared in the *Music Journal*. Reprinted by permission.

Chapters 1, 2, 3, 4, 5, 6, 7, 10, 11, 12, and 14 originally appeared in *Commentary*. Reprinted by permission.

Library of Congress Cataloging in Publication Data

Lipman, Samuel.
  Music after modernism.

  Includes index.
    1. Music—History and criticism—20th century.
  2. Music—Addresses, essays, lectures. I. Title.
ML197.L53   780'.904   78–73768
ISBN 0–465–04740–8

Contents

PART THREE: THE SCENE

Preface: The Need for Revaluation

USIC is in a bad way. Like an empire shorn of everything but its history, it scratches out a tenuous existence living on the capital of the explosion of creativity which lasted from before Bach to World War I; since then, only isolated flashes of genius have redeemed an artistic period notable in general more for controversy and provocation than permanent achievement.

The evidence for this pessimistic evaluation exists all around us. There is no audience—enthusiastic, wide, committed, and paying—for the music of the last sixty years. While performers, themselves subject to lessening enthusiasm from the audience, can make careers only by concentrating on the old and avoiding the new, composers exist only in the protective embrace of foundations, universities, and government arts funding agencies. So plain is the situation that it deserves description and analysis from more than the standpoint of those who, like Henry Pleasants (in *The Agony of Modern Music*), believe that the true musical culture of our time is popular music; a similarly insufficient answer may be found in the writings of Harold Schonberg (the senior music critic of the *New York Times*) who implies that the future of music lies in the revival of bypassed elements of its past. No more helpful is the musicological exegesis (as in the journal *Perspectives of New Music*) of contemporary and avant-garde composition; of perhaps the least value is the kind of crass boosterism retailed both by artists' publicity agents and by such self-serving institutions as the Metropolitan Opera and Lincoln Center.

The difficulty of all these approaches to the problem of music in our time is that they are based upon the false idea that people need only to be told what to like, and that, having been told, they will then like it. But in point of fact all these enterprises, if anyone notices them at all, preach only to the converted, to those whose musical tastes have already been formed. In a deeper sense, these attempts to further music in words are doomed because they make an argument about music which is better and always more cogently made by the music itself.

What is rather needed is a placement of the music which we know, as well as the music yet to be heard or written, in a new relationship to a possible intelligent audience—that is, to life and to the world of ideas. It is necessary to place music publicly where it has always actually been, as a constituent and interlocking part of culture and society. If this cannot be done by writing directly and narrowly about the music, how can it be done? It can be done by examining the relationship between music in its various serious forms and the public which listens or does not listen, which supports or rejects what it hears. This will have a threefold effect: it will relate the music to the audience; it will relate the audience to the music; finally, it will define the relation of members of the audience to each other. In this way, serious music may once again be taken seriously as a part of social and intellectual life rather than a mere worship of an unchanging past.

In order to accomplish this, one must attempt to suggest which areas of contemporary musical life—repertory, performers, and audiences—are still alive and which have become (or have always been) lifeless. A necessary part of this analysis is explanation of why performers play the music they do, of what differing people hear in the music they love, and of what wider influences composers have been and are under when they write music. And finally it is necessary, no matter how briefly, to suggest some possibilities for musical life in our new, post-modern age.

Part One

THE MUSIC

FOR EVERY MUSICIAN, in the beginning is the music. To write music is easy, to get it performed is harder, and to have it remembered seems almost beyond human capacity. Because music, unlike the novel, has little value as documentation, it lives or (mostly) dies on the basis of its individual artistic essence. A few names thus pass into history and the rest remain scribblers. The last half of the nineteenth century was dominated—perhaps in more than music—by the German colossus Richard Wagner, that unique combination of genius and charlatan, mock humanitarian and real monster. The division of his vast musical estate proved both difficult and contentious. His heirs included more than his fervent admirers, who, like Mahler and Schoenberg, saw musical composition all too often for their own comfort in Wagner's image. Also among the claimants were those—chiefly Stravinsky—who reacted to Wagner's overweening ambition with cynical and hostile disbelief; but it was the fate of even Stravinsky to fail in the attempt to bestride our century in the same way Wagner subdued his. In Russia Sergei Rachmaninoff continued a tradition of songful symphonism oblivious to either Wagner's pretensions or the dislocations of modernism. In America Aaron Copland created a kind of folk music for a people only recently established as a nation. And still closer to our time a group of intelligent men, armed by technology, have attempted to save music by going beyond it, to enshrine electricity and mathematics as twentieth-century muses. But, regardless of the innumerable composers at work in our time, the nineteenth century remains for the music-loving audience the century of choice and the very model of musical creation.

1

The Holy Family
of Bayreuth

THE FAMILIES of musical geniuses do not usually
amount to much. Even the happy exceptions—the composer
sons of J. S. Bach, Robert Schumann's pianist wife Clara—seem
ultimately to achieve only modest reputations, while someone
like Beethoven's nephew remains of interest solely for the light
his sufferings throw on his uncle's psyche. For the rest, the relatives of great composers have mostly played a supporting role
and then vanished into obscurity. But the case of at least one immortal composer's family is altogether different. The relatives of
Richard Wagner—including in-laws and "out-laws"—constitute a
family whose position in history seems secure, even if its contributions have not always been honored.

The saga of the Wagners, as a group with an identity separable
from that of the composer himself, began in the middle 1860s
with Richard's second wife, Cosima. This redoubtable woman, in
addition to fulfilling her duties as mother of his children and
manager of his extensive household, acted during Wagner's lifetime as secretary, copyist, and diplomat for the burgeoning world
career of the Master of Bayreuth. Upon Wagner's death in 1883,
she assumed the directorship of the festival established to perform his operas, and until her breakdown in health in 1906, she
ran the Wagner inheritance with an iron hand.

When she was no longer able to perform this task of preservation, her work was taken over by Siegfried, the youngest of the

three children she had borne to Wagner. While it could not in
any way be said that the son shared his father's genius, he was a
competent composer and creditable conductor; some of his performances of his father's works and one of his own as well, dating
from the mid-1920s, are available to this day on discs. But more
important than Siegfried's conducting may well have been his
ability to bring the Bayreuth Festival through the difficult years
of war, defeat, revolution, and inflation in tolerable artistic and financial condition.

It had been plain for some time that Siegfried's political sympathies lay—as did, finally, those of his father—with the nationalistic Right in German life. His public partiality to the Right during the 1920s may well have been due in some degree to the
influence of his wife, Winifred, English by birth and the adopted
daughter of Wagner's disciple, Karl Klindworth. Winifred was an
early admirer and personal friend of Adolf Hitler. And it was
Hitler's fanatic enthusiasm for Wagner, demonstrated by
frequent attendance at Bayreuth performances, that resulted in
the festival being made a ward of the German state, and that
guaranteed its survival during the Nazi era.

The inevitable result of this unholy alliance of art and the politics of murder was the total discrediting of Winifred at the end of
World War II, and her official removal from the festival which
she had run since her husband's death in 1930. Her place was
shortly taken by her two sons, Wieland and Wolfgang. They put
together the first postwar festival in 1951, with Wieland as the
major artistic influence and Wolfgang as business manager. The
rehabilitation of Bayreuth was quickly accomplished, helped
along in no small measure by the striking success of Wieland's
1951 stagings of the *Ring* and *Parsifal*. These productions, in
their departure from the Victorian realism previously associated
with the staging of Wagner, and in their conception of the operas
in terms of modern psychology, influenced future performances
not only of Wagner but of opera in general.

Upon Wieland's death of cancer in 1966, Wolfgang assumed
artistic as well as business control, and must be considered responsible for the choice of the controversial French producer,

Patrice Chéreau, to stage the *Ring* in 1976 at the centennial of the festival. Wolfgang's sister, Friedelind (who, in revolt against the family, had defected from Germany at the beginning of World War II and written an antifamily and anti-Nazi book, *The Royal Family of Bayreuth*), has made a relatively minor career, mostly in England, as a teacher of operatic production; it seems also that the fourth generation of Wagners continues to find itself drawn both toward Wagner's works and the carrying on of his reputation. And meanwhile, the crusty old Winifred remains alive in her eighties, and only recently was the sole subject of a five-hour film documentary in which she aired her still-friendly feelings toward Hitler.

Clearly, however, of all these strong-willed, talented, and intelligent people, pride of place must go to the matriarch, Cosima. She was the daughter of remarkable parents—the great composer-pianist Franz Liszt and his mistress, the French aristocrat and writer, Marie D'Agoult (who wrote under the pseudonym Daniel Stern). Cosima's parents were never married, and after her birth in 1837 she was brought at first under the supervision of Liszt's mother. Later she was put in the care of cold and unfeeling governesses, and long afterward felt that she had always been an orphan. In 1857 she married the pianist and conductor, Hans von Bülow, an artist of the highest seriousness, whose edition of the Beethoven piano sonatas was for many years the standard version used by students.

Bülow was a fervent acolyte of Wagner, whose works he conducted to the Master's musical satisfaction. He first met Cosima when Liszt's new (and final) love, the Princess Wittgenstein, decided to remove the young girl from her mother's presence in Paris by sending her to Berlin, where Bülow became her piano teacher. At a concert shortly thereafter, Bülow conducted the *Tannhäuser* Overture—which was hissed. Cosima consoled him, and at that moment, it would seem, they made their decision to marry.

The marriage was scarcely happy. Bülow was moody, petulant, and easily shattered. Cosima supported him in his career and had two children by him. She had already met Wagner when she was in her teens; she and Bülow visited Wagner on their honeymoon, and the next year the two of them were witness to the final collapse of his marriage, and of his affair with Mathilde Wesendonck (whose affections were the stimulus for the composition of *Tristan*). Wagner and Cosima, who was twenty-four years younger than he, became deeply attracted to one another. In 1863, while on their way to one of Bülow's concerts, they "sealed their vow to belong entirely to each other." The contrast between this vibrant, energetic girl and Wagner's wife Minna— from whom he had been estranged for some years—could not have been greater. In place of a nagging *petite bourgeoise*, Wagner now found a cosmopolitan, cultured woman, a sophisticate in art and literature, and above all—here the difference between Cosima and Minna was at its clearest—a fanatical believer in his music, his future, and his immortal mission.

At this point (1863), Wagner's position was a difficult one. The operas conceived after *Lohengrin* seemed as if they would be impossible to produce; he had suspended work on the *Ring* at the end of the second act of *Siegfried;* and he was on the run from an army of importunate creditors. But the next year a miracle occurred—Wagner was rescued from ruin by the eighteen-year-old King Ludwig II of Bavaria. Ludwig made it his life's sacred duty to enable Wagner to compose and have his operas produced. As a part of his royal support—which indeed lasted until Wagner's death—he lent the composer a villa at Starnberg. Here, if not earlier, Wagner and Cosima became lovers, and in 1865 their daughter Isolde—named, as all Wagner's children were to be, for a character in the opera he was working on at the moment—was born.

For the birth of Wagner's and Cosima's first child, the fiction was maintained that the father was Bülow. But in 1867 another daughter, Eva, arrived—in later years she was to become the wife of the notorious anti-Semite and premature Hitlerite Houston Stewart Chamberlain—and this time it could hardly be denied that Wagner was the father. Wagner had, indeed, already been driven out of Ludwig's capital city of Munich in 1865 not only because of his political intrigues but also because of his triangle with Cosima and the strangely complaisant Bülow, and in 1868, two years after the death of Minna, Cosima joined Wagner at Tribschen in Switzerland. They were to remain there until 1872, when they moved permanently to Bayreuth.

The Wagners' life in Switzerland and later in Germany was the subject of diaries kept by Cosima and covering the years from 1869 to 1883 in intimate and exhaustive detail. For a variety of complex reasons involving family squabbles and intrigues among the faithful, these diaries were never published or even made widely available to scholars, though they were selectively used in the 1900s by Carl Glasenapp to complete the final volume of his biography of Wagner, and in the 1920s by Richard du Moulin Eckart for his biography of Cosima. Both these works are, unfortunately, hagiographical and even sycophantic in tone and so of limited value. There was therefore a great deal of interest attending the first publication of these diaries in Germany in 1976; their appearance in English translation in this country can only be welcomed.

As might be expected from a journal so voluminous as to run to 600,000 words for the volume dealing with the years from 1869 to 1877 alone, the reader is presented with a fascinating look in depth at the early years of the Wagner family as seen from the most partial viewpoint imaginable, an account of personal and public events keenly felt and arbitrarily recorded. The most public aspect of the Wagners' life during this period—and the most important aspect of all, in that it was the underpinning of everything else—was the triumphant progress of Wagner from a *cause célèbre* and royal protégé to the rank of first composer in the world, a rank acknowledged by friends and enemies alike. Not only, by the end of this time, were his operas being performed in all the major cities of Europe—and in America as well—to audiences shaken by transports of enthusiasm; but as the statistics in the *Diaries* make clear, these performances had become money-making enterprises undertaken for profit as much as for art. The same financial success could not be claimed for the early years of

Bayreuth, but here what is breathtaking is the very audacity of Wagner's conception of the festival, an idea which has no parallels in the history of music: a platform specially created for one man's own musical works, established in his lifetime to worldwide attention and excitement.

Bayreuth was not founded without anxieties and moments of despair. In the end, Wagner's scheme of supplying the necessary funds through many individual subscriptions failed, and his own concert-giving activities in Germany and abroad also proved insufficient; the drain these put on his health is plainly apparent in the *Diaries*. What made Bayreuth possible in the end was the support of King Ludwig, and much of the Wagners' time was evidently taken up with keeping Ludwig attached to the cause, an enterprise made all the more difficult by Wagner's unwillingness to see his operas performed in Ludwig's own theater in Munich.

Occupying a great deal of space in these pages is the shocking story of both Wagners' virulent and committed hatred of Jews. The domestic revelations herein will give little comfort to those who still think that Wagner's anti-Semitism can be explained by his envy of the successful Jewish composers, Mendelssohn and Meyerbeer. Wagner was perfectly capable of ignoring or even admiring the successes of others; he did not become an Italophobe because Verdi was famous, and he did not hate his own Germans because of their worship of Beethoven. Even his contempt for the French and their civilization is not really cut from the same cloth as his feelings about Jews. His relationship with the French was one of rejected love, stemming most obviously from the scandalous treatment accorded *Tannhäuser* at the Paris Opera in 1861 by the bloods of the Jockey Club. Cosima quotes him as urging the burning of Paris during the 1870–71 war; yet in 1873, during a period of great uncertainty about Bayreuth, she writes:

He [Wagner] says he has a good mind to tell his joke in public (that it was his misfortune that Napoleon had not won, for then Napoleon would have become Germany's ruler, would have familiarized himself with German things at once and have built R's theater for him).

Wagner scarcely makes such jokes about Jews.

Among the true disciples of Wagner were, notably, several Jews, among them Hermann Levi and Josef Rubinstein. Levi, a rabbi's son who was the first conductor of *Parsifal* in 1882, put up almost uncomplainingly with the Wagners' anti-Semitism until his own death in 1900; something of what he faced is shown by Cosima's patronizing words:

At parting, Herr L tells me he is downright glad to be leaving, for he feels such a complete nonentity here, and will have to try and find himself again; a curious attitude—I should have thought one would only find oneself properly when one was confronted with a great man and could forget oneself.

Rubinstein first made his appearance to the Wagners in an 1872 letter from Kharkov beginning "I am a Jew" and, according to Cosima, "demanding salvation through participation in the production of the *Nibelungen*." Rubinstein served until Wagner's death as court pianist, coaching singers and playing Beethoven and Chopin for the family in the evening; his immense talent and doglike devotion to the cause were not enough to preserve him from racial slurs. But even then Rubinstein could not endure life without the Master, and scarcely one year after Wagner's death the Jew who had wanted to be saved by the *Ring* committed suicide in Switzerland.

In musical matters, it becomes evident from these journals just how much of Wagner's time was spent listening to the works of a wide range of composers, from Bach to Liszt. Of these it should come as no surprise that his favorite was Beethoven, who he felt was his only equal. All the rest had major defects in Wagner's eyes, though some, like Haydn and Mozart, he on the whole admired. Brahms he largely denigrated, and Cosima shared his feelings:

In the evening I make the acquaintance of Herr Brahms, who plays a piano quartet of his own making, a red, crude-looking man, his opus very dry and stilted.

Thus do the greats and their intimates speak of colleagues.

Their experience of the works of others was not limited to music. Many evenings were spent by Richard and Cosima reading aloud the masterpieces of world literature, with the repertory ranging from Sophocles and Aeschylus to Turgenev. In drama, Shakespeare was Wagner's choice, as Beethoven was in music. It is perhaps idle to complain that the Wagners' comments about literature often seem arbitrary and even simpleminded (and by extension cast doubt on their judgments in music). One should hardly expect critical depth or fair-mindedness from a composer and dramatist deeply involved in his own work. What is significant is the evident seriousness with which Wagner and Cosima regarded the entire enterprise of artistic creation; the conclusion can hardly be escaped that underlying this seriousness was Wagner's estimation of himself as already an immortal artist, the peer of all his forebears in the artistic pantheon.

The *Diaries* are also a chronicle of the many friends, admirers, and disciples Wagner collected during these years. One such friend and admirer, whom Cosima mistakenly thought a disciple, was Nietzsche. Many entries document the uneasy course of the Wagner-Nietzsche relationship. At first, when the philosopher read *The Origin and Aim of Greek Tragedy* out loud to her, Cosima burbled with "great delight" over the dedication to Wagner and added, ". . . in it one sees a gifted man imbued with R's ideas in his own way." Three years later the Wagners were registering their displeasure at Nietzsche's effrontery in speaking well to them of a work by Brahms. And even earlier than this, Cosima was disturbed by Nietzsche's dedication of his *Homer* to his own sister, after first promising it to her; after discussing it with Wagner, Cosima found Nietzsche's behavior on this occasion marked by "an addiction to treachery."

Family concerns occupy much space in the *Diaries*. Children's illnesses—such diseases as whooping cough and diphtheria were then ordinary, if frightful, occurrences—took up much of Cosima's time, as did worry about Wagner's physical and psychological health. She herself suffered from eye trouble, which occasionally interfered with keeping her diary. Money worries were always present; notwithstanding the large sums coming regularly from King Ludwig, and the ever-rising royalties from opera performances, expenditures always seemed to exceed income. And from time to time reminders of the past appeared in the shape of long-forgotten creditors demanding repayment for old loans. Wagner was never a good economizer. He lived in truly opulent fashion with a household of twenty-five, including the so-called Nibelungen Chancellery, disciples whose job was to copy the *Ring* score in preparation for its performance.

Throughout these pages, Cosima is obsessed by feelings of guilt over her abandonment of Bülow—and, for a time, of her elder children as well. She dreamed often of Bülow (as did Wagner), and blamed herself for all of Bülow's personal and financial troubles. It was, no doubt, her consciousness of her own bad behavior that was responsible for the special brand of suspicion and pessimism she reserved for Blandine and Daniela, her children by Bülow. She found them perverse in character and felt they mocked her for her infidelity. Toward her two daughters by Wagner she was more indulgent and even trusting. But like Wagner himself, she reserved her full parental love (and a large measure of fatuity as well) for the infant Siegfried, with whom she was pregnant as the *Diaries* begin. As Geoffrey Skelton suggests in his excellent introduction, the *Diaries* in some way seem to have represented to Cosima a justification of her conduct.

Deeply as she may have felt over her treatment of Bülow, Cosima's grand passion for Wagner was more momentous by far. Swept perhaps equally by sexual passion and her utter conviction of the value of Wagner's music and ideas, she was a wife heroically strong in dealing with the world, and at the same time putty in her lover's hands. For him she gave up family, religion, and nationality. His music caused her to lose control of her emotions; when she heard the love duet from *Tristan* her only feeling was, "to him, to him." She saw her existence in the extreme terms of the *Liebestod*. She wanted a photograph of the two of them, taken with her kneeling before him; when he died, for twenty-five hours she would not leave the body, and for days she refused to eat.

This love was remarkably joined to a deeply religious nature. Born a Catholic, Cosima could hardly remain one after her divorce from Bülow and remarriage to Wagner. She soon became a Protestant, defined as such more by her hatred of Jesuits and the Pope (which she shared with Wagner) than by any sympathy for Lutheran dogma. In any case, the real outlet for her religious bent was her husband and his cause.

It is this veneration of Wagner and Wagnerism which constitutes the endlessly repeated *leitmotif*—if not indeed the *idée fixe*—of the *Diaries*. She saw her love for him as renunciation, self-sacrifice, and rebirth. She found it "easy to believe that another age would have regarded me as a religious fanatic—now love has got me fully in its grasp. I know nothing else and am willing to suffer in and for it." In a euphoric mood after the birth of Siegfried, she rhapsodizes: "Could I but say a hymn to the godhead! R sings it for me, my hymn is my love for him." She calls him the "One and Only," and when he remarks that she should have married a god, she answers back, "Well, I did."

For Cosima, Wagner possessed "the divinely daemonic power of genius"; the notes on his penciled scores she thought "sacred runes." The *Lohengrin* Prelude was for her "such an ecstasy that I do not hear this music like other music, but experience it like a vision." A rehearsal of Wagner's music is "glorious, utter liberation of the soul." Nor are these isolated examples; the *Diaries* are full of such passages.

Wagner saw Cosima in much the same terms as she saw him. He thought her touch could bring back the dead, and told her that her love "meant the end of the world for him." Once, embracing her, he cried, "for my Redeemer liveth." Another time, kissing her, he said, "This is the holy Urdar Fount from which I draw wisdom." For him she was Eve and Mary. The divine character of the Wagnerian family milieu extended even to Siegfried: as he was being born, the sun rose in

> an incredibly beautiful, fiery glow which started to blaze with a richness of color never before seen . . . it was . . . reflected in the blue jewel box containing [Cosima's] portrait, so that this, covered by glass and set in a narrow gold frame, was transfigured in celestial splendor.

Their marriage seemed to her a reincarnation, a deliverance from a previous erring existence. When, in a moment that occurs at the very end of the first volume of these *Diaries*, Cosima asked Wagner whether he had not found a way of absorbing her into himself, he silently pointed to their grave—one of the first amenities he had seen to in the building of their new mansion in Bayreuth.

It is the revelation of these private attitudes which constitutes the value of the journals. Their significance quite makes up for the fact that these many words contain few passages of musical interest and little factual material hitherto unknown or necessary to an understanding of Wagner's career. Instead of such substantive disclosures, we are given here an account of the daily life of a holy family.*

The Wagners' feelings of holiness, which in our time would comfortingly be called delusions, were not restricted to their private view of themselves. When Cosima called the Bayreuth Festival Theater "the cross to which we are nailed, the temple in which we pray," she was not simply venting a personal opinion. She was also giving voice to the exalted regard in which Wagner

---

* It should be noted in passing that this holy family had room in it, in theory if not in practice, for the men whose wives had been annexed by Wagner; in some of the strangest passages in the *Diaries*, Wagner and Cosima seek financial support for Bayreuth from Otto Wesendonck, still the husband of Wagner's inamorata of *Tristan* days. Wagner himself cherished the hope that some day he and Cosima might be reunited with Bülow. Even more remarkably, the two cuckolds seem to have shared these feelings. Wesendonck did indeed pay his financial tribute, and Bülow, after Wagner's death, helped bring Cosima out of her trancelike state of mourning with the telegraphed words, *"Soeur, il faut vivre."*

was increasingly being held by the world of European culture. In 1873 a young businessman, anticipating the composition of *Parsifal,* introduced himself to the Wagners as a Knight of the Holy Grail; he was a member of the Munich branch of the Wagner societies then springing up all over Europe. Two years later a lady-in-waiting to the Empress of Austria told Cosima that she felt Wagner's art to be "like the creation of the world." People everywhere were beginning to talk of "pilgrimages" to Bayreuth, and by the turn of the century Colette could mockingly set one of her novels in Bayreuth, calling it the "holy city."

The practical effect of all this worship was that Wagner was taken as a source of ultimate wisdom on all manner of subjects— from the Jews to vivisection. His prose works were widely circulated in Wilhelminian Germany, and even appeared in 1911 in a cheap popular edition. In England, an eight-volume translation appeared in 1892 under the auspices of the London branch of the Wagner Society; it is still available in an elegant reprint edition.

What is often ignored today in the justifiable attempts to deflate Wagner's grandiosity and his intellectual flights is that their power is directly traceable not simply to his immense achievement as an artist. That achievement itself gained world recognition and carried Wagner's thought along with it only because of the lordship exercised by art over the nineteenth century, and because of the transcendental place accorded to music within that lordship.

The highest claim for the primacy of music within art was made, curiously enough, by a nonmusician. It was Schopenhauer who spoke for the *Zeitgeist* when he wrote in *The World as Will and Idea:*

Music . . . since it passes over the Ideas, is entirely independent of the phenomenal world, ignores it altogether, could to a certain extent exist if there were no world at all, which cannot be said of the other arts. . . . Music is thus by no means like the other arts, the copy of the Ideas, but the *copy of the Will itself.* . . . This is why the effect of music is so much more powerful and penetrating than that of the other arts, for they speak only of shadows, but it speaks of the thing itself.

The effect of all this on Wagner was dynamic. In 1870, as he was on the edge of completing the *Ring*, he paid his compliments to Schopenhauer as the first to "define the position of music . . . with philosophic clearness." (During the period of scandal surrounding their liaison, Wagner and Cosima signed their telegrams to each other "*Will*" and "*Vorstel*"—"Will" and "Idea"— respectively, presumably to avoid detection.) Under the influence of Schopenhauer, and obeying as well the dictates of his own estimate of his capacities, Wagner gave up a good deal of his previous insistence on the need for words to complete the music. For him, music now became the best way of apprehending reality.

Not only were the other arts to be explained by music, but music would replace religion as well. In 1874 Cosima writes, "The only possible church nowadays, R says today, is music, with Beethoven as the high priest." It was not just that Wagner felt, as he said when announcing his decision to write *Parsifal*, that "Art makes religion eternal." Rather, it seemed to Wagner that he in himself had superseded dogmatic religion, which he now disdained as a sop to the ignorant. Megalomania, never far from Wagner's mental state, could not have found clearer expression than in his proud boast: "When I write my treatise on the philosophy of music, church and state will be abolished."

Significantly, that other great megalomaniac of the century, Nietzsche, agreed at first with Wagner on the supreme importance of music. In *The Birth of Tragedy*, he wrote of the "renovation and purification of the German spirit through the fire magic of music." Nor was it only the Wagnerites who entertained this view. It was held also in circles deeply antipathetic to Wagner. In his new book (*Freud, Jews, and Other Germans*), Peter Gay quotes from the memoirs of Eduard Hanslick, the contemporaneous Viennese music critic who, in the name of absolute music, carried the banner of Brahms against the Wagnerites:

As we listened to Brahms' B-flat Major Sextet, after Wagner had in the afternoon performed various fragments from the *Ring* and from *Tristan,* we thought ourselves suddenly transported into a world of pure beauty—*eine reine Welt der Schönheit.* It sounded like a kind of redemption—*eine Erlösung.*

This same idea, now broadened to include the satanic as well as the redemptive force of music, underlies much of Thomas Mann's work, not only in the short stories with Wagnerian titles ("Tristan," "Blood of the Wälsungs") but also in his novel about a composer, *Doctor Faustus.* And in a sinister way it also underlies Wilhelm Furtwängler's remark, upon hearing from Toscanini that he would refuse to conduct under the German and Italian tyrannies: "There is always freedom where Beethoven's music resounds." This is music elevated beyond life itself, to the level of Isolde's *Liebestod:*

> *In dem wogenden Schwall,*
> * in dem tönenden Schall,*
> *in des Welt-Atems wehendem All,*
> *ertrinken, versinken,*
> *unbewusst, höchste Lust!*

> (In the surging swell,
>   in the ringing sound,
> in the vast wave of the world's breath,
> to drown, to sink,
> unconscious—supreme bliss!)

While it lasted—and it remained regnant at least until the outbreak of World War I—this attitude provided the ideological rationalization and the psychological underpinnings of the greatest flowering Western music has ever known. The years from Beethoven to Strauss, so neatly dubbed the Romantic era, have given us today the substance of our repertory and established the terms by which music written both before and after has unavoidably come to be heard and judged. Still today, commercial success is accorded only to those performers who specialize in the masterpieces of the last century.

Yet in the meantime the world has changed. Music, having succeeded religion for many as the cultivated medium of self-transcendence and salvation, has itself been replaced, first by science and perhaps now by popular culture. From being a world-redeeming faith, music has become a pleasure justified by its contribution to the quality of our leisure. Even the mecca of Bayreuth has become just another expensive way station on the European summer-musical circuit. And along with the decline in the public image of serious music has gone an erosion of self-confidence among its practitioners. No large audience has yet been found for the musical production associated with the last half-century.

The decline in the public image of serious music can only reinforce our present tendency to see the Romantic century as a sacred era, an age of special creation. This view of the nineteenth century as the holy—indeed, the biblical—period of music accords well with the Wagners' view of themselves, and with their contemporaries' view of the Wagners. All were engaged in a higher religious enterprise; a very few as prophets and saviors, and a vast cultivated multitude as followers. The results were, by common consent, immortal. So the problem for musicians in our time is both simple and difficult: after the old testament, what room is there for the new?

Wagner
on Broadway

THE PERFORMANCE of *Die Meistersinger von Nürnberg* mounted by the New York City Opera a few years ago made a considerable contribution to our cultural life, not only for the quality of the production but for the issues it raised; issues that might otherwise have remained unconsidered.

The performance represented the very pinnacle of the City Opera's achievement and its contribution to our cultural life. Fresh faces, attractive voices, excellent orchestral playing, authoritative conducting, and bandbox staging: taken all together, these virtues conveyed a conception of the opera which was in the best traditions of the American musical theater. Wagner's music was heavily cut, thereby enabling the performance to end a full fifteen minutes before the magic hour of midnight, at which the orchestra begins to collect overtime. The cuts naturally telescoped the action of the opera and speeded up the pace of the performance. The opera in this way became more palatable to an audience not schooled, as was the German audience for which the piece was written, in the virtues and duties of obedience and endurance.

The great innovation of this production was its presentation in English. The English version used is the work of John Gutman; I was struck by the fact that the libretto I bought in the lobby before the performance began—translation by John Gutman— coincided only partially with the words actually sung by the singers, and there seemed no obvious explanation for the many discrepancies. Many of the words, when they were sung against a thin orchestral background, were clear and perhaps would have been of help to someone who did not know the plot well. In any case, both translations—the one sold and the one sung—seemed adequate to the purposes of the production, which I took to be to present a pleasant, comfortable *Meistersinger*.

The problem of opera in the vernacular, involving as it does the relationship in opera between music and words, is a difficult one. Indeed, Richard Strauss made this relationship the subject of his last opera, *Capriccio*. His characters discuss, endlessly it sometimes seems, the question: First the music, then the words, or first the words, then the music? Who is to say? The balance shifts, as the talents of the contributors interact. The balance cannot and should not be defined, for in its vagueness lies the possibility of fresh creation.

No one would dispute the point that, for an audience which knows the piece, opera is ideally presented in the language of its composition. This is of course most obvious when the text is itself a work of literary art, such as Strauss and Hofmannsthal's *Elektra* and *Rosenkavalier*. It is probably even true when the text is only a peg on which to hang the tunes, as in the case of many of Puccini's masterpieces. For the composer cannot help but be influenced by the sounds of the words he is setting, the vowels and the consonants, the internal rhythms of the words and their order, the rhetorical associations of all the elements of his own mother tongue.

But this is, and must remain, a counsel of perfection. There is a long tradition of vernacular opera production, of *Aida* in German, of the *Nibelungenring* in French, of *Boris Godunov* in Italian. There was even a practice, now I think dead, of mixed performances—of artists in a single production each singing in the language in which he learned the piece. And the audience seems to become just as attached to the tunes when heard in the vernacular as when heard in the original. So, as a general rule, an argument can always be made for doing opera in the local language. If such a procedure enables the singers to feel more comfortable, the audience to follow the actors more easily, difficult problems of nationalistic dislike for a foreign language to be avoided, then one might feel justified in looking for a translation that works—that is singable, understandable, and accurate.

To be sure, opera in English is a special case, because English seems an unrewarding language in which to sing. It is difficult to enunciate clearly, and its vowel sounds do not easily lend themselves to the kind of Italianate vocal production now so much in fashion. The training of most American singers, furthermore, is mainly in the use of foreign languages, not their own. Still, one can say quite safely that the same rule applies to translation into English as it does for other languages: if it works, use it.

It remains to be seen, however, how well *Meistersinger* fits into this general rule of toleration. For this opera is a special case both in the world of opera and in the world of Wagner. The pragmatic question—does it work?—cannot so easily be asked of translation here as it can with so many other operas.

To see what makes *Meistersinger* special, we must ask what happens in the opera. Its plot is simple, as such things go. It is set in Nuremberg, an old German town of medieval houses, the historical Mastersingers guild, and the historical Hans Sachs. The story concerns an offer, made by a rich goldsmith, Veit Pogner, of his daughter Eva's hand in marriage to the winner of a singing contest to be chosen by the Mastersingers guild, of which Pogner is a leading member. He has been led to make this offer by a desire to show that contrary to what the bourgeoisie is accused of throughout Germany, the worthy burghers of Nuremberg value art over money. A young noble, Walther von Stolzing, who has fallen in love with Eva (and she with him), immediately sets about trying to win entrance to the Mastersingers guild in order to be eligible to compete. He is, however, rejected as unfit by the Mastersingers and particularly by Sixtus Beckmesser, their keeper of the rules, who himself wishes to compete for Eva. The wise shoemaker, Hans Sachs, also a member of the Mastersingers guild, but moved by Walther's talent, advises him on a suitable song for the contest; Sachs then tricks Beckmesser into stealing the song and palming it off in the contest as his own. Beckmesser makes such a botch of it that Sachs is able to get the assembled judges and people to allow Walther to show the way it should be sung. He does, wins by acclamation, and the opera ends with the lovers united and Sachs singing to the audience a plea for the preservation of German art.

Attractive stuff—almost a plot for a Broadway musical or an operetta: boy meets girl, youth triumphs over the spite of the mean through the help of mature wisdom. And that was what the City Opera production showed us—all the people as pretty as in a mail-order catalogue, and the music as tuneful as Lehár. But if that is the story of *Meistersinger* on the level of Broadway and the musical theater, it must be pointed out that another drama takes place in the opera on the level of those social, aesthetic, and political ideas to which Wagner devoted his life. The great arch of that other drama spreads from the speech in which Pogner offers his daughter's hand near the beginning of the first act—and which in Gutman's translation reads:

wherever German land I tread, I find with indignation,
we're rarely praised and have instead a miser's reputation.
I've heard it from both high and low; I'm sick of hearing it wherever I go
that we have bargained and sold our lives and souls for gold.

—to Sachs's peroration, written by Wagner in the decade of the Franco-Prussian War and the Prussian unification of Germany:

Beware! Us threaten evil days: If our great German realm decays,
When foreign powers rule the land, no prince his people will understand,
if foreign sham and foreign lies should ever darken German skies;
What's German and true could not abide, were't not for German master's pride!
I beg of you: honor your German masters, thus you will ban disasters!
And if you have their work at heart, though fall apart
the Holy Roman Domain, there still would remain
The holy German Art!

The keystone of this great German arch is Beckmesser, the keeper of the rules. Wagner, in creating Beckmesser, was making an attack—which he did not attempt to disguise—on the most famous and respected German-speaking music critic of his time, Eduard Hanslick. Wagner, like most of the musical world of the time, thought Hanslick to be Jewish (which he may or may not have been); this supposed Jewishness and Hanslick's rejection of Wagner's later music were for Wagner two sides of the same coin. The Jewish Hanslick's dislike of the German Wagner's music neatly illustrated Wagner's conception of the relationship between the Jews and Germany in general. Wagner went out of his way to point out this moral to Hanslick. In a late draft of the libretto, the character finally called Beckmesser in the opera is called Veit Hanslich, and Hanslick himself was present at a reading of this draft by Wagner in Vienna in 1862.

What makes Beckmesser loathsome in Wagner's conception is not that he is physically ugly, sings badly, or is old. His crime is that he has nothing of his own. So he must criticize, and what he cannot destroy by criticism he must steal, and what he steals he turns into nonsense. This is of course exactly how Wagner saw the Jews in his essay, *Das Judentum in der Musik* ("Jewry in Music"), which he first published anonymously in 1850 and then presented under his own name in 1868, the year of the first performance of *Meistersinger*.

The Jew, as Wagner portrays him in this notorious tract, possesses no culture of his own; at best he can only sing and talk in the language of the bazaar. Out of a mixture of tolerance and sloth, the Gentile world allows the Jew to compete for and win the highest prizes. Such tolerance is noble, but it is extended at the cost of bondage to the Jew and the degeneration of a once-pure civilization. What the lascivious Beckmesser wants from the Mastersingers and from the virginal Eva is precisely what the Jew wants from the Gentile world: domination and the joy of corruption. Thus Beckmesser is not only the villain against whom the beautiful lovers must struggle; he is the link between Wagner's homely story of young love and Wagner's sociopolitical ideas. It is the evil represented by Beckmesser upon which Wagner relies to unify the two strands of his opera.

This is the background against which it seems to me the New York City Opera production must be judged, if it is to be discussed not merely as a performance of music in the theater but also as an instance of the kind of attempt being made to realize a great work of art at this time and in this country. Against this background, then, the first aspect of the production to be questioned must be its use of English rather than the original German. *Meistersinger* is not only an opera in German; it is the supreme example of a German opera. It was seen that way by Wagner, and it has been seen that way ever since by the most diverse social, political, and intellectual groups, of whom the Nazis and the Communists are only two. It uses a deeply German cultural background; it bases itself on an old German situation; it glorifies the city of Nuremberg (which indeed has figured notoriously in the political history of this century): it contains many specific mentions of Germany; and it ends with a hymn to the German nation. For a character to speak in English of the Germany evoked by this opera as if he were a German is to be placed in a false position: that of a man who is seen to be lying as, with the greatest passion, he asserts his truthfulness.

This problem of being German in English arises most forcefully at the end when Sachs warns of the coming of evil days in which foreign princes who do not speak the language of their people will rise to power through lies and sham. The Sachs at the City Opera was spared most of the problem by the ruthless cutting of this final speech, Wagner's musical setting of his political testament. Whoever decided on the exact location of this cut accomplished the resulting joint in a structurally clumsy way not worthy of such otherwise fine musicians; more important, the loss of these emotion-laden lines, placed by Wagner against a thin orchestral background so that every word would be clear to the audience, also deprived the opera of its intended ending. All we had left as a remnant of Wagner's larger reasons for composing *Meistersinger* was one poorly declaimed, weakly sung, and orchestrally covered mention by Sachs of "holy German art" capped by an ending sung by the chorus, which—because of the limitations on clear enunciation inherent in any large group of singers—could only be rendered unclearly.

There can have been no purely musical justification for cutting a passage which is musically necessary, beautiful, and a traditional showpiece for great performers of the role. But other, extramusical arguments for this cut can be made. Leaving aside for later the problem of the sheer unpleasantness of the words, these arguments would seem to number three. The thoughts themselves, being German, are not properly conveyed in English; the passage is often cut in performance, even when it is done in German at the Metropolitan; Wagner himself wished to cut the passage, and only retained it at the passionate urging of his wife Cosima. The first argument is really only an argument against doing this particular opera in English. The second argument seems weak, because if a practice is a mistake it remains so regardless of the number of times it is made (as Toscanini is once supposed to have said: "Tradition is the memory of the last bad performance").

As for the argument about Wagner's real intentions, it is more difficult, for it immediately involves us in complicated questions of scholarship (who said what to whom, and how do we know it?) and psychology (what was Wagner's relation to his wife and to what extent was she capable of changing his mind?). These questions are fascinating, if only because their answers are unknowable. We do know that the passage is there in the final score Wagner approved for performance and publication; we do know that the music which clothes these words is a serious and distinguished example of his genius; we do know, as has been pointed out by Robert W. Gutman in his brilliant *Richard Wagner: The Man, His Mind, and His Music:* "Wagner wanted *Meistersinger* produced in the city it celebrated because he saw this ancient seat of German tradition as a bulwark against Jewish influences." Furthermore, far from seeming increasingly irrelevant with the passage of time, this speech has remained not only meaningful to audiences—witness the German reactions to it during the period of Hitler—but also to the artists who have sung it.

There are four large-scale historical recordings of *Meistersinger* which may illuminate this problem. These recordings are not historical simply because of their musical qualities, though these are high indeed; they are historical because they were recorded during live performances taking place at important moments of German political and musical history. The first recording, of extended excerpts, was made in 1928 on the 115th anniversary of Wagner's birth, at a performance in Berlin's *Unter den Linden* Theater. The Sachs was the great Jewish baritone, Friedrich Schorr, and the conductor was Leo Blech, a Jew who was allowed by Goering to remain as a performer in Germany almost until the outbreak of World War II. The second documents a performance at the wartime Bayreuth Festival in 1943 conducted by the famous Wilhelm Furtwängler. The third recording (the first complete *Meistersinger* on records) was made at the Bayreuth Festival of 1951, the first to be held after Germany's defeat. It was conducted by Herbert von Karajan and had Elisabeth Schwarzkopf as Eva; both of these great artists had, as is well known, been active in the musical world of Nazi Germany. And the last is a complete recording of the 1963 opening-night performance at the Munich National Theater on the occasion of its rebuilding after near-total destruction by an Allied bombing raid in 1943. Germany on the eve of Hitler, German musical performance during a period of heavy bombing of German cities, the first Bayreuth Festival after defeat, the reopening of a national treasure destroyed by enemy bombs: it was *Meistersinger* that served to commemorate these moments for Germany.

All these performances have an atmosphere in common—something composed of aggressive pride and noble arrogance. In all of them the final speech of Sachs is retained in full and serves as the climax of the drama. Each Sachs—Schorr (the greatest), Jaro Prohaska and Otto Edelmann in the Bayreuth versions, and Otto Wiener in the Munich recording—is betrayed by the music, the ideas, and the occasion into an excess of emotion on the

phrase *Was Deutsch und echt* ("What's German and true"); each
feels compelled to stress the word *Deutsch,* each time it appears.
This, one feels, is the real *Meistersinger,* the *Meistersinger* not of
Broadway and the United Nations, but of Wagner and Germany.
It is in being performed in the spirit of Wagner and Germany
that the opera becomes more than a collection of tunes and song-
birds, and becomes what all art aspires to be, a rival of life.

Of course a recording, while it can convey much of the musical
performance, can convey little of the acting through which an operatic character must also be portrayed. Beckmesser must be
acted more than he must be sung, and here lay perhaps the chief
weakness of the City Opera production. If the argument about
Beckmesser's significance which has been advanced here is right,
it follows that he must be presented as a villain, not only personally but socially, not only individually but as a symbol of the
crime of the Jews against the people. If this is done, all becomes
clear. It is then only proper that he is beaten up in the riot which
closes Act II; it seems just for Sachs to trick him into using
Walther's song as his own; it is inevitable that he should turn the
pure, lofty sentiments of the original into the kind of gibberish
which Wagner thought the fate of all Jewish imitations of Gentile
culture; his public humiliation, suffering, and disgrace at the
close of the opera may be seen as a triumph of restraint and humanity rather than an expression of spite. For against the enemies of the people all crimes are virtues, and all attempts at conventional virtue are crimes. These enemies of the people—and a
distinguished line from Wagner to Amin has thought the word
"Jew" described them all—are animal rather than human; as
Himmler put it in a speech to SS leaders in 1943, virtue itself lies
in the necessary crime:

It is completely wrong for us to offer up our ingenuous soul and spirit, or
good nature, or idealism, to other peoples. . . . Germans are after all the
only people in the world who treat animals decently, so we will also
know how to treat these human animals. . . . I can tell you, it is hideous
and frightful for us Germans to have to watch such things [execu-
tions]. . . . It is, and if we would not find it hideous and frightful, then
we should no longer be Germans. Hideous though it is, it has been nec-

essary . . . let us not weaken. . . . To have gone through this and—except for instances of human weakness—to have remained decent, that has made us tough. This is an unwritten, never to be written, glorious page of our history.

Of course, *Meistersinger* is not Bergen-Belsen; of course Wagner was not Himmler or Hitler; of course Beckmesser is only beaten and disgraced, not murdered. But those were gentler times, and the real audacity of pioneers often seems a cautious conservatism to distant successors. Is Wagner to be blamed for Nazism, for the murder of countless millions? He can only be blamed for what he did, not for what others did after him. What he did was to provide the shoulders on which others stood. Perhaps he could not have known what they would do when they stood there, but they were his shoulders.

How was Beckmesser performed at the City Opera? Not as a villain but as a fool, not as evil but as tormented, not as corrupt but as untalented, not as lascivious but as anxious. In short, as a figure of pathos mixed with fun, a clown, a pitiful, gently comic misfit. His fate—to be beaten, hissed, and rejected in love—was made to seem inexplicable, having been caused by none of his observed actions. For all he was shown to have done was lose a contest.

The City Opera production, then, misrepresented the social and political context of the opera in three ways: by performing it in English, cutting material of the greatest significance, and distorting the role of Beckmesser. By neglecting the ideas of the opera, moreover, the production inevitably transformed the music itself into a springtime frolic.

Why did this happen? How did this splendid group of musicians and theatrical people come to present so sanitized a version of *Meistersinger?* Certainly those responsible must have felt the force of practical considerations. The City Opera does have a reputation for bringing opera to the people, for making popular opera easily available and for making difficult opera popular. It has attempted to cast attractive young American singers in roles traditionally reserved for European artists of greater experience. As an American company it naturally is prejudiced in favor of English as a medium of expression. It is only reasonable for the City Opera to try to do what it does best—to bring the tradition and resources of the American musical theater to bear against the greatest of European opera.

The question then becomes why *Meistersinger* was seen as a proper field for the exercise of the company's undoubted virtues. There does exist a large area of the operatic repertory in which the City Opera has made a unique contribution to the history of operatic performance and production. That *Meisterisinger* was felt to belong to this area, notwithstanding the obvious nature of many of the considerations I have raised, says a great deal about our idea of the proper relationship in a work of art between elements of art and elements of life.

The New York City Opera was, I feel, unable to face the fact that *Meistersinger* is a blend of the beautiful and the horrid. It was unable to face the fact that both beautiful music and lofty sentiments could be inextricably mixed with implications of a political program which, in the hands of others, led to undreamed-of barbarities. They did not recognize that, in art as in life, the beauty often depends on the horror. Failing to recognize this, they attempted to disentangle the two, to leave out the horror and present only the beauty.

There was a previous, and much more thoroughgoing, attempt to accomplish this impossible task. Paul Rosenfeld, an important American music critic of earnestly modernist sympathies, in an article called "The Nazis and *Die Meistersinger*," written soon after Hitler came to power, accused the Nazis of taking what he saw as the healthy, democratic, individualistic nationalism of Wagner's opera as a justification for their tyranny. Wagner's nationalism, like all nationalistic art, Rosenfeld thought, was the expression of

the national superindividual entity at the moment that entity offers to form itself freely in the union of individuals, a formation inevitably flowing from the inner liberty of the individual.

For Rosenfeld, this blossoming of the individual led

> ultimately toward . . . the "anarchist commune." . . . For all artists are fundamentally "anarchists." . . . They touch material selflessly and shape it in accordance with its own nature and the idea to which it conforms; and work is a joy to them, an end in itself. And the social order to which they are natively directed could easily be an order based on the private ownership of the means of production, and the operation of those means for profit, in which labor got its just reward, and social, political, and intellectual advantages were shared by all. Such, then, is the social order adumbrated by *Meistersinger* and other great nationalistic pieces.

Such, rather, is the gospel of aestheticism—art is beautiful, art is truth, art will lead us to political, social, and moral salvation. But apart from whatever criticisms might be made of this position in general, the astonishing thing to notice is that Rosenfeld could only arrive at his reading of the ideological content of *Meistersinger* by entirely ignoring Beckmesser, whom he never once mentions. What Rosenfeld achieves by selection and distortion, the City Opera achieves by eliminating the whole question. They both transform Wagner's message of particularism and exclusion into a message of brotherhood and tolerance, a message the City Opera production reinforced by its prominent use of blacks and Orientals among the chorus and dancers without any attempt to make them up to look like members of the Nuremberg community.

Meistersinger is full of poison. It is also full of beauty. It represents the loftiest human sentiments, and implies the extinction of millions. In it, as in all the greatest works of art, there is not simply a necessary relationship between good and evil, there is an attempt at unity. It must be the purpose of artistic production and performance to present this unity in its full depth and intensity. Of course this does not, in the case of *Meistersinger*, mean that it must be performed with Beckmesser wearing a yellow star. What is implicit in Wagner's opera must not, in the fashion of certain politically conscious stage directors, be made explicit, for that, too, is distortion. It is only necessary that the work be presented with full awareness both of what it is and what it implies, no more and no less.

That the New York City Opera failed to do this derives from its inability—an inability characteristic of our time as a whole—to separate the realm of art from the realm of politics, to separate the fantasies of the artist from the proper goals of social policy. It is an inability to respect the integrity of art on the one hand and the political and social order on the other. Each of these realms has claims of its own and boundaries of its own, the observance of each being essential to the observance of the other. In its limited sphere, art must be total; in its total sphere, politics must be limited. All of *Meistersinger* must be fully performed on the stage; in our lives, we must resist all attempts of society at total control of man. We need not attempt to reconcile art and politics; we need only attempt to render both of them their proper due.

Schoenberg's Survival

THERE CAN BE little doubt that among the successors of Wagner I have mentioned, this century's most consequential reputation in the field of serious music is that of Arnold Schoenberg. His is the only name of our time to occupy the same kind of niche in the history of music as that of the greatest composers of the past 250 years—Bach, Mozart, Beethoven, Wagner, and Brahms—and it can be argued that his influence upon his successors has been greater than that of any of his predecessors save Beethoven and Wagner. For his work has done more than fundamentally change the course of music. The very act of listening to it has had the effect of altering the way in which all music, both later and earlier, has been heard. His compositions, moreover, have spawned not only fervent disciples and slavish imitators but, equally important, an opposition which by its ferocity and duration testifies to his power. And this is, and has been, consistently true despite the fact that, to this day, there has never existed any sizable audience for Schoenberg's major mature works.

This paradox ought to give us pause. One cannot easily find a similar separation of reputation and audience in the case of any other great musical figure. Of course, not every supreme master has been enthusiastically supported by the sophisticated audience of any given historical period. Fashions change, and complex works have often had tough sledding for some years after being written. The choral music of Bach—the St. *Matthew Pas-*

sion, for example—was slow in developing an audience; the late works of Beethoven took time to reach the devoted audience they now enjoy. But the audience for Bach's music developed *pari passu* with the widening consciousness of his general stature; Beethoven's *oeuvre* taken as a whole never lacked either influence or listeners. And in our own time there has been a rough equivalence between the fame of a Prokofiev or a Bartók and the desire of a concert-going public to hear their music. Even in the more complicated case of Schoenberg's only twentieth-century rival, Stravinsky, his reputation does not really rest on his relatively unpopular post-World War I pieces; he is mainly famous and was first influential precisely for those pieces—*Firebird, Petrushka,* and *The Rite of Spring*—which music lovers have always most wanted to hear.

With Schoenberg, it is different. From his first entrance into the public world of music with *Verklärte Nacht* (1899), a piece inspired by a poem of Richard Dehmel, he began to win the respect shading into awe with which he has been regarded by an intellectual class of musicians and a musical class of intellectuals. Yet only this first major piece has gained solid repertory status, and that status it probably owes in large measure to its use in Anthony Tudor's mid-1940s ballet, *Pillar of Fire.* Why this separation exists in Schoenberg's case between influence and audience invites analysis; such an analysis must of course be based upon a consideration of Schoenberg's musical career.

Schoenberg, born in 1874 to lower-middle-class Jewish parents in Austria, was as a musician largely self-taught. This fact may help to explain both the relative ease with which his personality was able to dominate and defy musical conventions so sacred to others, and also a certain feeling of personal alienation from the musical establishment which was never to leave him. He made maximum use of the limited instruction in composition he received, and with *Verklärte Nacht* he emerged at twenty-five as a fully developed master of the German romantic tradition of Wagner and Brahms, drawing with ease simultaneously upon

Wagnerian freedom of form and harmony and Brahmsian control of abstract structure and contrapuntal device. What was remarkable about *Verklärte Nacht*—beside the unforced melodic beauty of the music—was the originality Schoenberg demonstrated in writing it for string sextet rather than the full orchestra which Richard Strauss, among others, was then using for the musical treatment of programmatic ideas (though Schoenberg later did a version for string-orchestra performance which is now more commonly played).

This piece, with its relative economy of means, was succeeded by a work scored for something more than 150 orchestral instruments, consisting of 35 woodwinds, 25 brass, 4 harps plus celesta, approximately 80 strings, and 16 percussion instruments including iron chains. In addition, the score employs a solo soprano, a mezzo-soprano or contralto, two tenors, a bass, and a speaker, as well as three four-part men's choruses and an eight-part mixed chorus. This musical extravaganza, lasting almost two hours, the *Gurrelieder,* is a song-cycle set to poems by the Danish writer Jens Peter Jacobsen. In essence, it amounts to an unstaged Wagnerian music-drama, but it uses its grand forces with subtlety and elegance rather than with the striving for mass effect which often characterizes the work of the other giants of this period, including even Mahler. Schoenberg manages here to achieve, through the employment of innumerable small motives, a dense and at the same time broadly lyrical thematic texture. The work, though composed in 1900 and 1901, was not completely orchestrated until 1911. About its enormous success when it was first performed in Vienna in 1913, Schoenberg later (1937) wrote characteristically:

As usual, after this tremendous success I was asked whether I was happy. But I was not. I was rather indifferent, if not a little angry. I foresaw that this success would have no influence on the fate of my later works. I had, during these thirteen years, developed my style in such a manner that, to the ordinary concert-goer, it seemed to bear no relation to all preceding music. I had had to fight for every new work; I had been offended in the most outrageous manner by criticism; I had lost friends. And I stood alone in a world of enemies.

After *Gurrelieder* came the 1903 tone-poem *Pelléas and Méli-sande,* also written on a large scale and then, in 1905, the First String Quartet, which marked a decisive turning point in Schoenberg's compositional career. As turning points do, this one looked backward as well as forward. It looked backward in its length (almost one hour) and in its employment of extreme chromaticism while retaining the framework of conventional tonality—the piece began and was listed as being in D minor, and ended most properly in D major. What looked forward was the piece's tendency to compress the musical material in a way that gave every moment the highest possible polyphonic density— Schoenberg himself quotes Mahler as saying of this quartet: "I have conducted the most difficult scores of Wagner; I have written complicated music in scores of up to thirty staves or more; yet here is a score of not more than four staves, and I am unable to read them."

More importantly, however, Schoenberg here significantly advanced the revolutionary development of treating all thematic material motivically, and subjecting it to a process of continuous variation. Themes were thus freed from their former role as repeated and therefore recognizable melody and given the new role of bits in a mosaic. The end result of this process too was to concentrate attention on each moment rather than upon the long-term direction and structure of the piece. The effect upon even a knowledgeable audience was well described by the title of Alban Berg's brilliant 1924 article, "Why Is Schoenberg's Music So Difficult to Understand?," which uses the D Minor Quartet as its main example.

Thus by 1905 Schoenberg had, in *Gurrelieder,* exhausted the possibilities of the employment of enormous forces, and at the same time had, in the D Minor Quartet, exhausted the possibilities of internal complexity, if that complexity was to be achieved through the use of traditional musical means meant to be traditionally understood. If he wished to continue his forward progress, he would have to find a new direction. In his Second String Quartet (1907–08) he found it by adding, to the first quartet's

emancipation of the thematic material, the emancipation of dissonance from the former rules governing its use; in addition, he
now made it possible to hear these musical procedures in a quite
new way by presenting them in a clear and transparent texture.

The first two movements of the Second String Quartet, though
often on the border of tonality, are appealingly lyrical and very
much in the elegant tradition of the classical string quartet; only
the quotation in the second movement of the folksong *"Ach, du
lieber Augustin"* which its following line *"Alles ist hin,"* suggests
what is to come in the third and fourth movements. For both
these latter movements involve the addition of a soprano voice to
the strings of the quartet; the soprano sings two poems of Stefan
George, *"Litanei"* and *"Entrückung"* (ecstasy), poems which are
typical of George's style in their representation of depression issuing in ecstasy. And in the last movement, after a thin and skittish opening hinting at the abandonment of tonality, the singer
begins with the famous words, "I feel an air from other planets
blowing," to an accompaniment often fiercely dissonant and
always eerie. Though the piece ends both tenderly and tonally,
the point has been made: the new music of the spheres will not
possess the sweetness the astronomers traditionally had in mind.

Having felt this "air from other planets blowing," Schoenberg
was now ready to write those pieces of his expressionist phase
which Charles Rosen has correctly observed we have yet to come
to terms with. Perhaps that is only a polite way of saying that
these pieces—*Die Glückliche Hand* (1908–13), *Erwartung* (1909),
and especially *Pierrot Lunaire* (1912)—remain essentially unacceptable to an audience of nonmusicians, no matter how well-
versed. Be that as it may, these compositions share a common
climate of emotional disturbance, neurotic yearnings, and quasi-
psychotic transport (heightened by Schoenberg's use in *Pierrot
Lunaire* of *Sprechstimme*, a vocal style belonging more to the
realm of speech than of sung notes). All of these pieces attempt
directly to communicate emotional states seemingly unmediated
by normal artistic criteria of form, restraint, and balance; in this
the expressionist style of Schoenberg, most completely realized

in *Pierrot,* closely mirrors the expressionist style of painting ascendant during the same period in Germany.

Schoenberg himself, at about this time, began to paint seriously, and in the same expressionist style. His painting was much admired by Kandinsky, and was shown at the *Blaue Reiter* exhibition in Munich in 1911; to the famous 1912 *Blaue Reiter* almanac Schoenberg contributed an essay ("The Relationship to the Text") oddly denying the importance of the words to which music was written, a composition (the 1911 *Herzgewächse*), and two self-portraits. Kandinsky, in a 1912 book of tributes to Schoenberg, was prescient in seeing the similarity in spiritual content between Schoenberg's painting and his new musical works.

The atmosphere of emotional disintegration prevailing in those works was conveyed not only by the texts Schoenberg chose to set, but also through the apparent loss of any relationship between music and words or of any relationship between the resulting music and the traditions of the past. All seems illusion and specter; even the work of this period which has proven the most accessible and communicative—the Five Orchestral Pieces (1909)—suggests the same mood in its looming, threatening music and in three of the titles which Schoenberg unwillingly at his publisher's request gave the individual pieces— *Vorgefühle* (Premonitions), *Vergangnes* (That Which Is Past), and *Peripetia* (A Sudden Turn of Events).

Actually, far from being formless, the writing of this music is often devilishly ingenious, exploiting the most sophisticated orchestral techniques and the most abstruse devices of traditional counterpoint. In *Pierrot Lunaire,* for example, when one of the poems describes how Pierrot finds a spot on the back of his coat caused by a moonbeam—something he must have seen in a mirror—Schoenberg uses inverted and mirrored musical figures with the greatest formal mastery. Yet these and similar technical devices, because of their extreme subtlety and complexity, could hardly be appreciated by even the most educated of listeners. When to this difficulty Schoenberg added the "free atonality" of the music—the rigorous avoidance of tonal suggestion and resolution—he propelled himself into a public void, beyond even scandal. And the consequences were significant not only for the public but for Schoenberg himself. For deprived of the organizational possibilities of tonality, Schoenberg was now finding extended music unless supported by a long text very difficult to write—a fact shown by the extreme brevity of the Six Little Piano Pieces (1911), his last work without text for more than a decade.

Schoenberg now entered a time of retirement from composition. From 1912 to 1921 he completed only one piece, the Four Orchestral Songs (1913–16). About the beginning of 1915 he also started work on *Die Jakobsleiter*, a massive oratorio on the subject of the need for prayer. The music resembles Schoenberg's pre-expressionist writing more than his later work; melodies have a longer sweep, harmonies are more tonal, the orchestra supports rather than competes with the *Sprechstimme* parts. But *Die Jacobsleiter* remained unfinished.

For what Schoenberg was really involved in during this period was the systematic rationalization of a new kind of music altogether. By the summer of 1921 he was able to tell a pupil: "I have made a discovery thanks to which the supremacy of German music is ensured for the next hundred years." The discovery was "the method of composing with twelve tones related only to each other." This is what the world, against Schoenberg's objection, calls atonality. Music composed in accord with the tenets of this system is developed from an arbitrary succession of the twelve notes of the chromatic scale, this succession being available in four forms——its original order, its inversion (the turning of ascending intervals into descending intervals, and vice versa), its retrograde (the reversal of the notes, beginning on the last pitch and going to the first), and its retrograde inversion. The resulting succession of notes, called the series or row, may be transposed so that it begins on any step of the chromatic scale; from the possible 48 resultant series, the harmonic and melodic material for the piece is chosen and developed subject to the rule that all twelve notes or tones must be used before the series can be employed again.

It cannot in any ordinary sense be said that Schoenberg was

driven to this discovery—which involved the final sacrifice of his considerable lyrical gift—by an openly felt desire to be a revolutionary. On the contrary, he wrote to a Swiss music-lover in 1923:

I may say that for the present it matters more to me if people understand my older works. . . . They are the natural forerunners of my later works, and only those who understand and comprehend them will be able to hear the latter with any understanding beyond the fashionable minimum. . . . I do not attach so much importance to being a musical bogeyman as to being a natural continuer of properly understood good old tradition!

This attitude to the past was vividly manifested in the partially twelve-tone works that Schoenberg, armed with his new musical law and thus again able to compose, now wrote: the Five Piano Pieces and the *Serenade* for seven instruments and baritone voice (both 1920–23), and the Wind Quintet (1924). For these compositions are classical in their proportions and in the economy of their means if not in their harmonic configuration and sound. Not only in the *Serenade* but also in the Piano Suite (1921–23) and the Wind Quintet, moreover, Schoenberg seemed, as the French avant-garde composer Gilbert Amy has pointed out, concerned with proving the place of serial music in such classical formal structures as the march, the minuet, the theme and variations, and the waltz.

This desire for historical vindication perhaps clashed with Schoenberg's necessarily rigid early application of the technique in whose use he was now rapidly gaining virtuosity and ease. In his next two major instrumental pieces, however, the Suite for piano, three strings, and three winds (1925–26) and the String Quartet No. 3 (1927), Schoenberg not only retained his concern with classical forms but also began to employ his own discoveries in a way that now in itself seems classical. And in his first extended twelve-tone work for full orchestra, the Orchestral Variations (1926–28), he demonstrated a musical ingenuity reminiscent in its contrapuntal mastery of Bach's *Art of the Fugue;* indeed, as if in homage, Schoenberg quotes near the beginning of the piece the notes which are called in German by the letters of Bach's name.

The last years of the 1920s were to see only one more major work from Schoenberg—an opera *Heute auf Morgen* ("From Today to Tomorrow"), a topical lighthearted spoof of contemporary notions of marriage—before he undertook what was perhaps his most significant project, the quasi-biblical opera *Moses and Aaron* (1930–32).

Moses and Aaron represents the high point of Schoenberg's lifelong concern with the problem of Jewishness. Born into an assimilated Jewish family, he had had shown his inclination to religion by becoming a Protestant in his late teens. By the time he was forty, as his work on *Jakobsleiter* had suggested, he was growing more and more interested in religion and especially in prayer, and by the 1920s this concern had merged with his premonitions of the hellish torments in store for the Jewish people. An anti-Semitic incident at the beginning of his vacation in 1923 caused him to write his friend Kandinsky, in the course of turning down an invitation to teach at the *Bauhaus*, that in Germany the humanity of the Jews was being denied, and that he himself was unwilling to be one of the few Jews who because of intellectual distinction was tolerated. He was, he added, convinced that the Jewish people could "accomplish the task that their God has imposed on them! To survive in exile, uncorrupted and unbroken, until the hour of salvation comes!"

The first fruit of Schoenberg's thinking in this area was the play he wrote in 1927, *The Biblical Way*. The hero is a man named Max Aruns (i.e., Moses Aaron) who through personal force becomes the leader of a segment of the Jewish people and fails in his effort to establish a Jewish state because he fails to take the "biblical way" of complete reliance on the word of God. It was not a good play, but its main idea—the primary significance of man as the vehicle of God's word—was central to Schoenberg and was to achieve infinitely greater power and definition in the libretto he wrote for *Moses and Aaron* (first draft 1928).

In the opera, Moses is unable to communicate his knowledge

of the word of God; his stammer, a physical defect, exactly balances the people's spiritual weaknesses of superstition and susceptibility to magic. Thus Moses must depend on Aaron's corrupt version of the truth as a means of reaching the people. The climax of the second act, the Dance around the Golden Calf, is a victory for Aaron and a defeat for Moses. At the end of this act, Moses sinks to the ground exhausted saying, "O word, thou word that I lack." Schoenberg's music goes only as far as this point, but in the libretto for the third and final act (which Schoenberg did complete) Moses, having had Aaron arrested and bound, accuses him of betraying the idea of the one God and extends his charge to the people of Israel:

Whensoever you went forth amongst the people and employed those
    gifts—
which you were chosen to possess
so that you could fight for the divine idea—
whensoever you employed those gifts for false and negative ends
that you might rival and share the lowly pleasures of strange peoples,
and whensoever you had abandoned the wasteland's renunciation
and your gifts had led you to the highest summit,
then as a result of that misuse you were ever hurled back into the waste-
    land.

The last lines of the libretto belong to Moses and are addressed again to the people of Israel:

But in the wasteland you are invincible and you shall achieve the goal:
unity with God.

What Schoenberg does here is to present the conflict between Moses and Aaron as the essential battle which must be fought in every soul and at every time between the abstract and the concrete, between the eternal and the temporal, between God's word and man's words, and between God as an unimaginable idea and God as an all-too-palpable idol. To call this a dialectical battle which, properly approached, issues forth in a higher synthesis, as is so fashionable nowadays, is to ignore the fact that for

Schoenberg, no less than for the Bible, one side—Moses—is right.

There can be no doubt that *Moses and Aaron* occupies a central position in Schoenberg's *oeuvre*. What remains unclear is whether that centrality is due to its stature as opera, as music, or as ethical and philosophical tract. The received opinion, I think, is plain. For example, for both the literary critic George Steiner and the historian of twentieth-century music Karl Wörner, the music is primary. Steiner, after remarking on the importance of the work in the history of music, the theater, theology, and the relationship between Judaism and the European crisis, writes: "These aspects do not define or in any way exhaust the meaning of the work; that meaning is fundamentally musical." And Wörner rather more cautiously writes:

Schoenberg's text should not be judged by literary standards alone. The actions and the words are intended as a basis for music . . . like Richard Wagner, [Schoenberg] wrote poetry for music. . . . The musical conception follows the words, shaping them into musical structures . . . while retaining their spiritual significance, the words are dissolved in the higher amalgam of musical form. The higher unity permits no separation or isolation of single elements. Here words and music must always be appreciated as a synthesis.

What Steiner and Wörner seem to be saying is that in this work, while the words and the music are equal, the music is more equal than the words. Though this formulation is infinitely consoling to intellectuals more comfortable worshipping art than God, it fails to take into account the actual character and quality of *Moses and Aaron*, and still more important, the internal evidence of the opera itself.

For all the wizardry Schoenberg shows in organizing, complicating, and scoring his musical material, little about the music (always excepting the initial decision to have Aaron sing while Moses speaks in *Sprechstimme*) is in itself memorable or significantly adds to, goes beyond, or deepens the opera's words or ideas. In hearing the opera we remember the story, the characters, and the idea easily, but the music remains only an accompaniment, a background to the drama of ideas. To talk of this phenomenon as a "higher unity," as Wörner does, is to make an *ad hoc* argument, valuable in this case only—for no operatic masterpiece comes to mind in which the characters and the ideas so overpower the music; it is only here that the music cannot really take care of itself.

The internal evidence of *Moses and Aaron* supports much the same point. Schoenberg's inability to supply the music for the final act, though he had already written the words and though he lived for almost two decades after finishing the music for the second act, is an overwhelming indication of the relative weights in his mind of his music and his words. It is likely that his inability to finish the music was presaged in his decision that Moses (except for one short optional passage) would speak in harsh and unyielding accents while Aaron sings in seductive and mellifluous tones. This decision was of immense importance, for it meant that no one could miss the difference between the stark word of God spoken by Moses and the temptations sung by Aaron. The second act, which culminates in a victory for Aaron and a defeat for Moses, can only be an incomplete ending, given the context of Schoenberg's thought. For the presentation of the opera to stop here—as it does on the available recordings and generally also in live performance—is to be false to everything we know of Schoenberg's thought.

The third act fully represents Schoenberg's thought, for it gives the triumph to Moses and through him, the word. The message is plain. Moses's word has driven out Aaron's music. In the end the word of God, not the music of man, must be seen to prevail. It is of course quite possible Schoenberg hoped that he might find some way of reconciling this antinomy. Perhaps that is the meaning of his direction in the score that Moses *may* sing rather than speak the lines

> Purify your thinking
> Free it from worthless things
> Let it be righteous

—perhaps he had it somewhere in mind to put in melody some or all of Moses's final words about the destiny of Israel. This we can probably never know. What we do know is that Schoenberg could not or would not find the music for Moses's triumph, and as a result we are inescapably left with the primacy of the word amid the impotence of music.

As Schoenberg stopped work on *Moses and Aaron,* Hitler was coming to power. One of Schoenberg's first acts in response to this event was publicly to rejoin the Jewish religion and the Jewish community in a private but publicized ceremony in a Paris synagogue in July 1933. He was now an exile from Germany, and soon to be one from Europe. The rest of his life was lived out as a witness to the downfall of the civilization—and the musical tradition—he had so labored to continue. He emigrated to America, he composed, he taught, he sickened, and in 1951 he died.

The pieces he wrote in the United States in the last seventeen years of his life remain of interest, if only in the context of his entire career. They include the Violin Concerto (1934–36), the String Quartet No. 4 (1936), the Piano Concerto (1942), the String Trio (1946), and his last major composition, the Fantasy for Violin and Piano (1949). In addition, during this period he wrote several works set to texts which had great personal significance for him—the *Kol Nidre* (1938), Byron's *Ode to Napoleon* (1942), and his own text, *A Survivor from Warsaw* (1947).

These pieces of Schoenberg's American period do not follow an orderly line of development. They occupy several categories: some of them are rigorously serial in construction; some of them use twelve-tone procedures in such a way that tonality is often suggested; and finally a third category—including the Suite for string orchestra (1934), the Variations for organ (1941), and the 1942 Theme and Variations for wind band (also version for orchestra)—obviously aims at a more playable and listenable style. It is distressing, however, that whatever the stylistic approach, the verbal content or lack of one, or the general level of complexity of any of these pieces, the fate of all has been similar. They are admired from a musical distance not only by audiences but also by most musicians, they are either unheard or, once having been heard, are relegated to the area of virtuous tasks once performed, sufficiently performed.

The music written in the few years immediately before Schoenberg's death includes one other important category—that of three choral pieces on religious subjects set to biblical or quasi-biblical texts. The first of these is an *a capella* setting of Dagobert Runes's poem, "Three Times a Thousand Years," a work dealing with the destruction of the Temple and its presence in the memory of the Jewish people. The second is a six-part Hebrew setting of Psalm 130, "Out of the Depths." The third, and his last, though uncompleted, composition, is a setting of one of a series of meditations he had begun to write in 1950 and had originally called *Modern Psalms,* the title under which they were posthumously published against Schoenberg's wishes. It is to these words that the very last notes of music he wrote before his death were set:

O thou my lord, all people praise thee and assure thee of their faithfulness.
But what can it mean to thee whether or not I do the same?
Who am I that I should believe my prayer to be of necessity?
And yet I pray to thee, as everyone living prays, and yet I request mercy and miracles: fulfillment.
And yet I pray to thee. . . .

Since his death, the triumph of Schoenberg's reputation has become increasingly complete. To the numerous faithful students he taught during his lifetime—Alban Berg and Anton Webern being of course the most prominent—have been added posthumous (though partial) converts, Igor Stravinsky and Aaron Copland. Every tribute which scholarship can pay to genius has been paid; articles, archives, and anniversary observances abound. Almost all of his works have been recorded, the eight-volume set on Columbia Records being due, it is said, to the support of Stravinsky awakened by Robert Craft. The expanded English edition of his selected writings, *Style and Idea,* has now been published in this country at an outrageous price and in a large format suitable more to public reading on devotional occasions than to study by individuals with normal eyesight. But a nagging question remains: what is the place of the music around which all this activity centers?

It is clear that Schoenberg's music no longer scandalizes. The opposition he encountered—and from the time of his earliest major works it was fierce—has been assimilated into the twentieth-century history of that kind of resistance to the new which ends up sanctifying what it once hated. Schoenberg's dissonances no longer shock; the texts of his expressionist period are no longer considered depraved. Enough time has passed since the high period of Schoenberg's notoriety to provide us with both the distance and the material for an informed and dispassionate verdict on the present place of his music.

That verdict, for now at least, seems unavoidable. It is that Schoenberg's music, though it attracts the highest respect for its interest, craftsmanship, and nobility of purpose, has failed to compel immersion in its beauty. It will immediately be objected that this is a judgment not of the music, but of the audience, and of the performing musicians and critics responsible for providing the audience with enlightened leadership. There is some truth in this objection. Even sympathetic audiences generally know little about Schoenberg's pieces, about the wider area of contemporary music of which they are so central a part, or about the music of the nineteenth-century tradition out of which Schoenberg felt himself to be writing. Performances of Schoenberg in the concert hall—as well as on records—represent more often than not precisely that kind of dry, uninvolved, only technically adequate effort which is, alas, the hallmark of modern music performance. And critics writing about Schoenberg have frequently seemed more eager to display their learning and their labor than to communicate the power they must see in the music.

Yet it is in the end unfair to blame others for the failure of Schoenberg's music to be perceived as beautiful. The mark of great music is that it conquers all before it, performers, critics, and audience alike. It is, after all, hardly accidental that the word ravishing is so often used to describe the highest beauty.

Reluctant as one is to say so, then, the responsibility must lie in Schoenberg's music itself. In speculating on what may have gone wrong, one is led to observe that throughout his compositional career, Schoenberg's works were associated to a unique extent with ideas from outside the world of music itself. Not only were a large proportion of his pieces settings of texts rather than being purely instrumental; these texts were themselves often of the greatest power and resonance, in contrast to the sentimental literary clichés with which Schubert was so often associated, or they were highly controversial, as against the commonly accepted religious and cultural assumptions of the entire society which occupied Bach.

Weighing heavily upon Schoenberg, whether he was fully conscious of it or not, were the teachings of Moses, Herzl, and Freud. He was, for all his ultimate commitment to Jewishness, badly torn between Judaism and Christianity—one of his *Modern Psalms* is concerned with the failure of the Jews adequately to recognize Jesus. He combined in himself the modern sense of art as unconscious process with the modern compulsion to achieve a rational understanding of that process; the twelve-tone method is both an attempt to codify the workings of his imagination and an attempt, perhaps reminiscent of Mendeleev's Periodic Table of the Elements, to predict, through the manipulation of symbols, an as-yet-undiscovered (musical) reality.

The cumulative effect of this constant involvement with ideas may have been to place upon the music a weight it could not carry, to inhibit Schoenberg in his writing and the audience in its hearing. To the influence of ideas upon music we owe some of the greatest masterpieces of the nineteenth century, including many of the most stirring works of Beethoven and all the later works of Wagner. But in the twentieth century the consequences, not just for Schoenberg, have been less happy. Music has become the handmaiden of politics, as in the Soviet case; or it has become the handmaiden of science and mathematics, as in the case of electronic music; or it has become the handmaiden of the theater, as with the overwhelming majority of contemporary operas. Music has made a Faustian bargain, in which autonomy has been given up in return for inspiration coming from outside the realm of music itself.

But if, in Schoenberg's case, the role of their inspiring ideas has been to diminish the musical works, at the same time these very ideas may well guarantee Schoenberg's music its future place. It is not only that the pieces themselves, in their richness of musical material, in the complexity of their construction, in their high seriousness, will always attract the attention of the most gifted musicians; as long as the ideas with which Schoenberg was so deeply involved remain central in our sensibilities, the music which clothes those ideas will remain alive. And perhaps someday—predictions in this area are not worth making—his music will come fully into its own. He always thought it would. Schoenberg did, after all, identify strongly with Moses.

4

The Stature of Stravinsky

LESS THAN a decade after Igor Stravinsky's death in 1971, just two months short of his eighty-ninth birthday, the essential verdict on his music is in. That verdict, arrived at, as always, by audiences and performers alike, is really no different from the consensus about Stravinsky which had been developing for a half-century. Three pieces of his first maturity—the famous Diaghilev ballets written before the composer had passed thirty—have become components of the familiar repertory the world over; the music of his middle age is fairly widely performed, and found interesting by the intellectually cultivated but cold by the musically more enthusiastic; the work of his old age is almost unplayed except at ceremonial occasions in honor of the composer or at performances of modern music and ballet.

And yet, despite this longstanding and widespread judgment of his stature—a judgment which is, to say the least, a highly qualified one—during his lifetime, Stravinsky enjoyed a greater degree of celebrity and adulation than any other serious composer in our century, tremendous financial success, and the continual high regard of both music lovers and professionals. What was said about Stravinsky at his death had already been said many times before—that in him one saw the profession of master musician at its highest, in him one saw the rare intersection of talent, longevity, and well-deserved honors.

The extraordinary literary interest which Stravinsky evoked in the years close to the end of his life was symptomatic of the general view. Not only was he the admired subject of musical journalism, but he himself emerged as an author of repute. Beginning in 1959 and continuing for ten years, a series of books—six in the United States—appeared, containing his thoughts, table talk, obiter dicta, musical explications, and recollections of youth. The man portrayed through the medium of these hundreds of thousands of words is bright, witty, intellectually informed, waspish, nostalgic, unforgiving, even at times sentimental. Altogether, the books are both a tribute to the wisdom of old age and a remarkable example of a genius retaining his faculties intact long past the age when others are dead or senile.

These books, however, are not the work of the composer alone, nor were they ever claimed to be. They were co-authored by Stravinsky's constant companion since 1948, the American musician and writer Robert Craft. Indeed, the second half of each of the last three books to appear in American editions consists of diaries kept by the younger man during his association with the master; these diaries, amplified and with added material describing Stravinsky's very last years and death, appeared in 1972 under Craft's name with the title *Stravinsky: Chronicle of a Friendship 1948/1971*. What the composer came to mean to the young musician as employer, patron, tyrant, friend, and surrogate father is movingly described, and the cumulative effect of these accounts of prosperity and decline approaches the power of imaginative literature.

But history being the cruel selector it is, attention has inevitably come to be focused less on what Stravinsky meant to Craft than on what Craft may have meant to Stravinsky. From musical secretary and youthful presence, Craft became by an insensible progress both a ghost-writer and a performing collaborator who would prepare the orchestra and conduct part of the program during Stravinsky's increasingly frequent and profitable appearances. More and more he appeared as Stravinsky's spokesman, and toward the end he himself became a kind of public substitute for Stravinsky, conducting his works on recordings described (not always accurately) as having been made in the composer's presence and under his supervision. At Stravinsky's funeral in Venice, Craft was, next to the composer's wife, perhaps the chief mourner. Since then, he has become the louring presence of Stravinsky scholarship, with access, one assumes, to the material he knows better than anyone else.

The results of Craft's work are visible not only in the diaries but also in the range and breadth, the wit and energy, of those parts of the books cosigned by Stravinsky. The portrait of the artist presented by these productions is so captivating that perhaps only an exceptionally trusting reader could ever have fully believed they were true collaborations. In any case, what seemed doubtful to some on the basis at least of Stravinsky's creaky English and deteriorating health, and what had become the subject of much gossip in the music business, became a matter of open discussion in May 1969, when Donal Henahan published a famous noninterview with the composer in the New York *Times.* While Craft conducted the interview, the almost-eighty-seven-year-old composer sat silent, hunched, abstracted from the proceedings, seemingly immersed in some music he was writing. The general impression was of a man withdrawn forever into his own thoughts and beyond the capacity for verbal communication. Yet still the trenchant *morceaux* representing Stravinsky's very words continued to appear. The last may well have been an interview in the *New York Review of Books,* published after his death, in which Stravinsky discussed fluently—as late as four days before the end—his condition, medicine, music, and even life and death itself.

What can be said about the collaboration? According to Lillian Libman, who has described Stravinsky's last years from her standpoint as his secretary, business and household manager, and part-time companion, Craft had increasingly assumed an independent role in the relationship, and by the end the work was pure Craft, with Stravinsky only a passive and trapped onlooker, able, at most, to give approval to what was being done in his name. Her charges have in general been denied by Craft, who in any case might understandably plead the necessity of keeping

Stravinsky alive and functioning. Not surprisingly, discussion about the authenticity of the material produced under the joint by-line of the two men goes on to this day.

This controversy would matter less, and indeed be restricted to the question of the composer's last years, were it not for the remarkable fact that Stravinsky's final literary collaboration was by no means his first. His two earlier books—the reserved and distant *Autobiography* (1935–36) and the Norton Lectures at Harvard, *Poetics of Music* (1939)—were also not solely Stravinsky's productions. By the testimony of the third of his books with Craft, his *"Autobiography* and *Poetics of Music* [were] both written through other people—Walter Nouvel and Roland-Manuel, respectively—[and] are much less like me, in all my faults, than my conversations; or so I think." Elsewhere he acknowledged the help of the music theorist Pierre Suvchinsky in drafting the Russian original of the *Poetics*.

All in all, then, the evidentiary value of Stravinsky's large literary output seems diminished. Any citation from it, no matter of how "authentic"-seeming a statement, will inevitably inspire the question: is this what Stravinsky himself thought? Thus, whatever the great cultural and musical interest of these writings, the only sure testimony to Stravinsky's achievement and significance must be founded upon a consideration of his work as a composer, rather than as a littérateur or guru.

As a musician, Igor Feodorovich Stravinsky was not the product of routine academic training. He was born in the small Russian summer resort of Oranienbaum in 1882, and though his social origins were of the gentry, his father was a well-known bass and one of Tchaikowsky's favorite performers. The young Igor was hardly precocious musically, and the piano lessons he took went reasonably well if not brilliantly. Under parental pressure he studied law at St. Petersburg University, but he seems to have had little taste for any life but that of music. On his own he began to study counterpoint when he was eighteen, and in 1902 he asked Rimsky-Korsakov—the father of a classmate at the university—for advice about his ambitions to be a composer.

Rimsky-Korsakov seems to have taken the neophyte seriously, and offered to work with him privately and without fee in harmony and counterpoint. He was to be Stravinsky's only real teacher.

There are few surviving juvenilia of Stravinsky in which we may observe the man prefigured in the child. An early piano sonata (1903–04) seemed lost, and the earliest works we have known are the song suite—to words by Pushkin—*Faun and Shepherdess* (1906) and the Symphony in E-flat (1905–07). Both these compositions, though graceful to perform and pleasant to hear, are derivative, reminding the listener by turns of Wagner, Tchaikowsky, Glazunov, Debussy, Richard Strauss, and, of course, Rimsky-Korsakov. Much the same can be said of the *Scherzo Faniastique* (1907–08).

But the lightning strike which was to change Stravinsky's life was now close at hand. It came at the first performance in June 1909 of his new and very short orchestral fantasy, *Fireworks*. In the audience—in addition to the conservative Glazunov, who remarked at the end, "no talent, only dissonance"—was the legendary Sergei Diaghilev, the larger-than-life impresario of all the arts and the founder of the Ballets Russes. Today, it is possible to see Diaghilev's achievement in bringing Russian culture into the European world through France as the cultural analogue of the Franco-Russian alliance; at the time, his role in making dance the vehicle for primitive art and advanced thought in music and painting seemed both revolutionary and original. Diaghilev invited Stravinsky, on the basis of *Fireworks*, to write for the Ballets Russes. The first real fruit of this engagement was the famous *Firebird* (1909–10). The premiere starred the great Karsavina, with scenario and choreography by Fokine, and costumes and scenery by Golovine and Bakst.

In many ways *Firebird* is atypical of the mature Stravinsky, for it bears a large resemblance to the gorgeous orientalism of the Russian national school of which Rimsky-Korsakov was the leader. For its major melodic material it relies on Russian folk song, and the entire effect is traditional rather than modern.

Never again was Stravinsky to write a piece so clearly a part of nineteenth-century romanticism.

While working on *Firebird*, Stravinsky had conceived the idea for a ballet based on a primitive sacrifice in pagan Russia, but before he got to work out this idea, he decided to write a musical portrait of an ugly and downcast puppet who is rejected in love and finally momentarily resurrected in spectral triumph. At the outset, Stravinsky envisioned what was soon to become *Petrushka* (1910–11) as a kind of *Konzertstück* for piano and orchestra, and in the completed version the piano remains highly important. Though folk song remains influential in *Petrushka*, the impression it made—and still makes—is that of modern, i.e., dissonantal music. Particularly striking is its use of bitonality, in this case through the superimposition of two different chords, C and F-sharp major. And here for the first time the rhythmic movement, in its aggressive variety and complexity, can be called Stravinskyan.

But of course it was the *Rite of Spring* (1911–13) that made Stravinsky a famous international composer. The story of its notorious premiere has often been told; indeed, as a tale of the violent encounter of the avant-garde with the reactionary forces of bourgeois philistinism it constitutes one of the central myths of modernism. Several reasons for the famous ruckus can be identified; the story—one of barbarous religious practice—was shocking in itself, and so too was Nijinsky's choreography, at once original, clumsy, and incompetent. What has remained in the collective mind of our age, however, is the impact of the music, starting with the almost shapeless folk tune played above the customary range of the solo bassoon to which it is assigned. And from start to finish the pulse, both irregular and savagely insistent, broke new ground in the use of rhythm as a central structural factor independent of the particular notes and sonorities which carry it.

After the first scandalous success of the *Rite of Spring*, Stravinsky—never one to overwork an artistic mine—returned to complete an opera, *The Nightingale*, which he had begun in 1908. The long interruption in his work on this opera resulted in a sizable stylistic discrepancy between the earlier and later sections, the products respectively of the pre- and post-*Rite* Stravinsky. In this connection it is significant that when the composer later (1917) came to make a concert suite out of the opera, he dropped the entire first act, which in its opening measures had contained an almost literal quotation from Debussy's *Clouds* (1893–99); this borrowing, along with the resemblance between the opening of the *Rite* and the introductory flute solo of Debussy's *Prelude to the Afternoon of a Faun* (1892–94), demonstrates something of the influence of Debussy on Stravinsky's development.

He now began to write a number of works quite different from the three Diaghilev ballets in their smallness of scale, dryness of timbre, clarity of texture, and seeming simplicity of ambition. Especially consequential were the Three Pieces for String Quartet (1914), which foreshadowed the lean Stravinsky of the 1920s and 1930s. To a large extent this new emphasis on self-limitation was encouraged by the dislocations attendant upon World War I. Stravinsky spent much of the war in Switzerland, where he no longer had access to the great platform of the Ballets Russes.

Exile from Russia did not at first alter his interest in folk subjects; *Reynard*, a ballet with singing, was written in 1915–16, but not performed until 1922; its intimacy and its brevity have not proved helpful in securing it wide performance. The same could not be said of another Russian-inspired work, *The Wedding* (1914–23). In a daring innovation it uses four pianos and a large percussion section to provide the background for song and dance settings of peasant marriage customs. The combination of dry timbres and exotic ruralism has proved piquant without being unsettling to audiences.

More important—because it showed the composer's interest in going beyond even a new-sounding nationalist music—was the *Soldier's Tale* (1918). Though originally based on a Russian folk tale, this story of a soldier who sells his soul (in the form of his violin) to the devil was purposely broadened by Stravinsky and his

French-Swiss librettist C. F. Ramuz to make it international in meaning. And its clean sound and brittle atmosphere, so appropriate to a composition written during wartime in a neutral country, pointed the way toward Stravinsky's new aesthetic, which was to remain in many ways essentially unchanged for the rest of his life.

It was now clear that the same *Rite of Spring* which had brought great fame to Stravinsky had also been the last of his sonic blockbusters. The dilemma which faced Stravinsky was sensitively perceived, more than fifty years after the fact, by the American critic and composer Virgil Thomson:

After giving to the world between 1909 and 1913 three proofs of colossally expanding power—*Firebird, Petrushka,* and the *Rite of Spring*—he found himself unable to expand farther. And since, like Picasso, he was still to go on living, and since he could not imagine living without making music, he too was faced with an unhappy choice. He could either make music out of his own past (which he disdained to do) or out of music's past (which he is still [1967] doing). For both men, when expansion ceased, working methods became their subject.

The earliest clear sign of Stravinsky's new preoccupation with an already established music was his reworking of the compositions of Pergolesi, in the ballet *Pulcinella* (1919–20). Once again Diaghilev played a role in the composer's creative process, this time by actually recommending Pergolesi as a subject for Stravinsky's efforts. The result is one of Stravinsky's most delightful and ingratiating works. In an illustration of the ability of the present to reconstruct the past, much of *Pulcinella*, which sounded harsh and artificial on its appearance, now seems the very model of proper Baroque performance practice.

For the next three decades Stravinsky continued his attentions to the past. His sympathies were by no means confined to the pre-Romantic ethos, despite the implications of the term "neoclassicism" which is usually applied to Stravinsky's borrowings. His *Symphonies of Wind Instruments* (1920) was dedicated to the memory of Debussy; the opera buffa *Mavra* (1921–22) was mod-

eled on the vocal styles of his Russian precursors Glinka, Dargo-
mijsky, and Tchaikowsky. The works for piano—the Concerto for
Piano and Wind Orchestra (1923–24), the Sonata (1924), and the
Serenade in A (1925)—showed a deep interest in the keyboard
music of Bach and Scarlatti and a particular fondness for imitating
on the modern piano the timbre, articulation, and dynamism of
the harpsichord.

Most unexpected, considering Stravinsky's very real reservations about the romantic afflatus of Tchaikowsky, was his adaptation of many little-known piano pieces and songs by that hero of
musical self-expression, and his combining them into a full-
length ballet, *The Fairy's Kiss* (1928). In this piece, the identification with the spirit of Tchaikowsky is so complete that it is often
difficult to tell where the original leaves off and Stravinsky
begins.

His creative emulations were not limited to musical models. In
Oedipus Rex (1926–27), Stravinsky decided upon Latin for the
text of a large-scale dramatic work, because Latin was a language
partially ossified and associated as well with dogmatic religion.
Greek myth, sung in Latin, was yoked to a running commentary
in French, the whole written by the very modern and up-to-date
Jean Cocteau. This *aggiornamento* of the archaic Greek world
continued in one of Stravinsky's most lyrically beautiful pieces,
the ballet *Apollo Musagetes* (1927–28), and also in the less successful but equally attractive melodrama with song, narration,
and mime, *Persephone* (1933–34). At this time Stravinsky was involved, through his music, in the public proclamation of his deep
religious faith. His *Symphony of Psalms* (1930) was, in the words
of its dedication, "composed to the glory of GOD"; the three
psalms progress from fearful prayer to jubilation, and are expressed musically by modal harmony, a Bach-style double fugue
in the second movement, and a final radiant C-major chord.

Although the Violin Concerto (1931) is not easily traced to an
original, it was strikingly influenced by his own *Capriccio*
(1928–29) for piano and orchestra, itself a tribute to the pianistic
display of works by Weber and Mendelssohn. One of Stravinsky's
most influential and formally strongest works, the Concerto for

Two Solo Pianos (1931–35), combines melody and energy in the first movement while the second movement is a strongly Italianate *Notturno*, the third is a set of four variations, and the finale is a powerful fugue which appears at the end in an inverted form reminiscent of the close of Beethoven's Sonata in A-flat, opus 110.

The buildup of political and military tensions in the years immediately prior to the outbreak of war in 1939 seems hardly to have found expression in Stravinsky's music. The happy and light ballet *Game of Cards* (1936)—recorded by Stravinsky with the Berlin Philharmonic in 1938, the same year his music was condemned by the Nazis as degenerate art—is the story of a poker game, with the characters the important cards in the deck; the music sparkles with allusions to such composers as Rossini, Delibes, and again Tchaikowsky. The *Dumbarton Oaks Concerto* (1937–38), written, as was *Apollo Musagetes*, for an American commission, was described by the composer as "a little concerto in the style of the *Brandenburg Concertos.*" The *Symphony in C* (1938–40) commemorated the fiftieth anniversary of the Chicago Symphony; it too is optimistic, despite the almost concurrent deaths of Stravinsky's first wife, mother, and one of his daughters, and his forced exile from Europe in 1939.

Stravinsky's wartime pieces, written during the first years of his residence in Hollywood, present a picture of a lion trying to tame himself. He turned his hand abortively to movie music, including a film on the Nazi invasion of Norway and Franz Werfel's *The Song of Bernadette*. Neither project worked out; but some of the music was eventually used—the sketches for the film on Norway ended up as part of the *Four Norwegian Moods* (1942), and the *Bernadette* music saw the light of day in the *Symphony in Three Movements* (1942–45). Several works were written to improbable commissions; among these, the *Circus Polka* (1942), to be danced by elephants, was supplied for the Barnum and Bailey Circus, while *Babel* (1944) was paid for by the Hollywood composer and publisher Nathaniel Shilkret as part of a biblical suite by various hands, including Arnold Schoenberg and Darius Milhaud, with ideas (never realized) for other sections from Béla Bartók, Paul Hindemith, and Sergei Prokofiev.

About this time, Stravinsky once again became interested in jazz (he had earlier, in 1918 and 1919, written piano pieces based on ragtime, whose influence may also be noticed in the Piano and Wind Concerto); the *Ebony Concerto* (1945) was written for the Woody Herman Band. The *Concerto in D* (1946), dedicated to Paul Sacher's Basle Chamber Orchestra, marked Stravinsky's return to the European musical world. Lincoln Kirstein commissioned another ballet on a Greek theme, *Orpheus* (1947). And Stravinsky wrote a *Mass* (1944–48), not for the Russian Orthodox Church of his boyhood, but in Latin for liturgical use in the Roman Catholic rite. However much these pieces vary from one to another, and however imbued they all are with Stravinsky's typical freshness and life, they are little different in styles, scope, and musical purpose from the work he had been doing since the *Rite of Spring* thirty-five years earlier.

To summarize this long period of neoclassicism, one final work remained to be written. Into it went so much talent, effort, and even genius—and not from Stravinsky alone—that it seems a pity the resulting composition constitutes but one more sacrifice on the altar of the mythical great modern opera. *The Rake's Progress,* based on scenes from Hogarth paintings and written to a libretto by W. H. Auden and Chester Kallman, occupied Stravinsky from 1947 to 1951. In style it draws constantly on the formal devices of traditional non-Wagnerian opera, such as aria, recitative, chorus, and ensembles. It is also a conscious pastiche of the manner of several famous operatic composers, among whom Mozart, particularly in his *Don Giovanni*, occupies pride of place.

The libretto, though distinguished by much beautiful poetic writing by Auden and Kallman, suffers from pasteboard characters and an inconsistency between the setting—eighteenth-century England—and the authors' evident desire to incorporate elements of late 1940s existentialist philosophy. The resultant failure to integrate farcical and tragic elements is hardly unique in the history of opera; in this case, it is accompanied by a parallel unsureness in the music—a mixing of styles and an inability to write a music strong and compelling enough to convince an audience that the characters and their situations deserve attention.

Stravinsky's immediately subsequent compositions, the Cantata (1951–52) and the Septet (1952–53), both demonstrate a new concern with contrapuntal complexity. The Septet is particularly important for the composer's use of tone rows—although he employs them tonally rather than atonally. This practice was continued in several following works, among them the *In Memoriam Dylan Thomas* (1954) and *Canticum sacrum* (1955). These compositions illustrate Stravinsky's continuing drift to the serialism of the second Viennese school associated with the names of Schoenberg, Berg, and Webern, to which he had been introduced by Robert Craft. They illustrate as well his growing preoccupation with the subject matter of funerary observance and religiosity.

The ballet *Agon* (1953–57), based on a seventeenth-century French description of dances from the courts of Louis XIII and Louis XIV, shows Stravinsky poised between serial and nonserial writing, while the work's connection with Stravinsky's neoclassical past may be seen not only in its echoes of old dance forms but also in the Greek title. With his next work, *Threni* (1958)—a setting of the Lamentations of Jeremiah—Stravinsky at last wrote a fully twelve-tone composition. Remarkable for the work of a man so old in years is the size of the canvas on which the music is written, and the concentration and organization lavished on it. After *Threni* came *Movements* (1958–59); along with the later orchestral Variations (1963–64), this music marked Stravinsky's closest approach to the work of Webern, which in particular he had discovered through the good offices of Craft.

It is significant that the sparseness of texture typical of Webern seems more noticeable in Stravinsky's orchestral works, rather than in those compositions where the presence of a text and of the human voice demanded a more emotional musical expression. And even in his most "advanced" works he does not venture very far into the hothouse chromaticism of the atonal music produced by Schoenberg and his followers. Instead, he stays well within his own brand of diatonicism—a kind of partiality stemming originally perhaps from the regular arrangement of the keys of the piano, upon which he liked to compose, and which served him for his whole composing life.

The remaining memorials and works on religious subjects included tributes to Raoul Dufy, John F. Kennedy, and T. S. Eliot, as well as his last major composition, the *Requiem Canticles* (1965–66). Two years earlier he had completed a cantata, *Abraham and Isaac* (1962–63), a setting of biblical texts in Hebrew and dedicated to the people of the state of Israel; this work seems scanty and perhaps flagging in vitality. But it is otherwise with the unjustly maligned *Flood* (1961–62), choreographed by Stravinsky's long-time friend, collaborator, and exponent, George Balanchine—an attempt to write a work conceived in terms of television, to unite music and dance for the age of electronic technology, much as Stravinsky and Diaghilev had done for the early modern era. The attempt failed, due to a not unsurprising combination of oversell, commercial exigencies, and the limitations of television both in production and in home reception. But the music remains beautiful and clearly one of Stravinsky's great achievements. The aural impression is one of harmonic richness and expansiveness, notwithstanding the work's serial construction; it is altogether a convincing refutation of the accusation of unfeelingness that is so often leveled at Stravinsky.

His last musical activities, like so much of what he did during his last half-century, involved the recomposition of the music of others. These tasks were understandably only a pale echo of his earlier reworkings of the past. Only ten years before, again as a result of Craft's influence, he had become interested in the eccentric sixteenth-century polyphonic composer Gesualdo; he recomposed three madrigals for instruments, and part of this music, strangely romantic in sound, has been used by the New York City Ballet. His final published work seems to be an orchestration of two Hugo Wolf songs, and close to the end he was somehow working on some pieces from Bach's *Well-Tempered Clavier*.

No discussion of Stravinsky as a musician would be complete without some mention of his activities as a performer. In addition to the piano career he so assiduously followed in the 1920s and 1930s, he became with increasing frequency a conductor of his own works, performing them across America and—after the arrival of Robert Craft (and thanks to the managerial energy and ingenuity of Lillian Libman)—the world over.

Through his exclusive recording contract with Columbia Records, Stravinsky was able to compile a unique phonographic documentation of his preferred performance style. He himself expressed little but disdain for the tribe of star performers, reserving a special scorn for virtuoso conductors—whom in his books he accused of distorting and perverting his music in order to express themselves. If one bears in mind that in the last decade of his career much of the orchestral preparation was done by Craft, his own conducting on records is straightforward, unsentimental, rhythmically alive without being either rigid or hasty.

It is remarkable how Stravinsky's *oeuvre,* over all of his long music-writing life and with all of its different styles, remains a coherent entity distinguishable from the work of others in character and aesthetic quality. His absolute mastery is never in doubt, and neither is his ability to write music at all times conceived in terms of a sophisticated audience whose reactions he shrewdly knows and basically respects. Yet one cannot always avoid the disturbing impression that only part of his overall musical character is defined by the virtues of clarity, elegance, and vitality; some other part of it may well lie in his daring use of so many other people's work, and his appropriation of that work with so little violence to its creators. Seen in this way, his final apparent commitment to serialism constitutes less a conversion than merely one more way in which Stravinsky could be himself.

Yet what this self was, what Stravinsky's aesthetic purposes and motives really were, remains unclear today. In the passage quoted above, Virgil Thomson suggests that Stravinsky appropriated the music of others as a rational and even courageous solution to the failure of his own originality to develop. But such an explanation would not appear to take adequately into account the immense role of others, running from Rimsky-Korsakov through Debussy and Diaghilev, in the genesis of just those works which Thomson sees as proof of Stravinsky's expanding powers in his earlier years.

Another theory often advanced to explain Stravinsky as an artist applies as well to the whole modernist enterprise; this theory downplays the revolutionary and radically transforming side of modernism in favor of a view which places at least equal emphasis on the traditional and conservative impulses within the movement. It has been well stated by George Steiner, in *After Babel* (1975):

We know now that the modernist movement which dominated art, music, letters during the first half of the century was, at critical points, a strategy of conservation, of custodianship. Stravinsky's genius developed through phases of recapitulation. . . . In each instance the listener was meant to recognize the source, to grasp the intent of a transformation which left salient points of the original intact. . . . [Here as elsewhere] the apparent iconoclasts have turned out to be more or less anguished custodians racing through the museum of civilization, seeking order and sanctuary for its treasures, before closing time.

But this passage is more in the nature of a moving evaluation of our age than a real tribute to an immortal artist. Whatever the value of conservation in an age of dissolution, a high artistic price has to be paid by the conservators. That price, the penalty assessed for lack of originality, is the inevitable separation between an artist's self and the core of his art.

In the case of Stravinsky, this separation is expressed by the tendency of his music not to stick very well in one's mind. When one thinks of Stravinsky's compositions one sees yards and yards of excellent music, but that music is all too often attractive rather than memorable, a compilation rather than a creation, a musical individuality defined by its impersonality.

Not only Stravinsky, in our century, has modeled his music on the work of past masters. This trend is widespread among contemporary composers. But what makes Stravinsky special is the openness of his borrowing and the panache with which his actions have been defended. Other composers of less celebrated distinction, though they have borrowed from many—and not least from Stravinsky—have been rather more reticent and have given the impression of unconscious assimilation of a musical ethos rather than conscious appropriation. And it is unclear that this more muted process has been any the less effective in preserving the traditions of the past.

To find the secret of Stravinsky's great career and influence, one must go beyond his musical achievement, to the enduring image he represents of the artist as a central figure in the cultural life of the age, as a unifier of the arts. This image is not one that he himself invented, of course. In music it originated perhaps in the fantastic career of Richard Wagner, who convinced all of cultured Europe that through opera he had made all the arts one. In his own way, Stravinsky (following Diaghilev's lead) accomplished a similar feat in ballet. And in later years he was to serve as a symbol of that unification by composing music to texts by such central modern writers as Gide and Auden, and by having his likeness made by Bonnard, Chagall, Giacometti, Klee, Modigliani, and Picasso.

Stravinsky's image as a central and unifying figure in the culture as a whole slipped somewhat with his return to religion at the end of the 1920s, and it suffered badly through his separation from European intellectual life in the early years of his American exile. But it was restored in the 1950s and especially in the 1960s by the efforts of Robert Craft. Craft's achievement was simultaneously to bring Stravinsky up to date with the cultural and social world of the Kennedy years and to proclaim the continued vigor and artistic growth of a man in his eighties. By his intellectual and musical services to Stravinsky, Craft kept him alive in both public and personal terms.

In one of the several Stravinsky "interviews" dealing with his illnesses, a passage returning to the consideration of music is headed by the epigraph, *"Neue Kraft fühlend"* (feeling new strength), taken from the illness-inspired slow movement of Beethoven's Quartet opus 132; the pun seems fully justified. Craft has been belabored for having created a false Stravinsky, but perhaps he should be credited with a work of fulfillment. By his literary efforts in the books cosigned by him, and by his activities as social quartermaster for Stravinsky the celebrity, Craft brought to completion in Stravinsky that which his music alone is unable to supply—the total personality which does, in fact, stick in one's mind. Yet the final achievement will always be seen as Stravinsky's. For if, in his dependence upon others, Igor Stravinsky was a puppet, he was that rare puppet who chooses his own masters.

5

Copland as American Composer

HOUGH Aaron Copland has been an important figure in serious music for more than fifty years, he has remained, as Leonard Bernstein has said, "the best we have," and his career is the very model of the success to which an American composer may aspire.

Copland was born in Brooklyn in 1900 to Russian Jewish immigrant parents originally named Kaplan. In an autobiographical sketch dating from 1939, Copland seemed at some pains to present himself as his own creation rather than as the product of a milieu:

I was born on a street in Brooklyn that can only be described as drab. . . . I am filled with mild wonder each time I realize that a musician was born on that street. . . . In fact no one had ever connected music with my family or with my street. The idea was entirely original with me.

But there was, by his own witness, music in his house. His four older siblings took music lessons, though evidently without achieving excellence. And so the thirteen-year-old Aaron talked his parents into providing piano lessons. By fifteen he had conceived the idea of becoming a composer; two years later, in 1917, he began harmony lessons with Rubin Goldmark, a student of Dvořák and later head of the composition department at the Juilliard Graduate School, the predecessor of the present Juilliard.

Upon graduation from high school in 1918 Copland decided to devote his life to music. He continued his piano studies, working with Clarence Adler and Victor Wittgenstein. Soon he also began to compose in earnest, and these youthful pieces brought him into conflict with the academic conservatism of Goldmark, who had no sympathy for what he saw as Copland's "modernistic experiments." Finding the going without much honor at home, the young musician turned his eyes to Europe: not the Europe of his parents, but the Europe of French sophistication, spiced with a dose of the Slavic primitivism so beguilingly administered at that time by Lenin's Bolshevik revolution and Diaghilev's Russian ballet.

In 1921, then, Copland went to Paris, where he found both the foreign root of one side of his musical development and his first recognition. The story of the numerous American expatriates in Paris during the interwar period is familiar enough; exiles to a warmer cultural clime, they all seemed happier among strangers. But Copland was different. He had the good sense and the guts to learn what he could—which was a lot—and then to come back home. In France, he also had the good fortune to fall in with Nadia Boulanger, the patron saint of so many American composers of that time, including—in addition to Copland—Roy Harris, Virgil Thomson, and Walter Piston.

Still alive in the late 1970s, Boulanger embodied a unique amalgam of Fauré and Stravinsky, of French academicism and the prerevolutionary Russian avant-garde. She trained Copland in strict counterpoint and the other technical disciplines for which French musical education is famous, and she provided him with an environment in which he could discover the international world of musical modernism, of Stravinsky and Schoenberg, of Milhaud and Honegger, of Prokofiev and Bartók. She early saw Copland's promise, and arranged for the first real performances of his music in Paris; the response to these performances was greatly encouraging.

Still more important, Boulanger gave Copland his first boost back on home soil. She asked him to write a composition for organ and orchestra which she could perform in 1925 in her American appearances with Walter Damrosch and the New York Symphony and Serge Koussevitzky and the Boston Symphony Orchestra. The appearance with Damrosch was less than success-ful; at the end of the performance Damrosch turned to the audi-ence and said: "If a young man at the age of twenty-three can write a symphony like that, in five years he will be ready to com-mit murder." But in Boston the story was different. In Kous-sevitzky, just arrived in Boston from Russia by way of Paris, Copland found his first American-based champion. For Copland, this meant performances, and the best ones at that.

By the winter of 1924–25, Copland had thus been away, had come home, and had been performed under major auspices in perhaps the two most important centers of American musical life. And for all the influences of European and French musical life, he had returned to the United States filled with the conscious desire to become an American composer who composed Ameri-can music.

At first this meant for Copland the writing of pieces influenced by jazz. *Music for the Theater* (1925), the Concerto for Piano and Orchestra (1926), and the *Symphonic Ode* (1928–29): these jazz works represented Copland's first attempt to write a music of what he has called "conscious Americanism." But he was soon to find that jazz was both too limited in itself and too limiting to his work as a serious composer. He then abandoned the style of jazz, though not its feature of rhythmic freedom or some of its spirit, and in 1930 wrote the piece which established him as an influ-ence on American music.

The Piano Variations were not meant for a wide audience. First performed by the composer at a concert of the League of Composers in New York in 1931, they were short, dissonant, hard in sound, dry, and difficult. They shared certain features with Schoenbergian atonality, but where Schoenberg was pas-sionately warm, Copland was passionately cold; where Schoen-berg's writing was wilfully luxuriant, Copland's was painfully lean. With these Piano Variations he placed American music on one of the two tracks it was to follow for a generation, the evocation of steel girders and the skyscraper, of the world of the young industrial giant far removed from the European world of putatively effete passions and neurosis.

But it was also Copland who found the other track which American music was to follow in the years immediately ahead. If Copland's Piano Variations greatly influenced the most serious music, his pieces of the late 1930s provided a formative influence on American lighter classical music (though Virgil Thomson has claimed some priority for himself as an influence on Copland in this area). With *El Salón México* (1936), Copland began a search for a popular serious music, a style and content which, while employing the technics and some of the musical devices of modernism, would appeal to a "conventional concert-going public." His use in this composition of Mexican folk material associated in his mind with a well-known dance hall in Mexico City, Salón México, presaged his awakening interest in American folk music and the new kind of serious dance soon to be connected with the names of Lincoln Kirstein and Agnes de Mille.

From this new interest of Copland in folk music, dance, and a wider audience stem his three important repertory ballets: *Billy the Kid* (1938), *Rodeo* (1942), and *Appalachian Spring* (1944). These pieces make skillful use of Americana, including the cowboy song "Come wrangle yer bronco" and the Shaker tune " 'Tis the gift to be simple." In a somewhat similar vein is his movie music, most notably *Of Mice and Men* (1939), *Our Town* (1940), *North Star* (1943), and *The Red Pony* (1948). Another example of Copland's interest in a general audience was his writing of patriotic music. In this class are the *Lincoln Portrait* and the *Fanfare for the Common Man*, both completed in 1942.

Notwithstanding this opening to the masses, Copland resumed his interest in a more abstract music with the Piano Sonata (1941), the Sonata for Violin and Piano (1943), and the Third Symphony (1946). These lacked the extramusical associations of his "popular" music, and they have not been as widely played. After his tentative dip, soon abandoned, into atonal writing in the Piano Variations, his Quartet for Piano and Strings (1950) utilized the formal methods of serial construction while managing to sound quite like his non-twelve-tone music; his *Connotations*, written for the opening of Lincoln Center in 1962, continued his use of serialism, as did the later *Inscape* (1967). In the past few years, he seems to have composed little, confining himself to smaller-scale works. It is likely that, so far as major pieces are concerned, we are looking at a largely completed body of work.

No adequate summary of Copland's career could omit mention of his work as a performer of his own music as pianist and conductor both in concert and on Columbia recordings. His playing, on a piano of predominantly glassy sonority, has given pianists a clear aural image of what he as composer desires; his technical facility and rhythmic snap have been of great help in establishing the style in which his pieces are performed. As a conductor, however, he has been less successful in determining the way his works are performed by the famous conductors of our time.

But Copland's influence in music, though solidly based on his actual compositional achievement, goes far beyond the pieces he has written and their effect on the audience. From the time of his return to America in the 1920s, and as a teacher of composition at Tanglewood from 1940 to 1965, he has made it his business to befriend younger composers, to assist the performances of his contemporaries, and in general to be a stabilizing influence in the somewhat anarchic world of the creative musician. For a time he was perhaps our leading spokesman for serious music. He has given the Charles Eliot Norton Lectures at Harvard, later published as *Music and the Imagination* (1952); he has written an influential music-appreciation text, *What to Listen for in Music* (1939); and a history of modern music, *Our New Music* (1941; 1968 revised edition, *The New Music*); and his occasional writings have been collected in *Copland on Music* (1960). A fluent writer, he is by turns charming and reasonable.

But it is of course as a composer, regardless of the great energy he has lavished on so many related areas, that Copland's standing and relationship to our musical times must be judged. Too much has been made of the split between his serious and his more popular music, between his thorny, austere works and his lush, tuneful ballets and movie music. For whatever the audience to which he intends his music to appeal, his musical style remains individual and identifiable.

A great deal has been written in analysis of Copland's music. One of its most obvious characteristics—when one looks at it on the printed page or plays it—is its rhythmic variety and freedom. Frequent changes of time signature, many marked accents occurring off the main beats, many alterations of tempo make his music tricky to perform, requiring singers, instrumentalists, and conductors of strong nerves and secure rhythm. The effect on the listener of all this rhythmic complexity—even on the musician listener—is not always commensurate with the very real difficulty the music presents to the performer. For in Copland's music there is so much rhythmic variety and contrast that instead of rhythmic excitement one often gets an effect of rhythmic plainness. Perhaps also because of the fact that in his music, as in so much contemporary composition, the beginning of the bar is often determined more by notational convenience than by the demands of the music itself, the listener's expectations of rhythmic regularity are so consistently defeated that he sits back and takes everything rhythmically as it comes.

Copland's formal procedures, though musically solid, have broken little new ground. Rather than the traditional nineteenth-century development by expansion and growth, he has followed the widespread twentieth-century practice associated with the names of Schoenberg and Stravinsky, the device of separation of melodic and motivic material into parts which then are continuously reintegrated. His music is frequently marked by the use in fast passages of what Virgil Thomson has called "struggle-type counterpoint"; his employment of contrapuntal technique in quiet passages gives them an air of poignant tranquillity. His harmony, lean in his more abstract works, simple in his more popular works, often functions more as an accompaniment of the melody than as a feature of independent musical interest. Throughout his career he has been a brilliant orchestrator, showing a remarkable ear for orchestral balances and effects, and particularly adept at distributing the notes in chords in such a way that familiar harmonies sound fresh and dissonant harmonies sound clear.

Copland's real distinction is in the realm of melody. His specialty is long arching melodies of quiet intensity presented either unharmonized or against a slowly changing harmonic background. Whether the melodies are of his own invention or are of folk origin is not really important, for he has integrated what is his and what he has borrowed in a product entirely of his own making. In melody, perhaps more than in any other aspect of music, it is emotional effect, not exact authorship, that is important. Not only do Copland's tunes stick in the mind more than those of any of his contemporaries; they have the power to move audiences.

But Copland's true achievement lies not in his use of rhythm, harmony, counterpoint, or original musical structures; it lies in his ability, through the use of melody, to evoke a mood—the mood of America of the period from the Civil War to World War II. There is in this period of American life a combination of leanness and grandeur that Copland manages to capture. He does more: he catches the emptiness of the city and the quiet of the land. Having done all this, he has succeeded in fixing in the mind of a large public an aural image of what America, and therefore American music, sounds like. Copland sounds like American music, and music that is felt to be American sounds like Copland.

For Copland has managed to integrate his art and himself with his nation and his times. He would not have attained this integration without a passionate conviction that his country was worthy of proclamation, and that a composer like himself was capable of proclaiming it. He has, in other words, been the principal American representative of a long European (rather than American) tradition, the tradition of music as a symbol and expression of the national spirit, the composer as spokesman for the nation.

This kind of music, and the accompanying role for the composer, goes back to Weber's *Der Freischütz* (1821), the first implicitly nationalistic German musical work. The first explicitly nationalistic German opera was *Die Meistersinger* (1868), in which Wagner used not only a national story and a national locale but also at the end of the opera invoked the very name of the nation. But perhaps because in the German-speaking countries the tradition of absolute music had been so high in quality and so popularly successful, it was not in the German musical tradition that nationalism came to be most widely cultivated. For the greatest flowering of serious nationalistic music we must look to the countries of Eastern and Central Europe, Scandinavia, and Spain. Here great music was born of a condition in which the old order of state power, whether foreign or domestic, was on one side of the political and cultural fence, and the popular forces—represented by composers (as well as writers and painters)—on the other. Smetana, Dvořák, and Janáček in what is now Czechoslovakia; Glinka, Borodin, and Mussorgsky in Russia; Grieg and Sibelius in Scandinavia; Albeniz, Granados, and Falla in Spain: the works of all these composers stem from societies in a state of struggle, often with foreign overlords in a political sense, almost always with the pressure of foreign cultural influence hardened into academicism. Sometimes these composers chose national subjects; sometimes they directly quoted folk material; often they were content merely to evoke what they did not write about directly. But in every case their work was held high as the "true" music of the nation in contrast to the hated artificial product of foreign or cosmopolitan influence.

America came into the era of nationalistic musical culture late—not before the turn of the present century, at a time when the American nation was first beginning to see itself as having a mission outside its borders. The musical developments paralleled the political changes. Just as America was late in flexing its muscles in the world, so was it also late in developing any kind of competent professional musical environment, as such an environment was known in Europe. It was not until this century that

Americans became good enough to be participants—even at one remove—in European musical culture; American composers had previously not only been imitations of European masters, they had been poor imitations. It was not until Americans had won their spurs on the level of competence that they could set about the proper nationalist task of winning independence from European musical overlordship.

With Charles Ives, the battle was begun. But Ives's music, though deeply American in derivation, intention, and sound, was largely unperformed and unknown during the period of its writing—the first twenty years of this century—and for many years after. Because of its absence from the mainstream of musical life, Ives's work remained a beginning without possibility of a continuation. It was left to the young men of the 1920s—Virgil Thomson, Roy Harris, and Copland—to start the task from scratch. This they did, and with them a specifically American music first emerged into public notice. Although they were very late in coming—at least fifty years behind their colleagues in Europe— they were helped along by the atmosphere of the Popular Front of the 1930s—that curious alliance between populist nationalism and left-wing radicalism whose character was suggested with only a faint whiff of unintended irony by Earl Browder's famous formulation, "Communism is twentieth-century Americanism." Copland himself was deeply sympathetic to the politics of the Popular Front; and the political euphoria of those days almost certainly played a part in convincing Copland, as well as the others, that a mass audience did exist for the products of serious culture.

By the end of World War II they had each written pieces— Thomson's *Four Saints in Three Acts* (1928), *The Plough that Broke the Plains* (1936), and *The River* (1937); Harris's Symphony #3 (1938); Copland's Piano Variations (1930), *Billy the Kid* (1938), *Rodeo* (1942), and *Appalachian Spring* (1944)—which, taken together, established an independent American music, a music which was written to be American, and which was received as such by audiences. That Copland has overshadowed

Thomson and Harris in the public mind is a tribute to his wider scope, both emotional and musical. Leonard Bernstein was right. The story of Copland's music is the story of the best we in America have.

It is a story, however, that would seem to have come to an end. For nationalism in music has had its day. In Europe, nationalistic music flourished on the way up to nationhood; it was at its most alive during the fighting of the wider political, social, and cultural battles. When these battles were won—when nationhood and some semblance of stability had been reached—nationalistic music, if it was practiced at all, came to seem increasingly artificial and imposed. The most notorious example of such artificial imposition is of course the Soviet Union, where a strenuous attempt has been made for over forty years to force composers under the slogan "national in form, socialist in content" to act as if the nineteenth century in cultural history had never passed.

It is not simply that the larger goals of nationalism have been reached in the West, it is also that these goals have been overreached. The national and social units which have been achieved are proving too large and too indirect in their relationship to their members, too artificial in their supposed unity, to command assent. And so Western nationalism, which so recently seemed so successful, now suddenly seems senile. All over Europe, to many disaffected groups—whether the Basques or the Welsh, the Bretons or the Scots—the nation seems a lie; and once dominant groups are increasingly losing confidence in their own legitimacy. We in America, too, in our plenitude of power and luxury, seem to find nationalistic culture both superfluous and vulgar. Our most advanced intellectuals, when they are not busy promoting the old internationalism, urge on the new ethnicity. The attitude of our leading social classes is strongly against American nationalism in art no less than in politics. Only a lingering nostalgia for a simpler time keeps the memory of the old Americana even so much as faintly respectable.

Copland has himself written in his usual gentle and tolerant way of the sad outcome of his hopes for an American music. In reevaluating Roy Harris in 1967, Copland wrote:

In rereading my 1940 discussion of Roy Harris's music, I am suddenly aware of a curious dichotomy; Harris the composer has remained very much what he was, but the musical scene around him (and us) has radically altered. . . . My prognostication that the California composer was writing music on which "future American composers will build" now strikes me as downright naïve. I had completely lost sight of the fact that a new generation of composers, at a distance of thirty years, would have its own ideas about where a usable past might be found. As it turned out, the young men of this new crop show no signs of wishing to build on the work of the older American-born composers, the generation of the 20's and 30's. Today's gods live elsewhere.

And where do they live? Copland had seen the answer several years before:

. . . certain tendencies are discernible. The most striking one is the return, since 1950, to a preoccupation with the latest trends of European composition. This comes as a surprise, for, from the standpoint of their elders, it is retrogression because it places us in a provincial position vis-à-vis our European confrères. The older generation fought hard to free American composition from the domination of European models because that struggle was basic to the establishment of an American music. The young composers of today, on the other hand, seem to be fighting hard to stay abreast of a fast-moving post–World War II musical scene.

Copland's diagnosis seems even more applicable today, almost twenty years later. From Elliott Carter on the (musical) Right to John Cage and his followers on the (musical and political) Left, American music is now a branch of the world musical scene. Our composers have been as interested in post-Webern serialism, the music of chance, and up-to-date electronics as their European counterparts. If our leading composers are importantly creative (as Carter undeniably has been), it is as international figures, not as Americans. We may not quite be, as Copland has implied, once again a dependency of the Old World, but neither are we distinctive. We have come to the end of a chapter in American music, as we have come to the end of a chapter in our national life. In music, if nowhere else, internationalism has triumphed, and we are all homogenized. Whatever the future shape of American music, it will not follow in the directions toward which Aaron Copland's work once seemed to lead.

The Mahler Everyone Loves

USTAV MAHLER, it would seem, is our most successful twentieth-century composer. Despite the fact that the century is now almost eight decades old—and that Mahler died in 1911—his is still the newest name to penetrate the consciousness of both musicians and nonmusicians, of committed fans and casual concert-goers alike.

The frequency of concert performance of his music is itself impressive. In the number of times his works have been played by the New York Philharmonic, we are told, he shares third place with Tchaikowsky, behind only Beethoven and Brahms. Not too long ago, the New York Philharmonic spent the month of September at Carnegie Hall doing a Mahler Festival which included most of his compositions; and this itself was only a replay of the Bernstein-Mitropoulos Mahler celebration of 1960, which may be said to have made Mahler big time in the American musical world. And even in the Soviet Union, where Mahler's music had fallen under the Stalinist ban, by the 1960s no secret was being made of Dmitri Shostakovich's high regard for Mahler, and Yevgeny Svetlanov, the conductor of the State Symphony Orchestra of the USSR, could say: "I personally consider Mahler the greatest genius of all peoples and all times."

On records, the story is the same. Important conductors—among them Bernstein (Columbia), Bernard Haitink (Philips), Rafael Kubelik (Deutsche Grammophon), and Georg Solti (London)—have, by their complete sets of the Mahler symphonies, furthered their careers as such careers have always been furthered: by convincing audiences that they are hearing personal interpretations of vital and relevant music only recently come to public attention and recognition. As for recordings of the individual symphonies, one of the *least* popular—the Seventh—was recently available in no fewer than five separate stereo versions. Of the more popular works, the First and Fourth symphonies were available in thirteen performances each, and the Second in twelve. And in an attempt by a record manufacturer to serve an even larger market than is made up by the lovers of serious music, works of Mahler have been packaged on one of the releases in London's "Orphic Egg" series under the title "Mahler's Head," with liner notes by Dave Marsh, the editor of *Creem* magazine.

Not only is there a rush to perform those pieces of Mahler which are by now familiar, but his forgotten early works are exhumed, and one of them—his ballad *Das klagende Lied* ("The Wailing Song")—has been recorded for Columbia by no less a musical figure than Pierre Boulez. At the other end of Mahler's life, there have been the variously successful attempts to complete and render performable the entire corpus of his Tenth Symphony, left unfinished at his death.

In addition to recordings and concerts, Mahler has captured the imagination of moviemakers. Ken Russell has included Mahler in his collection of artistic subjects, and Luchino Visconti, having discovered that Thomas Mann was thinking of Mahler while working on *Death in Venice* in 1911, turned Mann's hero, the author Aschenbach, into a composer and used Mahler's music for the film score. The liner notes for the Deutsche Grammophon recording of this score call it "the most beautiful film music ever written."

The fourth and final underpinning of Mahler's present popularity is the emergence of a Mahler literary industry, ranging from musicological studies through biography to large new gift books splendidly illustrated and printed on expensive paper. The musicological works subject Mahler to the kind of musical analysis heretofore reserved for the music of Bach and Beethoven, and among the increasing number of treatments of Mahler's life are two volumes (so far) by Donald Mitchell and the excellent short biography by Kurt Blaukopf, which appeared in Germany in 1969 and in English translation in 1973. In that same year, the numerous previous biographies were crowned by the publication of Henry-Louis de La Grange's ineffably detailed *Mahler;* this work, whose second and possibly concluding volume seems eagerly awaited, constitutes the most ambitious and exhaustive book written about the life of a musical figure since Ernest Newman's four-volume study of Richard Wagner was issued over a thirteen-year period from 1933 to 1946. And not even Newman, no slouch when it came to searching out and recounting minutiae, displayed the consuming passion for intimate facts and buried references which characterizes the work of the indefatigable de La Grange.

For display on the proverbial coffee table, the new presentation books on Mahler* demonstrate, in their similarity to two recent works celebrating Wagner and the centenary of Bayreuth (and even brought out by the same publishers, Oxford and Rizzoli), just how great a composer Mahler is presently seen to be. The Oxford volume concentrates on documents, often reproduced in facsimile, and illustrations of Mahler and his friends in their musical and geographical habitats; the Rizzoli volume confines itself to fairly long articles—among them an introductory essay by Boulez—as well as illustrations covering Mahler's career in Vienna before, during, and after his engagement as Director of the Vienna Opera.

All this present activity and reclame surrounding Mahler and his music contrast oddly with the bleak, depressing picture of pain and failure one carries away from most of the literature about him. For it is a literature that represents him as obsessed, oversensitive, born to suffer, and above all doomed by a cruel

---

**Mahler: A Documentary Study*, edited by Kurt Blaukopf, Oxford University Press; *Gustav Mahler in Vienna*, edited by Sigrid Wiesmann, Rizzoli.

fate which begrudged him the happiness and success properly
owing to a supremely great artist.

Mahler was born in 1860, in his own expression a Bohemian
among Austrians, an Austrian among Germans, and a Jew among
the nations. His parents were ill-matched and poor. Of his eleven
siblings, five died in infancy, one died at the age of thirteen, and
one committed suicide at twenty-five. Gustav, the eldest survivor, did poorly in school but seemed greatly talented in music.
At fifteen, he entered the Vienna Conservatory where he had a
checkered career. Upon graduation in 1878, however, he won a
prize for composition and formed a sympathetic relationship with
the outcast Anton Bruckner (of whose Third Symphony he had
helped make a piano transcription).

Mahler's professional career began in 1880 with a position as
conductor in a tiny summer theater where the standards were
mean and the duties unsatisfying. But from there he went on to a
series of other conducting jobs, each one more important than
the last. As he gained in experience and authority, his reputation
also grew, so that within fifteen years he had become a serious
contender for the most important post of all and the one of which
he had always dreamed—Director of the Vienna Opera.

This dream of a triumphal return to Vienna was aided by the
support of such figures as the already mythic Brahms, Eduard
Hanslick, the greatly powerful critic of the *Neue Freie Presse*, and
Rosa Papier, an influential singing teacher and mistress of both
political intrigue and a high official in the Imperial and Royal
Court. As against all this, Mahler had an almost crippling disad-
vantage—his having been born a Jew. But he let it be known that
he had been (rather freshly) converted to Roman Catholicism;
with the obstacle of Jewishness out of the way, he was named a
conductor at the Vienna Opera in 1897 and shortly thereafter its
Director.

The decade he spent in Vienna was considered a golden age by
his admirers, but as the years passed, the Viennese opposition to
him (which contained a strong anti-Semitic component) quick-
ened. Thus he welcomed the offer made him in 1907 to become
principal conductor at the Metropolitan Opera House. He

opened in New York with *Tristan und Isolde* and scored heavily. Soon, just as the possibility arose at the Met of conflict with the newly arrived Arturo Toscanini, the constitution of the New York Philharmonic was altered to permit him to become its director with absolute control. This was the last post he was ever to occupy.

All this time, of course, Mahler had also been composing. Unlike Richard Strauss, he found it impossible to write music during the winter when he was busy as a conductor, but he did manage to set aside the summers for composing. Moving on from the grandiose dimensions of *Das klagende Lied*, he converted the experience of an unhappy love affair into the *Lieder eines fahrenden Gesellen* ("Songs of a Wayfarer"), based on his own adaptation of texts drawn from the early-nineteenth-century collection of German folksongs, *Des Knabens Wunderhorn* ("The Youth's Magic Horn"). These poems of doomed love provided Mahler with the literary framework for the musical mood he was to cultivate all his life—a melancholia simultaneously abject and lofty, disturbed by frequent interjections of coarse peasant humor, and saved by the prospect of redemption both sublime and certain.

Although more and more celebrated as a conductor, Mahler the composer was forced to suffer rebuffs from critics who disliked the few public performances he was able to arrange (sometimes with his own funds) and—much worse, of course—from those great men whom he most admired and who were his greatest supporters as a conductor—Brahms and the famous pianist and conductor Hans von Bülow. He felt Brahms had, when serving as a juror for the Beethoven Prize in 1881, blocked him from winning with *Das klagende Lied;* and Bülow had exclaimed after Mahler played for him part of what was to become his Second Symphony: "If what I have just heard is music, then I no longer understand anything about music!" When Bülow died in 1894, Mahler was finally able to complete that symphony, and in 1895 he began a third.

By the time of his death in 1911 Mahler had composed nine symphonies, with the Tenth existing in a far-advanced sketch. He had also added to his works for voice and orchestra *Das Lied von der Erde* ("The Song of the Earth"), a cycle written to poems from the Chinese, and the *Kindertotenlieder* ("Songs for Dead Children"). These last, settings of Rückert poems, though begun before the arrival of his first child in 1902, and completed two years later, eventually became his memorial to the death of that child from scarlet fever and diphtheria in 1907.

Mahler's own death four years later seemed to put paid to his career both as conductor and composer. In an era before recordings, his conducting would only be quickly forgotten, and his music could no longer profit from the performances his power as a conductor was able to garner. Not only did the predominantly conservative audience of the day find his music too modern for its taste as compared to the great Viennese masters, but music itself was changing; the decadent and overblown romanticism which Mahler seemed to typify was being replaced by the new aesthetics of expressionism, primitivism, and neoclassicism. In 1908, Schoenberg had, in his Second String Quartet, followed a quasi-atonal passage with a setting of the famous words of Stefan George, "I feel an air from other planets blowing"; in 1911, the year of Mahler's death, Stravinsky began work on *Le Sacre du Printemps* and Strauss started *Ariadne auf Naxos*. Then came World War I which, with its four years of unprecedented slaughter and destruction, was everywhere felt to mark the burial of the world of nineteenth-century sentimentality and self-indulgence.

So the brief spurt in Mahler performances in Vienna immediately after the war, no less than the Amsterdam Mahler Festival in 1920, seemed no more than a limited nostalgic survival. His music remained fitfully popular in German-speaking countries, and even that limited fame vanished in the avalanche of Nazi anti-Semitism. As far as Anglo-Saxon countries were concerned, it was only the influx of refugee conductors—and, one suspects, refugee audiences—in the 1930s that led to any widespread programming of Mahler's music.

After World War II the phenomenal development of recording based on magnetic tape and the long-playing disc made possible—at first monaurally and after 1958 still more effectively in stereo—the presentation of Mahler's music as he had conceived it, full of clearly heard polyphony distributed among the instruments of the orchestra by novel scoring and the separation of textures through actual physical spacing. From this point, it was only to be expected that he would quickly reach his present eminence; had not Mahler been told by an irate listener whom he was admonishing for booing a work of Schoenberg, "I hiss your symphonies too"? Thus, at long last, justice was done, and Mahler's prophecy about himself—"My time will come!"—was fulfilled.

This impression of martyrdom and resurrection, of personal tragedy and artistic survival, of public error redressed by public adulation, is the idea of Mahler we get not only from his biographies, or even from such a painstaking effort as that of de La Grange. On an artistic and philosophical level far surpassing a mere recounting of the facts of the composer's life, we find Pierre Boulez beginning his piece on Mahler—the introductory article to *Gustav Mahler in Vienna*—with the words: "How long it took until he stepped forth, not from the shadows but from purgatory! A long lasting purgatory that held him prisoner for a thousand reasons. . . ." And more than sixty years earlier, just after Mahler's death, the same note was sounded by perhaps the seminal figure of twentieth-century musical thought. For Arnold Schoenberg

Gustav Mahler was a saint.

Anyone who knew him even slightly must have had that feeling. Perhaps only a few understood it. And among even those few the only ones who honored him were the men of good will. The others reacted to the saint as the wholly evil have always reacted to complete goodness and greatness: they martyred him.

They carried things so far that this great man doubted his own work. Not once was the cup allowed to pass away from him. . . .

Rarely has anyone been treated so badly by the world; nobody, perhaps, worse.

It is clear that what Schoenberg is propounding here is a myth of Mahler as Christ. But the problem with this myth, as perhaps with all religious stories, is that its emotive force does not guarantee historical exactitude. At the least, as we learn from the facts if not from the mood of the Mahler biographies, the history is vastly more complicated and ambiguous than the myth. Arguably, what we have in the case of Mahler is a life in many ways closer to a fabulous success story than to the martyrdom of Schoenberg's homily.

Consider those facts: A poor Jewish boy from a provincial Central European backwater, born to a family barely participant in even such limited emancipation as the nineteenth century allowed to his people, without outside material assistance, without effulgent charm, nonetheless in a short life of fifty years goes from smaller to ever larger assignments, from the shadow of his father's near-poverty to a leading position on the world artistic stage. As Director of the Vienna Opera, the most important opera house in the world, he is able to refuse a personal request concerning the hiring of an artist from the Emperor Franz Josef himself, from whose purse the Opera subsidy is drawn. His conducting is greeted by wild enthusiasm in a most significant part of the European press, and he is made a handsome offer to come to America, where again he scores triumph after triumph.

As a composer, Mahler's success was less flamboyant, but his works were earning enough royalties by the end of his life to support the publication of the music of Bruckner. By then, too, Mahler's works, considering that they required such extravagant forces, were being performed reasonably close to the time they were written: his Eighth Symphony—called the "Symphony of a Thousand" because of the number of performers needed—was finished in 1907 and performed in 1910. The young Bruno Walter and the already established and famous conductor of the Amsterdam Concertgebouw, Willem Mengelberg, were both avid proselytizers for Mahler.* In addition, his music received the public support and approval of Richard Strauss, the most successful

* Fortunately, both these conductors recorded some of the works of Mahler: the Fourth Symphony performed by Mengelberg was available on Turnabout until recently, and the Walter recordings of five Mahler symphonies and the *Kindertotenlieder* have been available on Columbia/Odyssey, as is his performance of *Das Lied von der Erde* on London/Richmond.

composer and one of the most powerful conductors of the day.

Plainly, the evidence exists to support either a triumphant or a tragic interpretation of Mahler's musical career. Why, then, does the tragic interpretation prevail in most of the literature about Mahler? To answer this question one must proceed to an assessment of his achievement, and use that standard to evaluate both how he fared while alive and how he has been seen in the years since his death.

Perhaps the easiest aspect of Mahler's career to evaluate is his conducting. There can be little doubt that he was one of the greatest figures in the rather brief history of that branch of musical performance—the founder of the twentieth-century tradition of the virtuoso music director as a creative musical force.

Musically, by claiming the right in the classics not only to change tempos and dynamics in ways not indicated in the score but also and more importantly to alter in ways large and small the very written notes themselves, Mahler contradicted the sober and respectful approach of his admired predecessors and colleagues in Vienna. To this willingness to alter the written notes, he added a sense of rhythmic flow which depended upon fluctuating tempos rather than classical steadiness; in this he has been followed by such conductors as Wilhelm Furtwängler, and in our time Leonard Bernstein, rather than the literalist school popularly exemplified by Toscanini and Pierre Monteux. His choice of repertory, and its alertness to new music (even to music which he disliked) and its revivification of acknowledged masterpieces, provides a model worthy of study, particularly today. Regrettably, however, it is his personal behavior, so demanding as to verge on cruelty, that has been taken up as a model by too many of his successors. Perhaps as a result of that behavior, he was able to extend into the area of orchestral music that ascendancy of the performer over the music which had been earlier accomplished for the piano and the violin (and of course the voice) in the nineteenth century.

Much the same verdict can be passed on Mahler's work both as a musical administrator and opera producer. Throughout his career, wherever he had the chance, he enforced the idea that the director of a musical institution ought to combine managerial and artistic control, and that such control rightly belonged to the institution's chief performing artist, the conductor. He also reformed contemporary notions of opera production by diminishing the role of star singers in favor of the ensemble as a whole, and by allowing new ideas of staging and design to begin the process of destroying nineteenth-century operatic naturalism. He was thus the spiritual forebear of the revolution in operatic staging associated with Wieland Wagner and post–World War II Bayreuth.

But it is of course as a composer that Mahler's achievement must finally be judged. And here it must be said that an assessment of Mahler written from this time and place cannot substantiate a ranking of him on the level of the very few immortals of classical music. His output is much smaller than theirs, it is restricted almost solely to orchestral music instead of the enormous variety of musical media characteristically used by the immortals, and its narrow concentration on disappointment, depression, and despair contrasts sharply and unfavorably with the vast emotional range of a Bach, a Mozart, a Beethoven.

Viewed strictly in formal terms, Mahler's pieces fail to achieve the perfection one associates with the work of the highest masters: the perfect relationship between means and ends. Each piece—the slow movements excepted—is full of starts and stops, of strains and anticlimaxes. And most important, his music often lacks stylistic assurance and integrity—the ability to convince the listener that the composer is speaking with his own voice, and that of no one else.

For Mahler's compositions are those of a late-nineteenth-century Romantic, a continuer and developer of the tradition of Austro-German music. This tradition contains, in the music running from Bach to Brahms and Wagner, the most widely and strongly appealing serious music ever written. In the operatic world it is challenged only by the Italianate works of Verdi and Puccini which, however, it deeply influenced. In the world of orchestral and instrumental music it is unchallenged and is today the backbone and by far the largest part of the repertory. What a general audience hears and loves in Mahler is precisely his membership in that tradition, and his ability to draw, most especially in his beautiful slow movements, on the legacy of Beethoven, Wagner, Liszt, Brahms, and Bruckner. If Mahler cannot be considered a great melodist—notwithstanding the affective power of his melodic writing—it is because his tunes are evocative of the old rather than newly creative in their own right.

Nor is this reliance on the past limited to Mahler's slow music or to his relation to his great predecessors. It is implicit in all his material, so much of which is drawn from trumpet and horn calls, and from folk music. A particularly interesting example of this process, because it is at the same time so obvious and so little remarked, is the extraordinarily close resemblance between much of the posthorn solo in Mahler's Third Symphony and one of the themes of Liszt's *Spanish Rhapsody,* written in 1863; significantly, Mahler's work was written in June and July of 1895, and we learn from de La Grange—though he does not mention the connection—that the great Italian pianist and composer Ferruccio Busoni was soloist in his own arrangement of the *Spanish Rhapsody* with Mahler as conductor in Hamburg in October 1894. And even Liszt's usage of the theme is secondhand, for it is in origin part of a well-known *jota* from Spanish Aragon.

Another and very significant characteristic of Mahler's melodic writing is the instrumental function these melodies serve even when they are scored, as so often happens in his work, for voice and accompany a text. Beethoven made a revolutionary alteration in the conception of symphonic music when he ended the Ninth Symphony with a solo vocal and choral setting of Schiller's "Ode to Joy." But two widely divergent paths were taken as a result of this revolution. One was to use the orchestra as a means of extending and completing the work of the voice, as in the music-dramas of Wagner. The other road—chosen by Mahler and his successors—was to use the voice, and even the sound of the text itself, as an acoustical and thus instrumental component of the orchestra.

It is here that one may find the most satisfactory answer to the persistently asked question of why Mahler, the greatest of opera conductors, never composed an opera. The answer is implicit in his vocal writing; no matter how much he needed the stimulus of a verbal text to fire his musical imagination, he did not view the voice as the embodiment of a character. For Mahler, the voice was a sound of great beauty to be orchestrated, not the expression of a human being with an independent existence. The practical consequence of Mahler's treatment of the voice is that singers are chosen for Mahler performances today not for their ability to project the text but rather for their beautiful creamy sound and its capacity to blend with rather than stand out against the orchestra.

Yet to judge Mahler so harshly is to say no more than that he falls short of six or so individuals out of the tens of thousands who have composed in the past three centuries of the flowering of Western music. Below that level of exalted, quasi-divine genius there are many composers who wrote music of beauty and force. In the symphonic tradition in which Mahler worked there were several such composers writing at roughly the same time. Coming slightly before him were Dvořák and Tchaikowsky—whose *Symphonie pathétique* resembles in its fundamental pessimism much of the mature work of Mahler. And coming slightly later were Rachmaninoff and the composer Mahler replaced in the affection of English and American audiences, Sibelius. Though there are of course significant differences in the nature and quality of these men's music, they remain linked as epigones of the nineteenth-century greats. Mahler's relation to Strauss is a more difficult matter; certainly one cannot know whether Mahler would have followed Strauss in his retreat after the dissonant modernism of *Elektra* into the enclosed garden of classicism, or instead have gone along with Schoenberg into the rejection of an easily comprehensible music.

If this assessment of Mahler as a composer is correct, it follows that there was, even in his lifetime, a rough equivalence between his musical worth and his career. No one expects the path of new serious music to be easy, and naturally a famous performer is more generously remunerated than a composer. And if his reputation as a composer grew after death while the memory of him as a conductor faded, that too does not seem unnatural. Why, then, is he seen today as a specially tragic figure?

There are at least two parts to the answer. The first is perhaps less important; in any case, it is trite, cruel, and to the artist deeply offensive. It is the idea that an artist must pay for his creative powers with his life. One sees this delusion in the nineteenth-century view of the artist as either tubercular or syphilitic; Thomas Mann played on both these ideas, most directly in *The Magic Mountain* and in *Doctor Faustus*. In our time this idea satisfies, by its crude retributive justice, the fans of great movie and rock stars like James Dean, Janis Joplin, and Elvis Presley—and it may well have been the prospect of just such a denouement which inspired the camp followers of Maria Callas. Not only does this view of the artist's suffering and death enable the audience to master its otherwise overwhelming envy; it contributes to the comforting feeling that the artist by dying has more fully lived for others. It is thus the tragedy of Mahler's life, including his career failures and personal miseries, which "proves" the authenticity of his art, whereas it is the success of Richard Strauss's life—his longevity, acclaim, and contentment—which "confirms" the basic falseness of which his music is often accused.

More interesting, however, is the way Mahler's life is conceived by musical intellectuals like Schoenberg and Boulez who see their own role as creators of the new in opposition to a superseded tradition. Though to a wide audience and to those musicians who primarily serve that audience, Mahler's general popularity rests on the appeal of his melodic writing, for the intellectuals his melodies and their rhetorical setting are initially embarrassing in their old-fashioned and vulgar sentimentality, their naked evocation of the passions of love and death. What the intellectuals have singled out as valuable in Mahler is his "modern" side—his violation of classical and even romantic bounds of length and permissible scale, his tendency to mockery and burlesque, his rapid alternation of wildly contrasting material, and his use of orchestral instruments in unaccustomed ranges and timbres.

Yet while it is true that these "modern" features can loosely be seen as adversary in the context of Mahler's time to a traditional conception of music—though no more so than much of the music Richard Strauss was writing during Mahler's lifetime—and thus responsible for much of the dislike with which Mahler's music was originally received, it is obvious that today they have lost their capacity to shock. Not only are they no longer seen as adversary, but they actually seem to the general audience to define the very nature of romantic music.

In any case, it is as a martyr to the new that musical intellectuals tend to revere Mahler—a tendency that can be explained only in the context of the predicament of new music in the past half-century. This predicament, for a long time called a crisis, can now fairly be called a collapse. Not all the government and foundation support, not all the tenured positions in colleges and universities, and not all the performances extorted in the name of the musician's duty to one's time can conceal the fact that there is not now, and has not been for decades, any intellectually admired new music being written which anyone outside a small educated group, highly conscious of its presumed historical role, has any desire to hear. Indeed, the major use of the word "contemporary" in music today refers to popular and "rock" music and not to classical music at all.

This verdict of failure has been passed despite an unprecedented burst of publicity from the most intellectually respected salesmen of culture to the masses—salesmen who in literature and painting have been fairly successful in communicating the gospel of the new. There is no point in denying that the sense of this failure, notwithstanding the mutual reinforcement musicians and composers have freely given each other, has bitten deep. No less than other hurts, the misery of public rejection loves company. What better company can there be than Gustav Mahler—so interested in the work of the young pariah Schoenberg, so conscious of the failure of his own music to elicit universal acclaim, and so confident of future vindication—when that same Gustav Mahler is now so plainly the darling of something approaching a mass audience?

It is this conjunction of the audience's love for what it hears as a deeply romantic and therefore essentially conventional music with a life which it is possible to see as martyrdom in the service of the new in art that is responsible for the current unanimity of opinion about Mahler. Here may be found the explanation of the otherwise incongruous appearance of Karlheinz Stockhausen, the *enfant terrible* of postwar avant-garde music, as the writer of a hagiographical introduction to de La Grange's biography of Mahler; here may also be found the meaning of Pierre Boulez's eagerness to secure the first complete recording rights to *Das klagende Lied,* despite the evident distaste Boulez shows for Mahler's grandiosity; here may also be found the reason for the use of Mahler quotations in the work of ambitious American contemporary composers. It is as if they were all saying: "My time, too, like Mahler's, will come."

Though Mahler's present success and his contemporary image can be described and analyzed, it is obviously impossible to forecast the future rank his music will occupy. There is much truth in the motto which is so often quoted as describing the right of new art like Mahler's to be accepted—"To each epoch its art, to art its freedom." One cannot say whether the needs which his art fulfills today will be fulfilled in the same way in the future, or indeed whether these needs will even continue to exist. But one can point out the shaky nature of a reputation which depends upon a double weakness—in this case the desire of an audience for satisfactions from music which can artistically be better provided by the music of other composers, and the need of frustrated composers and musicians to reassure themselves about their own future by the arbitrary interpretation of the life of a man long dead.

7

And Still Rachmaninoff

THE 1978 appearance of Vladimir Horowitz with the New York Philharmonic and Eugene Ormandy in Carnegie Hall—interesting for so many reasons both historical and contemporary—provided yet another manifestation of the present gulf between public taste and advanced musical opinion. No exponent of the advanced himself, Horowitz chose as a vehicle for his first performance with an orchestra in twenty-five years Sergei Rachmaninoff's Third Concerto (1909), not only one of the longest and toughest, but also perhaps the last famous piano concerto written in the nineteenth-century tradition.

Close to the end of this spectacularly romantic work, piano and orchestra join in a mighty anthem, developed out of earlier and relatively simple material. When this point in the Horowitz performance was reached, the audience seemed to lean forward—as it always does at this moment in the piece—and give every visible sign of being ready to burst into enthusiastic song. Faces were radiant and taut with absorption in the music. At the close, the predictable pandemonium broke out, a tribute both to the soloist and to the work he had just played.

As the excitement mounted, one of America's most respected modernist composers was heard to remark: "That's the worst piece of trash I've ever heard." Obviously, the audience disagreed. And yet it was an audience composed almost entirely of Philharmonic subscribers, which meant that it was a veteran of nearly a decade's training by Pierre Boulez, the orchestra's former music director and perhaps the most widely known champion of musical modernism in our day.

The popularity of Rachmaninoff's music with a wide public goes back to his C-sharp Minor Prelude, written in 1892, when the composer was nineteen. Uncopyrighted and sold to a publisher for forty rubles, it achieved world fame in 1898, when the pianist Alexander Siloti, Rachmaninoff's cousin, played it in London. Its popularity subsequently dogged the composer, who found himself obliged to play this favorite of struggling piano students at every one of his innumerable piano recitals.

Rachmaninoff's Second Concerto is perhaps the most frequently performed of his pieces; as played by Artur Rubinstein it was the background music of a late 1940s Hollywood tearjerker about a concert pianist and the source as well for a hit song of the period, "Full Moon and Empty Arms." Slightly later, the eighteenth variation from the last of Rachmaninoff's works for piano and orchestra, the *Rhapsody on a Theme of Paganini*, provided American jukeboxes with still another smash hit.

As for the Third Concerto, it remains the most surefire vehicle available to a virtuoso pianist today. It has been a favorite with Horowitz for many years, and its power was demonstrated by the very fact of his having chosen it for this important and highly publicized concert. So, too, when, twenty years ago, Van Cliburn chose to perform it, along with the shorter and technically easier Tchaikowsky B-flat Minor Concerto, in a sensationally successful New York appearance after his Moscow contest triumph.

Rachmaninoff's strictly orchestral works are also popular. His Second Symphony remains a conductorial showpiece, and his symphonic poem, the *Isle of the Dead*, though played less often than in the past, is still familiar to audiences. Two of his songs, "Lilacs" and the wordless "Vocalise," come as close to being hackneyed as any art songs written in this century. Just about all his compositions are available in modern recordings; many appear in new performances almost every year.

Critical reaction is plainly pained and embarrassed by all this public favor. The authoritative *New Oxford History of Music* in its concluding volume (1974) simply dismisses Rachmaninoff's "polished superficiality." The respected English chronicler of modern music, Wilfrid Mellers, writes that Rachmaninoff's life-long conflict between the desire to be musically creative and the wish to be financially successful "finds an echo in our hearts, living as we do in a society dedicated to material gain."

The object of these disparate judgments by the few and the many was easily one of the most versatile musical figures of the recent past—a pianist and conductor of world stature as well as a composer. In fact, his entire career may be said to represent the final flowering of the Russian musical culture which was to come to maturity uninfluenced by the Bolshevik Revolution and the ideologies of artistic and political radicalism which followed it.

Rachmaninoff was born on a small estate near Novgorod in European Russia in 1873, the child of gentry adapting poorly to the winds of change which had come with the recent abolition of serfdom. By the time he was ten, the family had been forced to leave the rural estate for a crowded flat in St. Petersburg. There the boy, who had always been deeply interested in music, was sent to the conservatory where he did excellently in musical subjects but poorly in everything else. Later he was sent to study the piano with a famous Moscow master, Nicolai Zverev. Zverev's pedagogical system was both simple and draconian. Although he supported himself in grand style by giving lessons to the rich, his serious work was done with young boys of immense talent whom he taught without charge. These few Zverev required to sever almost all ties with their families and live in his house, "submitting completely to his discipline." Here they were to absorb the piano as a life rather than as a mere profession. Whatever Zverev's actual piano-teaching abilities—no one seems to have heard him touch the piano during a lesson—his successful protégés included not only Rachmaninoff but also Scriabin.

Through Zverev, the young Rachmaninoff experienced much of the rich musical atmosphere of Moscow. At Zverev's, he first met Tchaikowsky, then at the height of his fame. Because Rachmaninoff was by now taking classes at the Moscow Conservatory, he was also invited to play for the *doyen* of Russian music, Anton Rubinstein. Rubinstein, a legendary pianist and (at that time) popular composer, was giving his 1886 series of "historical concerts" in St. Petersburg and Moscow. Rachmaninoff twice heard these surveys of keyboard literature from Couperin to the then present, and they no doubt helped to form his idea of the pianist-composer as conquering hero and master of the musical world.

As part of his musical education, Rachmaninoff, now in his early teens, was allowed to get away from the piano enough to study theory and harmony. His work in harmony caught the attention of Tchaikowsky, and thus encouraged, he began to show more interest in composing than in playing the piano. This led to his expulsion in 1889 from Zverev's hothouse. But within two years, he had finished his First Piano Concerto (heavily revised in 1917), and a tone-poem, *Prince Rostislav*, written for his teacher, the composer Anton Arensky. The next year, as one of the tests for graduation from the Conservatory, he was assigned the task of composing a short opera, *Aleko*, based on a poem by Pushkin. He finished it in eighteen days, and the result, added to his piano playing, won him the rarely awarded Great Gold Medal of the conservatory. His *Aleko* was accepted for performance by the Bolshoi Theater, and Zverev—with whom he was now reconciled—arranged for his music to be published.

Confirming Rachmaninoff's increasing reputation as a composer, Tchaikowsky proposed that *Aleko* be performed as part of a double bill with his own *Iolanthe*. Rachmaninoff continued to compose, writing in 1893 his First Suite for two pianos and a second symphonic poem, *The Rock*. To make some easy money, he also turned out many small piano pieces and songs, all of which are still performed today. But his major compositional effort now was to go into his First Symphony. Performed for the first time in 1897, it was a ghastly failure, more (or so Rachmaninoff thought) for the way it was conducted than for any intrinsic musical shortcomings.

During this decade Rachmaninoff often found himself severely depressed. He was hit hard by the deaths in 1893 of the two great

influences on his life, Zverev and Tchaikowsky, and he suffered,
too, from a chronic lack of money. He managed to support himself—but only just—by giving lessons. For a short time, he also
worked as an opera conductor in a somewhat sleazy company
supported by a Moscow millionaire; here he gained valuable conducting experience and met his lifelong friend and collaborator,
the great basso Feodor Chaliapin.

In 1898 the success of the C-sharp Minor Prelude in London
brought Rachmaninoff an invitation to conduct and play. The
result was such that he was invited to return, and he promised to
come back with a better piece than the First Concerto, which he
had just performed. But unable even to start the Second Concerto, he fell into a depression which a visit with Chaliapin to the
great Tolstoy did nothing to lighten. After hearing Rachmaninoff
play his works, Tolstoy asked him: "Tell me, is such music
needed by anybody?" Though Rachmaninoff managed a saucy answer when Tolstoy attempted to apologize, his self-regard had
been even further damaged. As a last resort, Rachmaninoff underwent treatment by a hypnotist. Thanks to this therapy, he was
at last able to compose the Second Concerto. It was a resounding
public success in its first Moscow performance in 1900, as it was
to be later in Vienna, London, and the rest of the world.

In 1904 Rachmaninoff was appointed to the conducting staff of
the Bolshoi Theater, but he soon left to devote himself to composing and went to live in Dresden, where he worked on his
First Piano Sonata and the vastly more significant Second Symphony. The *Isle of the Dead* followed in 1909. That same year, in
preparation for his first American tour, Rachmaninoff completed
the Third Piano Concerto which he first played in New York
with Walter Damrosch and the New York Symphony, and then—
to his much greater satisfaction—with Gustav Mahler and the
Philharmonic.

Throughout the years before World War I and the Revolution
of 1917, his triple career as composer, pianist, and conductor
prospered. His compositions of this period included two religious
works, the *Liturgy of John St. Chrysostom* (1910) and *Vespers*
(1915). In lieu of another symphony he wrote a large work for

chorus and orchestra to a Russian translation of Poe's "The Bells" (1914). And, for the piano, he completed his second set of preludes (1910), the thirteen of which, when added to the ten of the first set—and of course the C-sharp Minor—placed him with Chopin as a composer of one piano prelude in each of the twelve major and twelve minor keys.

As a pianist, Rachmaninoff devoted himself, after Scriabin's death in 1915, to playing that composer's works. Here he aroused controversy, for Scriabin's adherents felt that Rachmaninoff's approach was too severe and old-fashioned for this mystical and revolutionary music. But as a conductor, his triumph was near complete: in Moscow he was called by the press a God-given leader, an equal of Nikisch and Mahler. And in general, something of the aura which surrounded his career and public position in the years just prior to the end of the traditional Russian world may be seen in the composer Glazunov's remarks during Rachmaninoff's visit to the St. Petersburg Conservatory, of which Glazunov was the director: ". . . this is a day to be marked no less than a day when the school is visited by a member of the Imperial family."

Without doubt the Bolshevik Revolution in November of 1917 was the great watershed in Rachmaninoff's life. Though he had signed a petition demanding reforms during the 1905 revolution, he never forgot his quasi-aristocratic social origins. He had held office under Czarist patronage, as a high officer of the Imperial Russian Musical Society. Furthermore, as an estate owner deeply interested in agriculture, Rachmaninoff was heavily involved in traditional landlord-peasant relations. A petty irritant, but one he must have felt prophetic of the future, was enforced attendance at Bolshevik-imposed house-committee meetings. It was plain to him that the freedom and the repose he needed for his work, and indeed his very physical existence, had been placed in jeopardy by the Communist accession to power. So it was that Rachmaninoff left his beloved Russia at the end of 1917, never to return. From now on he would support himself and his family as a concert pianist.

Given both the trauma of exile and the demands of a keyboard career, his new compositions became fewer. Moreover, they were generally less successful. His Fourth Concerto, written in 1926 and revised more than a decade later, was a public failure, as were his Third Symphony (1935–36) and his last major composition, the *Symphonic Dances* (1940). Indeed, only one work of his last years, the *Rhapsody on a Theme of Paganini* (1934), proved an immediate public success.

Throughout the 1920s Rachmaninoff combined residence in America with an evident inability to give up the Russian world he had lived in so long. He kept up a busy correspondence with musicians who had remained in Russia, and he frequently sent his old friends money. Both in this country and later in Europe, he associated mostly with Russians. Thus when he signed a letter to the *New York Times* in 1931 protesting conditions in the Soviet Union, he was perhaps unprepared for the consequences. These included a boycott of his music and meetings in Moscow and other Russian cities to accuse him of anti-Soviet behavior. By the end of the 1930s—probably because of Stalin's desire to build up Russian nationalism—the music was reinstated, and Rachmaninoff himself was rehabilitated as a person after Hitler's attack on Russia in 1941. For his part, Rachmaninoff supported the Soviet war effort, and made several large contributions to Russian war relief.

He died of cancer in Beverly Hills in 1943, several weeks after becoming an American citizen, and a few days before his seventieth birthday. He had been concertizing until almost the end. How much he saw himself as a pianist may be gathered from his touching and often-quoted words in the hospital as he lay near death: "At my age one can't miss practice. . . . My dear hands. Farewell, my poor hands. Farewell, my poor hands."

And Rachmaninoff's piano performances are supreme examples of the art. Many of them have been preserved on records, and often reissued in the years since his death. At present they are available in a complete set, constituting documentation of a pianistic achievement which may well rank in excellence if not in scope with that of Franz Liszt and Anton Rubinstein. Most of his recordings are of his own music; in their simplicity and easy technical mastery they have set a high standard for his successors. The only recordings he ever made of extended works by other composers—the B-flat Minor Sonata of Chopin and the Schumann *Carnaval*—are simultaneously imaginative, idiosyncratic, and willful. In these recordings, as in the many he made of smaller Chopin pieces, he has often been accused of revealing more of himself than of the composer. While this criticism may well be justified, it ignores the fact that the immanent tendency of virtuoso performance is self-exhibition rather than self-abnegation.

As a composer, Rachmaninoff was not prolific in the fashion of the greatest masters, but it is not generally realized just how much music he actually wrote. Five works for piano and orchestra, three symphonies, a choral symphony, three symphonic poems, three short operas, two religious services, two piano sonatas, a host of songs and smaller piano pieces; it is an output comparable in size to that of such coevals as Sibelius, Mahler, and Schoenberg, though certainly not in influence to the last two.

In quality, the *Rhapsody on a Theme of Paganini* and the four piano concertos—including the lesser-known First and Fourth—comprise the most important body of work for piano and orchestra since Brahms. Their appeal to a wide audience is nicely balanced by the difficult but surmountable technical challenge they offer to pianists. The same can be said about his twenty-four preludes, and to a large extent of his other solo piano pieces as well.

Of Rachmaninoff's three symphonies, the Second not only seems to me more consistently interesting in its musical material than the Second Symphony of Sibelius (the best-known of the seven written by that composer); it even compares favorably to the symphonies of Tchaikowsky, being both of equal melodic power and rather less harmonically obvious. A similar verdict can be passed on *The Bells,* which was Rachmaninoff's favorite of all his works; unfortunately it requires forces too large to permit frequent performance. Among his symphonic poems, the *Isle of the Dead* easily stands with the comparable productions of Richard Strauss as a masterfully integrated and sensuously beautiful example of late-nineteenth-century orchestral writing.

No such high claims can be made for Rachmaninoff's operas, though *Aleko,* the product of his youthful facility, seems the most successful in its combination of gypsy love and jealousy, well-drawn characters, and attractive melodies. On the other hand, his neglected church services contain some of his most beautiful music. What is most striking about Rachmaninoff's achievement here is his ability, particularly in the *Vespers,* to write freely and originally within the strict rules which governed music composed for the Russian Orthodox Church. Because of his disciplined submission to these rules, and the religious devotion he clearly felt, this music seems rather plainer, purer, and more inward than his other works.

These religious pieces aside, the most obvious of Rachmaninoff's musical virtues are his broad, long-lined, and easily remembered melodies. His orchestration—especially in its use of the strings—also easily catches the listener's ear; in this area his effectiveness was so great that his detractors have often pointed accusingly to the use Hollywood and other commercial composers have made of his characteristic orchestral sound.

But music is more than melody and orchestration. Less obvious is the role played by Rachmaninoff's other compositional virtues in supporting and setting off his melodies. There is, first, his rhythmic energy and the excitement it invariably generates. His work is also rhythmically complex, as is shown by the tendency of his melodies to find their final climax off the strong beats of the bar. All this vitality, expressed technically by the syncopations with which his music abounds, makes Rachmaninoff both interesting and tricky to perform.

Like the academically well-trained Russian composer he was, Rachmaninoff found counterpoint fascinating. His music is full of inner voices and depends for much of its harmonic richness on his habit, especially noticeable in the preludes, of filling in every blank space on the staff with melodies. An overlooked example of this luxuriant contrapuntal writing may be found in his G Minor

Prelude, opus 23 no. 5. Here the slow central section simultaneously combines in its second half three separate strands: the melody of the first half of the section, a motive drawn from the outer parts of the piece, and an additional related melody as well.

Harmonically, Rachmaninoff belongs to the very end of the nineteenth century. Despite a few attempts in the Fourth Concerto and the *Symphonic Dances* to assimilate some twentieth-century developments, any dissonances he used were merely "false notes" employed in addition to and not as substitutes for clearly consonant chords. These chords functioned within a strong and simply tonal, diatonic system.

It is a paradox that Rachmaninoff, whose music seems so Russian to us, belonged, with his mentor Tchaikowsky, to a more cosmopolitan group of composers than those who, like the "Five" (Borodin, Cui, Balakirev, Mussorgsky, and Rimsky-Korsakov), formed a consciously nationalistic school of composition. Despite his attachment to Russian culture, Rachmaninoff looked to the West for his formal musical models. He admired non-Russian composers and performers; he felt that American orchestras in general, and the Philadelphia Orchestra in particular, were the best in the world. Nevertheless, his melodies do have a Russian cast about them; and at the bottom of his harmony one can always find a fully articulated bass line, drawn from the timbre of the Russian bass voice with its distinctive richness and cutting edge.

As far as the guardians of musical opinion have been concerned, the status of Rachmaninoff as a performer has never been in doubt. Their dislike of his compositions, however, has often taken the form of a ferocious attack on Rachmaninoff's principled and total rejection of modernism. Rachmaninoff accepted neither the twentieth-century dissolution of traditional harmonic practice nor the new idea of music as social provocation. Not only did his own works hew closely to nineteenth-century aesthetics and techniques, but he spoke freely of his dislike of the direction music was taking around him. He thought the new music heartless and ugly, a product of the disordered contemporary world. As long ago as 1906, he said he liked Richard Strauss's *Salome* only when "it wasn't too discordant." When the young Henry

Cowell brought him a new work for evaluation, his only remarks concerned the number of wrong notes he had found in it. One can only regret that his specific comments about Arnold Schoenberg and his school were never preserved.

Some of the critical attack on Rachmaninoff has made its point by simply denying him any role at all in either nineteenth- or twentieth-century music. He is not mentioned, for example, in Alfred Einstein's classic history of nineteenth-century composition, *Music in the Romantic Era*. And Joseph Machlis, consigning him to the past in his standard college text, *Introduction to Contemporary Music* (1961), emphatically states: "Although certain of his works have enjoyed a phenomenal vogue with the public, Rachmaninoff has no proper place in a work on contemporary music." Even where he is included, he is often dismissed as a mere follower: Paul Henry Lang, in *Music in Western Civilization* (1941), finds him "entirely under [Chopin's] spell . . . [but] not able to derive from Chopin's heritage more than ephemeral compositions, dated at the time of their creation. . . ."

Critics more sociologically oriented than these have found in the character of his music something even worse than a turning away from the proper course of artistic development. They have seen Rachmaninoff's music as both representative and expressive of a decadent, outmoded, and discarded society. When Rachmaninoff had the temerity in 1919 to call himself a "musical evolutionist"—in contrast to the revolution and anarchy he saw going on around him—the American modernist critic Paul Rosenfeld answered:

His music is evidently wanting in boldness. On the whole it is cautious and traditional. . . . The school of which Rachmaninoff is perhaps the chief living representative is . . . the work of men essentially unresponsive to the appeal of their compatriots . . . [they] did not hear the appeal. They sat in their luxurious and Parisian houses behind closed windows.

Because he had never been a modernist, Rachmaninoff did not suffer the hatred and personal obloquy reserved for the renegade Richard Strauss; and in any case, these criticisms of his reactionary cultural identification are, at least as description, accurate. He called himself "a ghost wandering in a world grown alien." He did indeed find in the world of his birth a social environment which he thought made autonomous artistic creation possible. More generally, he saw that world as gentler, more civilized, and, despite its flagrant abuses, more merciful and hopeful than all the "utopias" which succeeded it.

Foolish as this notion of bourgeois melioration and social peace may sound in a liberated age, millions of people—among them the vast majority of music lovers—seem to share with Rachmaninoff precisely such a vision of a tolerable and indeed happy past. Whatever Rachmaninoff's exact rank as a composer, it was his achievement to reflect his own world—simply, honestly, and directly. The public has perceived this in his music; which is why that music, regardless of the demands of advanced opinion, will continue to be played, heard, and loved.

Yesterday's New Music

ALTHOUGH the situation of music at the end of World War II was undeniably chaotic, there were important if superficial reasons for optimism. The days in which public musical life had been curtailed or even halted by bombing and bombardment were safely past. Music, with other kinds of culture, seemed to belong to the new world of peaceful construction. In undamaged and prosperous America the influx of refugee musicians, composers and performers alike, had changed the domestic musical scene, and a parallel strengthening of audiences by the cultivated émigré public was providing both aesthetic approval and material support of concert activity. And in Europe, a whole new generation of artists, denied access to the world stage for almost a decade by the dislocations of war, was ready to come forward. Perhaps most important, a new electronic technology, based upon the German-invented magnetic tape recorder and (after 1948) the American-developed long-playing phonograph record, were available to provide the possibility of a hitherto unimagined diffusion of the great works of music.

It might have been supposed that all these phenomena, which were to prove so beneficial to the performance of existing music, would benefit new creation as well. For while musical composition had indeed shown marked signs of autumnal decline in the interwar period, it was hardly denied that some important works had been written in the 1920s and 1930s, and had been widely accepted as such by a cultivated audience.

Of the most important composers who had made their mark in the preceding two decades, only Berg was dead at the end of the war. While Bartók was to die shortly thereafter, even the nineteenth century survivor Richard Strauss, still alive at the age of eighty-one, was in 1945 in the middle of writing some of his most beautiful and affecting music. The two most widely respected modern masters, Arnold Schoenberg and Igor Stravinsky, were musically active; Schoenberg would continue composing until his death in 1951, and Stravinsky, his conversion to twelve-tone writing several years in the future, was still involved in the neoclassicism which was to culminate in his opera *The Rake's Progress* of 1951.

Among those newer figures whose downplaying of modernity was compensated for by greater public acceptance, Prokofiev and Shostakovich were prolific as ever, and only their difficult political situation in the Soviet Union seemed to stand in the way of the highest achievements. In England and France the erstwhile *enfants terribles* William Walton and Darius Milhaud (the latter an alternate-year resident in the United States) continued to write, and the very American Aaron Copland was consolidating and extending his reputation as our most considerable musical figure.

It is possible in retrospect to see that all this activity in composition, though hardly as central to the wider culture as the works of earlier composers had been, belonged to the mainstream, a kind of writing traditional in both aesthetic and technique. One can even see this kind of middle-of-the-road art as a loyal product of bourgeois society—nowhere more so, paradoxically, than in revolutionary Russia, where Stalin and Zhdanov were trying to resuscitate the corpse of Victorian aesthetics. But whatever the social system in which these moderate composers worked, and whatever their past innovations, by 1945 they seemed neither to be breaking new ground in the character of their music nor to be disturbing their essentially accommodating relation to the audience and to society.

This mainstream activity, in the work of such newly important figures as Benjamin Britten in England and William Schuman and Leonard Bernstein in America, was to continue, and remains until the present day a possible choice for contemporary composition. But the survival of a past way of writing into the present does not alter the fact that for at least the past thirty-five years the word "new" in composition had two uses. Its ordinary use has been simply to convey that a work has just been written; its more important use has been to convey the ideological message that the work in question possesses qualities of style which place it in the avant-garde, a movement revolutionary in purpose, historically unparalleled in technique, critical in reference to the past, and audacious in regard to the present.

The history of this advanced music since World War II is the story of the development, at first separate but later merged, of two conceptions—freedom and order. The freedom sought was the possibility for composers (and later for performers) to use any resource they might find attractive at any point from the writing of the music to its reception by the listener. The order sought involved the subjection of the musical material by the composer to the most rigorous and conscious intellectual control in the writing and to similarly conscious physical control in performance; this control was to be based both upon the generation of the composition from musical elements as carefully delimited as possible and upon the exclusion from their treatment of structural accident or sentimentality.

The roots of both these ultimately metaphysical goals lay, as might be expected, in prior developments going back to the early 1900s. To a significant extent these goals were both exemplified in the life and music of the most intellectually significant composer of the past century, Arnold Schoenberg. From his beginnings as a lush hyperromanticist extending the swollen forms of Wagner, Strauss, and Mahler, Schoenberg had exhausted the possibilities of complexity and sheer size alike; after the First Quartet (1905), he ventured increasingly into expressionism, into the uninhibited depiction of previously repressed emotions through musical means of hitherto unimagined dissonance and seeming formlessness. Though in fact ingeniously constructed, this music—best known in *Pierrot Lunaire* (1912) was written in a style significantly called "free atonality," and struck listeners as madness and anarchy let loose on the world.

But this kind of writing did not satisfy Schoenberg's restless craving for order. So in 1921 was born his great theoretical contribution to music: "the method of composition with twelve tones related only to each other." In this innocent-sounding phrase was contained both the destruction of tonality—the euphonious world of chords and keys which underlies what we hear as "classical" music—and a new system rigorous enough to attract and satisfy the most scholastically inclined of modern composers.

Given Schoenberg's propensity toward theory and discipline, it was ironic (though perhaps fitting in the light of his basic unruliness) that his most consequential pupil during his years of American exile should have been the composer, writer, and sometime mycologist John Cage. Under Cage's benign exterior lies a streak of aesthetic nihilism which has not only influenced the kind of music today's up-to-date composers write, but also our very idea of what it means to be an avant-garde composer.

Indeed, in the words of Schoenberg himself, Cage was perhaps not a composer at all but rather "an inventor of genius." Following upon his early interest in percussion music, in 1938 he invented the prepared piano, by which the insertion of metal, wood, and rubber objects between the piano strings produces exotic pitched and unpitched sounds different for each note so treated. His search for new sounds led him further, along the lines explored by Edgar Varèse and by Cage's own teacher Henry Cowell, the inventor of the tone cluster, in which the keys of the piano were smacked by palm, fist, arm, or—so that even more notes might be sounded at once—by a board. Whereas Schoenberg had aimed at—and in the eyes of his supporters succeeded in—the emancipation of the dissonance from the tyranny of what was accepted as consonance, Cage now, as early as 1937, sought the liberation of acoustical phenomena themselves from what he regarded as "so-called musical sounds."

For Cage, the future of music lay with the vast body of sounds in the past called noise. As musical instruments seemed at the time incurably specialized for the production of musical sounds— notes and harmonies—Cage began by working with electrical sound sources, writing in 1939 *Imaginary Landscape No.* 1 for two variable-speed phonograph turntables playing frequency re- cordings along with muted piano and cymbal. Twelve years later he had advanced to *Imaginary Landscape No.* 4, for 12 radios, 24 players, and conductor. The really revolutionary aspect of this work is demonstrated by the fact that its initial failure in perfor- mance—by the time Cage's piece was gotten to on the evening's program, too few radio stations were left on the air to provide the necessary sound material—hardly bothered the composer and confirmed for him (as failure in revolution always does for its supporters) the conceptual superiority of the enterprise.

As can be seen from his use of radios to provide material, Cage had become interested in the possibility of freeing composers from the necessity to choose and write down each individual note on the basis of its relation to the preceding notes. Thus, in the same year as his piece for radios, he composed *Music of Changes,* a work for piano solo in which the notes to be played by the pianist were determined in their pitches, loudness, duration, tempos, and sequences by consultation, through the mediation of coin tosses, with the Chinese oracle book *I Ching.*

One year later, in 1952, Cage achieved the ultimate chance composition and perhaps not quite by accident thus reached a level of public notoriety granted to few artistic creators in our time. Deciding that the noises which inevitably surround us are at least as interesting as anything a composer might write, he conceived the notorious *4'33",* a work in three movements of pure silence for any combination of instruments whatever, with only exact durations and absence of sound specified. This was not music but pure theater, as the "performance" by pianist David Tudor proved; Tudor simply sat at the piano, closing its fall board (the lid which covers the keys) at the beginning of each of the work's movements in accordance with the composer's directions in the otherwise empty score.

At about the same time Cage became further involved in electronic music, composing *Williams Mix* for eight-track tape. By 1958 he had married tape music to chance in *Fontana Mix,* described as "(a) a score for the production of one or more tape track(s) or for any number of instruments, or (b) prerecorded tape material to be performed in any way." Chance techniques were applied to purely instrumental pieces as well; in *Variations I* (1958), for "player(s) on any kind and number of instruments" the performer(s) is (are) required to choose notes and rhythms with regard only to charts containing schematic notation and written instructions. The later *Variations V* has no musical score at all; in its place the performer is given a general description of past performances, among them one (according to an article on Cage by his follower Christian Wolff) containing "dance by Merce Cunningham, film material by Stan Vanderbeek, special electronic equipment including electric eyes so that the movements of the dancers would trigger sound sequences, television material by Nam June Paik, and lighting and scenery by Robert Rauschenberg."

In the meantime, avant-garde music in Europe had started out after 1945 by choosing a compositional aesthetic based upon the other side of Schoenberg, his concern with order. Only in the very first years after the war was the influence of Schoenberg, through the teaching of his pupil René Leibowitz, anything like directly felt. Soon Schoenberg was being decisively overshadowed—as was his most distinguished disciple Alban Berg— by the music and even more the example of Anton Webern, also Schoenberg's pupil and with Berg and Schoenberg a member of the Viennese serial trinity. Webern's small body of mature work consisted of short, sparse sounding works of the most complex and ingenious organization; his later works were carefully written according to Schoenberg's method of twelve-tone organization.

But whereas both Schoenberg and Berg had composed works

of essentially romantic sensibility, direct in their open emotionality and unabashed self-indulgence, Webern constantly pared down his rhetoric, eschewing massive combinations of instruments in favor of individual fragmented melodic lines. Webern's few notes, written in a style utilizing preclassical contrapuntal devices, seemed a world small, perfect, and totally controlled. Webern thus became a heaven-sent model for the widely felt musical reaction against both classicism and romanticism. And not only was Webern validated as a hero for the new generation by the neglect he and his music had suffered; as if to set an eternal seal on his martyrdom, he had been killed in 1945—but after the war was over—by an overeager American soldier who mistakenly thought the gentle composer was attacking him.

These general considerations of Webern as an example of the artistic predicament aside, what seemed so useful to young European composers about his work was what they saw as his attempt to build his compositions out of a very few "preformed" elements, so that the entire composition seemed the inevitable outcome inherent in its constituents. In Webern these constituents were largely melodic, and thus based on pitch; but they also included color, dynamics, and rhythms. Now composers attempted to treat all the parameters of music—among them pitch, duration, amplitude, timbre, and articulation—as Schoenberg had required pitch alone be treated. Thus in a quasi-mathematical way, each element of music could be assembled into its own series, with each unduplicated pitch, duration, etc. assigned a numerical value based upon the order in which it was first stated; the series and its parts could be inverted, retrograded, and transposed according to a predetermined scheme which governed to as great an extent as possible what occurred and where such occurrences took place.

The first attempt (though only analogically serial) at such preformation was made in 1949 by the French composer Olivier Messiaen, in his etude *Mode de valeurs et d'intensités*. Messiaen was vastly more influenced musically by his French Catholic religiosity and fondness for birdsong than by any aesthetic sympathy for Schoenberg and Webern, and so he did not follow up his first experiment. In any case, the influence of the experiment hardly stemmed from its artistic achievement. Rather it was the fate of this short work to be noticed by the two seminal minds of the postwar avant-garde, Pierre Boulez and Karlheinz Stockhausen. In their separate ways—Boulez savagely polemical and passionately intellectual and Stockhausen inclined toward technological innovation and personal mysticism—these two men personified the early search for total determinism in music.

The rationality with which they worked now seems both artificial and terrifying. For example, Boulez's most totally preformed composition, *Structures I* (1951–52)—based on the pitch order of Messiaen's 1949 *Mode de valeurs*—was written following the preparation of matrix tables consisting of the numerical values of the original series of notes, its retrogrades and their inversions, and their transpositions. These tables were then used to determine all note durations, dynamics, and modes of attack, as well as to determine the order in which the note series themselves were used.

Though Boulez was to be influential—among many other reasons precisely for his achievement of total control—he himself soon abandoned the rigorous application of his own former principles. Stockhausen, by contrast, remained for many years (perhaps because he was not interested, as Boulez deeply was, in the performance of the music of others) committed to the role of the composer as dictator over both his compositions and the musicians who play them. More seduced by the possibilities of magnetic tape than Boulez ever was, Stockhausen saw in tape a medium which offered total control to the composer.

For on tape, though working with it in these early years was inefficient and horribly time-consuming, pitch could be controlled both by the signal the tape was electronically fed and by the speed at which the tape was run by the playback heads; rhythm and duration were not only matters of tape speed but even more conveniently of tape length to be determined by measurement with a ruler; timbre was a matter both of signal generators and frequency filtering; and dynamics were simply determined by settings of the gain controls. In fact, the composer could now be the performer, and once his tape was made, it contained its own permanent and unvarying realization.

It is difficult to avoid the impression that what animated Stockhausen and his followers—whether they worked with tape alone or, as Stockhausen often did, with conventional instruments used in such a way as increasingly to resemble electronic sources—was the desire to create a new-sounding music from scratch. Stockhausen put it well in the first issue of *Die Reihe*, a periodical devoted to the new music which appeared from 1955 to 1962:

A sound which results from a certain mode of structure has therefore no relevance outside the particular composition for which it has been intended. For this the same "prepared" element, the same sound or the same "object" can never be utilized in different compositions, and all sounds which have been created according to the structural pattern of one composition are destroyed when the composition is completed.

Not only does this apply to the individual work of one composer; the destruction of which Stockhausen wrote could be applied in a wider sense to musical memory itself and the block it always presents to the acceptance of anything new. This position has been brilliantly and sympathetically put in a recent history of avant-garde music by the English composer and writer Reginald Smith Brindle:

In the post-war years, one of the most difficult obstacles to our "beginning again" was our own musical memories. Our minds normally create only out of what memory suggests. Thinking subjectively, we tend to reassemble familiar musical patterns. To avoid this needs deliberately objective reasoning and the use of thought processes into which memory cannot obtrude. This was precisely the main reason for the flourishing of integral serialism. It was, in theory at least, a system of composition which obliged composers to think objectively and eliminate memory, so that the musical heritage of the past was blotted out and a completely new music created.

It needed little imagination to predict the reaction of the musical public to the demand that it participate in the destruction of musical memory. But even within the avant-garde movement itself, this fantasy of total control, no matter how logically impeccable and psychologically satisfying, could hardly last. Upon composers it laid the obligation to be thinkers rather than instinctive musicians; from performers (when they were allowed into the picture at all) it demanded absolutely faithful execution of the minutely detailed notation of the extreme complexities required by serialization. And upon even the most favorably disposed listeners it placed the burden of hearing and discriminating among sound events whose very complexity and differentiation made them seem both opaque and isolated.

For all of Stockhausen's commitment to intellectual control—he has during his career subjected other, non-specifically musical phenomena to such manipulation, including comprehensibility and confusion, density and complexity, as well as symmetry and asymmetry—he too realized the nature of this cul-de-sac; by the mid-1950s he was looking for a way to bring back some important role for variation and imagination in composition and performance alike. It was clear that this way out could not involve a return to the past. How impossible such a return was perceived to be can be gathered from a 1957 comment of Herbert Eimert, co-editor with Stockhausen, in *Die Reihe:*

There is little to choose between "advanced" expressionist music and the stagnant bourgeois reaction to it; today, either music exists as it is in the vanguard, or it does not exist at all. This is not a "totalitarian" alternative; it is the simple truth.

But while it was thus neither possible nor desirable to give up the characteristic sound of atonality as perceived by the listener, it was possible to substitute the new indeterminacy associated with John Cage for the total rigor of the disciples of Webern. In 1956 Stockhausen had already developed, in *Klavierstück XI,* the idea of mobile form. Here the performer is allowed to choose the order, determined by wherever his eye has happened to light in the music, in which any of the work's nineteen sections are played; when one of these sections is met with for the third time, the performance is over. More than order is left to the discretion of the performer: he is directed to begin the "first" section at a tempo, loudness, and attack of his own choice; at the end of this section he is given performance instructions applying equally to whichever section he chooses to continue with.

Though Stockhausen's use of chance as described above was hardly epochal, the effect of chance in the extreme form adopted by Cage in the 1950s and soon to be picked up in Europe was to complete the process begun earlier in $4'33''$ of transforming music into a form of theater. This kind of theater was of course far removed from traditional performance of either the classics or the ordinary new well-made play. The theater in which composers were now involved was much closer, in its emphasis on improvisation, to the idea of action painting as a process stemming from the painter's unconscious and performed by the body upon the canvas. Indeed, an attractive model for music was the "happening," first performed by a Cage-organized group at Black Mountain College in 1952, which included Charles Olsen, M. C. Richards, David Tudor, Robert Rauschenberg, Merce Cunningham, and Cage himself.

Stockhausen actually wrote a kind of happening, described by himself as "musical theater." *Originale* (1961) consists of a hodgepodge of elements, among them people doing what they usually do in real life. Two musicians play *Kontakte*, an earlier score by Stockhausen; actors act; a technician makes recordings; a street singer sings street songs, and a newsvendor comes in to sell papers. Even in works of Stockhausen where the performers' actions do not seem in context quite so bizarre, the element of theater still came to occupy an important place. In *Musik für ein Haus* (1968), for instance, a collective composition by members of his composition class at the Darmstadt Vacation Courses for New Music was conceived to be performed by instrumentalists assigned to each of fifteen composers in a cluster of rooms of various sizes on two floors connected and acoustically isolated by a network of passages. Each listener comes and goes in his own time and is able to change his listening perspective within the House at will.

What the instrumentalists play is picked up by microphones in each room and relayed at varying amplification over loudspeakers. Each of the four rooms is linked by a loudspeaker with the three others. The players not only react to one another, but also to the music emanating from the other room. In a fifth room (*"Klangbox"*) may be heard a continuous relay of the music from all four rooms over four separate speakers.

It is precisely this profusion of visual and theatrical elements which makes any evaluation of avant-garde music as music so difficult. And yet since these pieces go under the name of music, they clearly require evaluation in musical terms. So it is fortunate that this period was comprehensively documented on records. Some of the most characteristic works of the late 1950s and the culminating decade of the 1960s have been preserved by Deutsche Grammophon on a series of discs issued between 1968 and 1970. Consisting of 18 individual records released in three groups of six each, the series was simply called the *Avant-Garde.*

The history of these records turned out to be a short one. Though the critic of the English record magazine *Gramophone* referred to the release of the last group of six as "an annual event, something a reviewer can look forward to as winter closes in on him," no further records were to follow in the series, and those already issued were soon being discontinued and (at least in the United States) remaindered. By 1978 no trace of any of them remained in the American Schwann LP Catalog, and only two were still listed in Bielefelder, its German equivalent.

Strikingly produced, with each jacket save one bearing (in different colors) a handsome cover in the style of the American color-field painter Kenneth Noland, the records are centered around the music of Stockhausen; to him are devoted three complete discs and a part of another. Hardly less space—two complete discs and parts of two others—is given to the Argentine Mauricio Kagel. Single records are allocated to the German

Bernd Alois Zimmermann, and the French Luc Ferrari, while the Hungarian György Ligeti receives parts of three records. The rest of the series contains smaller selections from the music of twenty-two other composers (among them John Cage), and one group performing improvisations.

The series begins almost apologetically with conventionally modern-sounding music for that most bourgeois of combinations, the string quartet made up of two violins, viola, and cello. The longest of the three pieces on this disc is the String Quartet (1964) by Witold Lutoslawski, a Pole best known for his showy two-piano work, *Variations on a Theme of Paganini* (1941). His inclusion in the avant-garde is explained by the fact that most of the *Quartet* is written as completely independent parts, "each player [performing] his part as though he were alone." The second composition on the disc is the String Quartet (1960) of another Pole, Krzysztof Penderecki, whose most popular work has been *Threnody* (1956), dedicated "to the victims of Hiroshima." Though his quartet begins with a jumble of harsh sounds (obtained by treating the instruments as if they were percussion devices), nothing in the piece, except perhaps for the composer's intentions in writing it, justifies the jacket's comment that its significance lies in features "whose insistent irreconcilability crystallizes the composer's resistance . . . to forces dominating culture." Nor does the final piece on this record, the Japanese Toshiro Mayuzumi's Prelude for String Quartet (1964), bear up well under the jacket's Hegelian analysis of its structure and methods; what seems attractive about this piece is rather its obvious orientalisms and quiet effects of instrumental color.

Whereas the first record seems historically tentative, the second plunges directly into the vortex of the avant-garde. Here are two of Stockhausen's most influential and talked-about works, *Gruppen* (1955–57) for three orchestras, and *Carré* (1958–59) for four orchestras and four choruses. Both works are examples of Stockhausen's "spatial music." *Gruppen* is meant to be performed, for instance, with the three orchestras separately stationed on three sides of the hall, conducted by three conductors. This division of forces makes possible the simultaneous performance of several different tempos, a feat enormously complex with one orchestra playing under one conductor on one stage.

While the explicitly notated and involved serialism of *Gruppen* must, in the words of a commentator, have required "fanaticism to write out," the composition of *Carré* was assisted by Cornelius Cardew, Stockhausen's then disciple. Cardew, though he attempted to follow the composer's general instructions, seems to have had no real idea of what he was to write; the doubt, in the words of still another commentator, was "all to the good in preventing creative conflicts." Whatever the value of Stockhausen's novel methods of working, listening to this music can only for most musicians produce amazement that sounds of such seeming shapelessness could have been conceived and performed, and even more compel respect for the personal will which could see such a project through.

The next record features the organ playing of the German Gerd Zacher performing compositions by Kagel, Ligeti, and the Chilean Juan Allende-Blin. Kagel's *Phantasie* (1967) can be seen, from one standpoint, as the continuation of a historical crime upon the organ. By combining, as he does here, electronic techniques with the characteristic organ sound, Kagel is following in the footsteps of Laurens Hammond, who introduced the electric organ bearing his name in the 1930s. Kagel's bright idea here was to mix composed music played on the organ with recordings of the environmental noises of the organist's daily life. The sounds on these tapes—some of them made by the organist, some by Kagel—include the flushing of a toilet, the train carrying the organist to work, excerpts from wedding, christening, and burial services, and so on. And the notes actually written by Kagel do their part by sounding like electronically produced material. The other pieces on this record seem less like sound effects, and perhaps for that very reason seem less advanced. Allende-Blin's *Sonorités* (1962) is a collection of mainly static throbbings and sounds like an improvisation calculated to show off the timbres of the organ. Even more static for the most part are the Ligeti works, *Volumina* (1961) and *Etude #1* (1967). The first work manages at its end to get away from the tendency of so many avant-garde works to sound canned, but the second seems mainly distinguished for being performed with a vacuum cleaner instead of the normal organ blower in order to produce a pale and weak sound.

The fourth record consists of unaccompanied choral music, and begins, in contrast to some later works in this series, by using the voice in a fairly traditional manner. The English composer David Bedford's *Two Poems* (1966), written to words by Kenneth Patchen, are pleasant even if some of the work's pleasantness stems from its brevity rather than its incorporating of "sections in which the singers are instructed to fill a fixed space of time with a certain number of notes, *ad libitum.*" Ligeti's *Lux Aeterna* (1966) is slow beyond belief, and the Swede Arne Mellnäs's *Succsim* (1964)—the title is a combination of "succession" and "simultaneously"—uses no words; instead one hears vowels, whispers, hisses, and whistles. The Czech Marek Kopolent's *Matka* (c. 1967) seems more communicative than most of the pieces on all these records: for the composer's pains, the work has been called by a distinguished English critic "disguised bubble-gum music, simple and unprovocative."

The next record contains music for the trombone as played by the well-known virtuoso Vinko Globokar, one of whose own pieces is included here. This disc is significant for the example it provides of an important trend in avant-garde music—the use of instruments in nontraditional ways involving hitting or rubbing them in order to produce sounds, and in the case of winds and brass, singing, humming, and speaking into them at the same time as tones are being blown. For all the skill involved in the production of sound by such means, the total effect resembles nothing so much as a tuneless one-man band. Globokar's *Discours II* (1967–68) for five trombones has all its parts performed on this recording by the composer alone, through the superimposition of five separately recorded tracks; this is a demonstration of the assignment frequently given to avant-garde performers to play with their recorded selves. The Italian Luciano Berio's *Sequenza V* (1966) has energy and some humor, but even then only seems to show just how ugly sounding an instrument the trombone can be. Stockhausen's *Solo* (1966) presents a tape commentary on the trombonist's earlier performance simultaneously with that performance, and finally the Argentine Carlos Osuna's *Consequenza* op. 17 (1966) has as its goal the writing of music of such difficulty that the player is finally forced to give up out of exhaustion.

On the sixth record, the last of the first group, Kagel begins with a viable theatrical idea. *Match* (1964) for three players is written for one cellist scraping on the left, another on the right, and a percussionist who goes from side to side acting as an umpire. This sonic volleyball contest has obvious possibilities for stereophonic recording, and indeed is acoustically effective when reproduced on good equipment. But as music it is utter thinness. Lacking even theatrical effect is Kagel's long work on the other side of the record; *Music for Renaissance Instruments* (1965–66) is played on, among many other instruments, krumhorns, recorders, bombards, curtals, theorbos, and violas da gamba. The music provides a prime example of how neoclassical music sounds when deprived of quotations from the classics.

The second group of records begins with improvisations by the Italian *Gruppa Nuova Consononza* done in 1969. Given the penchant for thinking in extremes so popular in the late 1950s and the 1960s, it was only natural for the retreat from total compositorial control to suggest the practice of improvisation in performance. And consistent with the political ideology of the late 1960s, this record's jacket states that the group aimed at "a collective achievement" in which "the figure hitherto known as the composer is completely robbed of the myth which has surrounded him." But more is lost in this combination of conventionally instrumented and totally electronic works than the *amour propre* of the composer; the fashionable eclecticism of this group's procedures, drawn from jazz and Indian influence as well as chance music, sounds like an unmitigated mess, at once fragmented and boring.

The second record in this group, while perhaps ideologically regressive, sounds more interesting. Zimmermann's *Présence*

(1961) is a piano trio—played, that is, by a piano, a violin, and a cello. *Intercommunicazione* (1967) employs a piano-cello duo. The instruments are used fairly normally, and the piano parts, which sometimes sound like the pieces of Messiaen based on birdsong, provide a refreshing texture. But here again, as in so much of this music, discontinuity remains a problem, one which all Zimmermann's quotations from Strauss, Debussy, Prokofiev and even Stockhausen(!) do little to ameliorate.

The third record in the group returns again to the very center of the avant-garde. The first side contains a long effort by John Cage, as confused in its title and indeterminate in its writing as it seems anarchic in sound. The flavor of the piece, title and instrumentation alike, is best conveyed by the notes accompanying the record:

John Cage: Atlas Eclipticalis (1961–62) for 1–98 orchestral players (86 possible parts) and *Winter Music* (1957) for 1–20 pianists may be performed simultaneously, like so many of Cage's works.

All or some of the instruments can be fitted with contact microphones whose outputs can be controlled by a special interpreter, the "assistant to the conductor," according to the graphic notation of Cage's *Cartridge Music* (1960), by means of adjustable electronic amplifiers.

Atlas Eclipticalis uses maps of stellar constellations as if the star markings were notes printed on music. *Winter Music* is made up of 20 pages performed in this verson by groups of five pianists playing 4 pages simultaneously; the musical notation is ambiguous, and what is notated is unplayable.

As music this makes no impression at all. But as a sonic environment it conjures up a world without plan, purpose, meaning, or value. The sounds suggest a Rorschach test devised and administered by a Dada psychologist; its meaning is in the eye (ear) of the beholder (listener), and its wit can be fully appreciated only by those who are hostile to the idea of organized social life. All this might well make Cage content, for his "music" is a joke as seriously intended as it must be mockingly hostile. And the butt of the joke is that audience which in the bourgeois past has taken music seriously.

The reverse side of this record presents a vocal and instrumental piece by the German Dieter Schnebel called *Glossolalie* (1959–60, version 1961). Once again, any description other than that on the record jacket could only seem unfair. According to the jacket, the title is the

"definition of music for speakers and instrumentalists" on 26 unbound pages: a simple material definition of remarkable elasticity. Any composition conforming to this would be a version of the work, and everybody has the right to produce one. The recording on this disc is of Schnebel's own compositional realization . . . .

Just how a nonexistent composition can have a version is a conundrum perhaps never to be solved by traditionalists. In any case, for such traditionalists the piece, with its quasi-nonsensical text spoken and sung in hysterical voices, sounds like the ravings of madmen, just as did the speaking in tongues so popular among the religiously inclined young at the end of the last decade. The jacket comments that the "incomparable significance" of this work "is in the fact that composers setting themselves the task which is necessary today of politicizing music can learn from this work's technique the elementary manipulations of this absolutely new *metier.*" If this be so, it is clear that underneath whatever politics such art espouses lies the cult of insanity.

The same subverted ground is covered in the next record, which contains choral pieces by Kagel and, again, Schnebel. Kagel's *Hallelujah* (1967) for 16 unaccompanied solo voices is meant to be "understood as a masterpiece of rabbinical expounding"; but *Hallelujah* as a song of praise "is in view of the state of the world today an expression of utter scorn." While *Hallelujah* perhaps contains more real music than is usual with Kagel and the rest, this content can only seem an inadequate reward for the philosophical barbarism a listener must endure at the same time. Schnebel's *Für Stimmen* (1956–58, 1964–68), carrying similar ideological baggage, is a collection of the fashionable whimpers, groans, and sobs which made up so much of avant-garde vocal writing.

The next disc is devoted entirely to tape music. The German

Gottfried Michael König's *Terminus II* (1966–67) derives all of its sounds from one original electronic noise, the *Urklang;* the sounds succeed each other in the composition in the order in which they were originally produced, or backward. Though the piece often has a rhythmic beat, it remains lifeless. Konig's *Funktion Grün* (1967) sounds like a stormy-night broadcast over shortwave radio with, it is true, some oriental noises toward the end. The Hungarian Zoltán Pongrácz's *Phonothese* (1965–66) sounds more refined, but also contains birdbeeps, growls of thunder, siren glissandos, and wind murmurs. Finally the German Rainer Riehn's *Chants de Maldoror* (1965–66, revised 1968–69) is a thin collage, unrelated to Lautréamont's poem, which scatters many long silences among its usual fragments of storms and radio interference.

The last record of the second group is again devoted to Stockhausen. His *Telemusik* (1966) was composed in Tokyo on a six-channel tape recorder in the studios of Japan Radio; its realization on this disc is a two-channel reduction, as are the recorded versions of the other Stockhausen multitrack works in this series. In *Telemusik* the composer writes that he wanted to compose "not 'my' music, but a music of the whole world, of all countries and all races." Toward this end he included music from Japan, Bali, the Sahara, Hungary, the Amazon, China, Vietnam ("what a wonderful people!") and "who knows where else." This material is transformed, with the addition of studio-produced material, by electronic manipulation. The result seems varied and perhaps less dependent on tape music's usual reliance on weather effects and the sounds of nature, but again in this case the work's relative brevity is a considerable virtue. *Mixtur* (1964), based upon orchestral sounds as modified by electronic signal generators, is sufficiently imaginative and polished to be judged by aesthetic criteria; what is missing here, as in *Telemusik,* is the possibility of gaining from listening any warm musical satisfaction,.

The third, and last, group of the *Avant-Garde* series begins with a long piece by Kagel, *Der Schall* (1968)—"The Sound." It is scored for such instruments as foghorn, spaghetti tube with trumpet mouthpiece, plastic tubing, garden hose, rubber bands, telephone, nose-flute, and a few conventional winds as well. The result is 37 minutes of mildly interesting drones and rattles with some very peculiar gasping sounds adding a sinister touch. Because Kagel is here raising basic questions as to "proper" composition and performance, one can readily forgive the absence of the wit which has marked the use of such "instruments" by Hoffnung and Schickele. Unfortunately, Kagel's questions are not raised to be answered, but rather themselves constitute the answers—answers as unproductive as they are unacceptable.

The second record in this last group presents the American Earle Brown's String Quartet (1965), in which the players follow a prescribed series of events whose details are determined by the performers' choices. The piece is only 11 minutes long and makes a wispy, tenuous impression. Here as in the other pieces on this disc—Ligeti's Quartet No. 2 (1967–68) in five mostly delicate movements, and the Quartet No. 3 (1960–61) of the German Wolf Rosenberg—the reliance upon conventional instruments, even if they are not always conventionally used, is itself welcome.

Immediately following is a record containing another of Stockhausen's better-known and important works, *Stimmung* (1968). The title is a word with many many meanings in German, among them "tuning," "voicing," and "mood." The work's six unaccompanied singers sing one chord—a dominant seventh on B flat—for seventy-three minutes, in ways calculated to stress certain overtones as directed by the composer. In a combination of the efficient new and the comfortable old, the singers are assisted in finding the exactly correct pitches by softly sounding electronic reminders on tape; but as they sing, they sit cross-legged in a circle around a low light, much like a campfire. In addition to the vowel sounds they sing, one hears lines of amorous poetry written by Stockhausen, and the repetition of "magic names" of gods and goddesses from many religions, as well as erotic terms. The repetitive, droning effect creates an atmosphere of contemplation, self-absorption, and even passivity; the music serves as background for that ideal trip which seemed in the late 1960s paradise itself.

The next record conceives paradise in rather different terms. The Italian Luc Ferrari's *Presque Rien No. 1* (1970) is a taped sonic environment describing daybreak at the beach. Sounds of birds, dogs, and faintly lapping waters, and muted, indistinct voices can be heard; through the magic of stereophony the "composer" presents a truck driving off from the right speaker to somewhere past the left speaker. It all resembles a sound track for a Jacques Tati film. And yet this vaguely nostalgic boredom is more satisfactory than what has gone before on these records, for it makes no pretense to being music. Unfortunately, that pretense makes its return on the other side of this record, for it is devoted to Ferrari's *Société II* (1967), subtitled "and if the piano were a female body." Here the tedium is occasionally relieved by the interpolation of real music, including welcome snatches of Liszt's famous *Liebestraum*.

The fifth record of this last group begins with the American Lukas Foss's *Paradigm* (1968). This combination of notation, improvisation, and chance is divided into "Session—Reading—Recital—Lecture," and is performed with "notes to play and words to speak, whisper, or shout" by a sextet including percussion, electric guitar, violin, clarinet, cello, and tape recorder with other electronics. The result combines loud frenetic passages marked by a heavy jazzlike beat with quiet, almost inaudible withdrawals. The composition is sometimes entertaining but mostly dull.

Not even this much can be said for the work of another American: Lejaren Hiller's *Algorithms I* (Version I and Version IV—both 1968). These collections of beeps, buzzes, and bangs were composed by means of programs fed into computers and transcribed, on their reemergence, into notation to be played by conventional instruments assisted by the ubiquitous tape recorder. However this music was assembled, it lacks all vitality, and remains heavy, turgid, and meaningless. Filling out this all-American record is Elliott Schwartz's *Signals* (1968), a duet with shouts for trombone and double-bass. Here the only achievement might be the provision of suitable background music for Hobbes's pessimistic view of the life of man.

The final record of all begins with still another piece of electronic music bearing a pretentious title, *Cybernetics III* (1969) by the German Roland Kayn. Here the acoustical material is fashioned entirely out of vocal material subjected to almost complete transformation. The result, as is typical of so much tape music, is the replication of the sound of weather, jet planes, and water running down the drain. The series as a whole ends with the Italian Luigi Nono's *Contrappunto dialettico alla mente* (1968)— "Dialectical Counterpoint for the Mind." Nono has made no secret of his Communist sympathies, and this work has an explicit political program based upon such crimes as the murder of Malcolm X and imperial aggression in Vietnam. To dramatize the presentation of his concerns the composer uses electronically transformed voices along with material produced by square- and triangular-wave oscillators. Though the piece does have a vague tonality, as a whole it resembles old-fashioned radio drama sound effects, this time yoked to agit-prop purposes. Perhaps the significance of Nono's compositions—this work just as much as his other similar political efforts—is the realization of just how much the effectiveness of program music depends on the appeal of the program.

The Deutsche Grammophon *Avant-Garde* series has passed into history, and it is hardly too much to say that the entire musical movement which it documented is in process of suffering a similar fate. Audiences the world over continue their chestnut-worshiping ways, closely followed by their leaders, the best performers. The dream of the avant-garde that it might entice a complete generation of alienated and affluent youth to tune in the new has proved chimerical, as has the idea that music can be revolution by another name. And although related music— sometimes called by new names and often written by new figures—continues to be produced, the intellectual excitement seems gone, and the classical avant-gardists themselves appear dispirited and disunited. Their own corrosive dissatisfaction with what they have done in the past generation is convincingly demonstrated by their restless search—always so marked in the cases of Cage and Stockhausen—for ever newer, ever more outré ways to reach any kind of audience at all.

What went wrong to dash the high hopes of so many young, bright, and talented minds? Why has so much effort left so little of permanent value in its wake? One cannot but be aware of the danger of making sweeping judgments on the basis of even as generous a sample as that contained on these eighteen records. Of course hundreds and hundreds of composers wrote advanced music in the postwar period without having their works represented on the Deutsche Grammophon series. And as has already been mentioned, mainstream music—a category probably wide enough to include someone as involved in the past with the avant-garde as Pierre Boulez—continues to be written and performed and even to some extent appreciated. But the Deutsche Grammophon series nevertheless does cover the main post-war modernist trends of control, chance, improvisation, theater music, and nonmusic; it is furthermore fairly eclectic in its choice of composers and brilliantly recorded.

The most striking evidence these records provide, it seems to me, is the failure of electronic means of musical composition and performance. After 1945—and for Cage even earlier—it seemed as if electricity was an Aladdin's lamp, capable of providing composers with total control over the production of music and its realization. But in place of this grandiose dream of unimaginable power eternally wielded, the reality of electricity's coldness and lifelessness, and the horrid invariability of sounds fossilized on tape became clear—at least to all those not professionally involved. Not only did the tape composer's ability to make any sound he might desire—now become so convenient with the new keyboard synthesizers—prove destructive of the hierarchy of sounds which had previously divided music from noise; performers now found that easy amplification of their efforts, divorced from physical labor, devalued performance. So electronic music has become a vehicle for Walter Carlos's gutting of the classics, for rock bands and movie sound tracks, for sonic environments, TV commercials, and white noise to sleep by.

No more successful has been the attempt to force normal instruments beyond their conventional use. Though the range of possible sounds has in general been greatly increased, the new techniques on wind and string instruments have mostly proven either hard to hear or no more than mere eccentricities. Furthermore, the use of the inside of the piano as a playing field, so attractive to children and to people who don't play the piano conventionally very well, has produced effects of limited variability, weak audibility (unless amplified), and musical sterility. And the whole panoply of performance techniques based upon aggression—hitting and banging instruments under the guise of using them as percussion—reflects only the widespread dissatisfaction and anger with traditional music among the avant-garde.

It is significant that there has been some attempt made to conceal the extent to which this movement has been a real, albeit failed, revolution. Like most revolutions—especially those in trouble—this one has increasingly looked for roots in the past, finding forebears in Bach and Mozart, Liszt and Wagner, Debussy and Mahler. And the revolution's fellow travelers, consistent with their nature, manage to approve the most shocking provocations on the grounds of the necessity of the new, while always being quick to defend the provocateurs' backsliding on grounds of their reconciliation with tradition. And as has so often happened with revolutions in the past, the results of the avant-garde movement turned out to be the opposite of what had been intended. The desire for logical organization of musical material turned into a total serialism which left no room for creative contingency. The desire for freedom from serialism produced random sounds; the writing of continuously varied notes produced monotony. The return to some sort of recognizable harmonic structure produced the boredom of *Stimmung's* one chord. New musical sounds turned out to be noise. Freedom from vagaries of performers produced improvisation, in which nothing remained except performance. And most unhappily, the reaction against the extramusical associations of romantic program music left composition almost wholly dependent upon conceptual schemes and written explanations.

Something of the extent of the avant-garde's failure can be seen from a sad and ironic little record, now also out of print, containing Mauricio Kagel's contribution to the Beethoven bicentennial celebration of 1970.* Though Kagel seems to have felt that the best tribute would be not to play this music at all, he nonetheless had the idea of making an avant-garde collage from passages in some of Beethoven's most beautiful and familiar pieces. Treating Beethoven's music as he might treat his own, on this record the passages, subjected to every structural indignity, are combined, mixed up, and torn almost apart. Yet these samples of Beethoven, momentarily intact in melody, rhythm, and harmony, continue to resonate, casting their spell across the centuries. Thus regardless of his own ambivalence, Kagel has taught us something about the nature of musical immortality. No friend of new music can be happy with the implications of such a lesson.

---

*Ludwig van. Deutsche Grammophon 2530 014.

Part Two

THE PERFORMERS

IT IS TEMPTING to say that where music slackens, performance steps in. An important result of the atrophy of musical creation in our time has been the tendency to replace the composer by the performer, to substitute star performers for star composers. Our living musical heroes are no longer drawn from the ranks of those who write music; gone are the days when countless thousands of Viennese could turn out for Beethoven's funeral procession, or when Verdi could seem the very embodiment of Italian national unification.

Instead, the performer has now come into his own, and our musical superstars are creatures velvet of voice, fleet of finger, or, in the case of conductors, strong of nerves. But while composers may be immortal, performers are all too mortal, though like the famous athletes they are, our famous executants prosper; also like athletes, they age and are replaced. The Lhevinnes—the husband transmitted by the wife—are part of my own past. Vladimir Horowitz has more nearly attained superstar status than any other musical executant of the last two generations. And Yehudi Menuhin bears the sad distinction of being the last child prodigy to have fulfilled the quintessential requirement of that species—that the child be a greater artist than his adult colleagues.

But this new prominence for the performer has been achieved not only through, but because of his separation from the new music. This separation has created severe difficulties for performers; never before have they been so dependent on the past for the music they play and the way in which they perform it. This parasitic relationship to the past has produced both a codified repertory and interpretative style. Nowhere is this more true than in the case of the formerly all-conquering piano (in the words of Busoni) that "discredited, indispensable, and most comprehensive of instruments." And now, due perhaps to the existence of recording and the consequent diffusion of past masterpieces, performance itself seems less significant in the transmission of those masterpieces than ever before.

The Lhevinnes:
Four Hands
at One Piano

JOSEF AND ROSINA LHEVINNE, the deeply Russian subjects of Robert K. Wallace's admiring, but hardly inspired biography,* were, to an extent nonmusicians can scarcely realize, formed and given meaning by the piano which they spent their lives practicing, playing, and teaching. He was born in 1874, the son of a Jewish trumpet player, and died in 1944; she was born in 1880, the daughter of a Dutch diamond merchant of Jewish origin and French cultural sympathies, and died in 1976 at ninety-six. They were both raised in Moscow, they both studied with Safonoff at the Moscow Conservatory, and both received the coveted gold medal on graduation, he in 1892 and she in 1898.

By this time, he was a rapidly rising virtuoso; from the age of thirteen his playing had attracted the attention of the great Anton Rubinstein, and it was only fitting that in 1895, one year after Rubinstein's death, he should win the international piano prize awarded in the master's name. His wife-to-be, though her playing had won fulsome praise from important musicians, had smaller—though quite definite—accomplishments and ambitions.

* Robert K. Wallace, *A Century of Music Making*, Indiana University Press.

They were married in 1898 in a Dutch Reformed ceremony (they both had been baptized) and on their honeymoon they engaged in a small contest to see who could win in learning a Mendelssohn étude. She got the notes faster, but he played them better. And she now found out that he loved to go fishing—an activity where her presence was tolerated only if she remained silent.

Upon their marriage she had made a decision to resign her embryonic solo career in his favor; from this time until his death forty-six years later, her public piano-playing was generally limited to joint appearances with her husband in works for two pianos. Unfortunately, a year's compulsory military service had cost him the impetus gained in his career by the winning of the Rubinstein prize, and upon his return to civilian life he found himself in that situation so depressingly familiar in today's concert life—he was a former contest winner. In order to do without her parents' support the young couple moved for a short time to Tiflis, where Josef could teach. It was however plain to Rosina that a solo career for her husband could not be made from a base in Tiflis. She was already deeply involved in that combination of encouragement, hectoring and coaching which was to characterize her role in their marriage both personally and musically.

The years before the First World War found him touring in Russia, Europe, and the United States. Mostly he was highly successful, but no matter how much he won the respect of critics, his colleagues, and the lay sophisticates of piano-playing, he never hit the jackpot of show business fame. After some years of teaching at the Moscow Conservatory they lived awhile in the United States and then finally in 1909 moved—they thought permanently—to Berlin.

Gradually Josef won a secure place in Berlin concert life; he continued to give concerts in Europe and the United States. He also began to teach a large class of piano students, and during his frequent extended absences Rosina took over his teaching, becoming every day less his assistant and more his colleague. From the outbreak of war they were, as enemy aliens, subject to a mild form of police supervision, but the chief inconvenience they faced (in addition to the growing food shortage) was the ban placed on their musical activities and on their earning money. But this they got round, and Josef even played in support of the German war effort—which cause he, according to a student, rather favored.

At first Josef had trouble after the war regaining his earlier form, for the years of relative inactivity had not only left him rusty but had also intensified a certain tendency toward musical aloofness and noncommunicative introspection in his playing. As is the case with many highly regarded artists whose careers are below the highest level of success, teaching became an increasingly important part of his income; the Juilliard Graduate School was founded in 1924, and the Lhevinnes were among its original faculty. At the beginning of the 1930s, Rosina showed her independence by going off, with their two children, to Austria to teach at Mondsee; she returned there in 1932 when Josef came to Salzburg to play and teach. If at this time there was a certain strain in their marriage, it was paradoxically accompanied by a growing musical closeness, for in the last years of his life they gave twice as many recitals together as he did by himself—their joint concerts did contain some solo pieces for Josef, but the bulk of the recital was devoted to two-piano works.

His death in 1944 found Rosina financially unprovided for, a fact not made clear in this book. She was, to her surprise, asked to remain at Juilliard, and she was soon receiving preferential treatment from William Schuman and Mark Schubart, the new administrators of the school. Her many students began to win contests right and left, and when Van Cliburn won the Tchaikowsky Competition in 1958 she was propelled to a kind of world fame as a trainer of champion pianists, and a direct link between the golden age of nineteenth-century Russian music and the hopes being entertained in the 1950s and 1960s of a musical "romantic revival."

She was not content merely to teach. She began—in her seventies!—a belated emergence as a solo pianist. She played several important orchestral engagements, most notably a series of performances of the Chopin E Minor Concerto with the New York Philharmonic in 1963 when she was almost eighty-three and no longer in anything like robust health. Her last appearance took place in 1964 at the Aspen Music Festival when she played the Mozart Concerto in B-flat K 595 (and not the Mozart C major K 467 as stated in this book). She supplemented the meager list of records made by her husband with discs of the Mozart K 467 for Columbia in 1960 and the Chopin E minor for Vanguard in 1962.

All of her playing was marked by a sturdy technique, a comfortable musicality, and old-fashioned charm. Her students have continued to win prizes, and several since Cliburn have made major public careers. She continued to teach as long as she lived, indeed remaining on the Juilliard faculty until six months before her death.

In his biography of husband and wife, Professor Wallace makes abundantly clear the strong differences between the Lhevinnes as personalities. He was quiet, socially reserved, something of a dreamer, gullible, and easily swindled. He disliked the routine of practicing, touring, and almost everything else about being a concert artist. He loved the outdoors and had quite an admiring eye for the ladies. She, on the other hand, never looked at another man; she was practical, deeply interested in the business of music, gregarious, and greatly attracted to public performance and exposure. Had he not married her, he well might not have become a famous pianist, but he probably would have been a great deal happier. Had she not married him, one suspects she would have lived her life much as she did, save that she might have preferred to play more and teach less.

As far as it goes, this book is adequate, and gives evidence of much time and effort spent in interviews and libraries. The book's origin as a doctoral dissertation is demonstrated by the author's tendency to add unnecessary material, by a somewhat homely style, and by a lack of ease in dealing with many minor details outside his personal experience; nonetheless, it is good to have this serious attempt to document the Lhevinnes' careers and lives. It is a pity (or so it seems to this writer, who was a sometime student of Mme. Lhevinne at Juilliard and is married to Jeaneane Dowis, one of her young assistants in the 1960s) that he fails to go beyond the fine public success enjoyed by the Lhevinnes to consider the significance of their lack of participation in the new currents which so profoundly affected music in their lifetimes, not only in composition, but also in the revitalization of the classic piano repertory.

For it does not seem quite enough that Josef Lhevinne's chief claim to being a twentieth-century pianist lay in his unwillingness to tolerate personal mannerisms in performance at the expense of the composer's text. There can be no doubt that his playing, in its steady rhythm and its avoidance of distortion, was "modern" rather than "romantic."

But all this is a kind of negative virtue; his cool style, which the *New York Times* called that of a "sympathetic but detached observer" tended often, in spite of his brilliant mastery of notes, nuance, and color, to leave colleagues, students, and audiences alike with respect and admiration rather than that transforming emotional experience which music must be in order to influence ideas and lives.

More important in terms of his lack of relationship to his times is the depressing evidence this book provides as to how little, save for the addition of Debussy and the near-elimination of Anton Rubinstein, Josef Lhevinne's repertory changed from the day he left the Moscow Conservatory as a student in 1892 to his death in 1944. It was a repertory composed (in addition to the numerous obligatory transcriptions) largely of what were then and remain till now the most popular and least problematic works of Beethoven, Chopin, Schumann, Brahms, and Liszt. It was largely inherited from his mentors; it ignored the early works of Prokofiev, the extended works of Rachmaninoff, and the later works of Scriabin, to name only the music written by his countrymen before Lhevinne himself had gone very far into middle age. He seems to have played, early in his career, some of the late music of Beethoven, but as he grew older even these pieces were banished from his repertory in favor of what was called after his Carnegie Hall recital in 1924 a "box of unarguably pretty trinkets," a "flower garden of simple, familiar delights." If today's virtuoso programs differ greatly in the seriousness of the music they contain from the programmes of seventy-five years ago, it is a change in which Josef Lhevinne played no part.

And similar questions may well be raised about Rosina Lhevinne. She was able through her talent and industry to replicate in the America of the mid-twentieth century the musical values and the pianistic procedures of the Moscow where as a child she had been schooled during the 1880s and 1890s. Her students did, in point of fact, play a wide range of music for her; but when she taught the music of Bach and Beethoven, of Mozart and Schubert, as well as that contemporary music which she was willing to hear, she was all too often content with correcting wrong notes and rhythms, and advising a seemly adherence to the text and the successful live and recorded performances of others. It is true that when she taught Chopin and Liszt, Tchaikowsky and Rachmaninoff, she spoke on the basis of her ears, not her eyes. Here she was cogent, personal, and creative, and it is no accident that the careers of her most successful students, as in the case of Cliburn, have been made largely in this music.

It would be wrong to place the blame for this lack of major consequence on the Lhevinnes alone. For it is likely that much of the less permanently distinguished aspect of the Lhevinnes's achievement may be traced to its origin in the Russian academic conservatory tradition of piano playing and music performance. This tradition has always emphasized, as did the Lhevinnes, technique as prior to artistic expression, the need to please rather than cause controversy, contests as the prime vehicle for the evaluation of performers, and the subordination of the performer's individuality to some imagined pure spirit of the composer. Along with this attitude of caution toward the individual expression of the performer and the distrust of original interpretative conceptions goes a worship of the past and a cult of its famous personalities. Revealingly, this book quotes Emil Gilels as telling Rosina Lhevinne in 1955 (which for either her or the author, or both, was "in the days of Stalin"): "Not only I but everybody with anything to do with music in Russia knows Josef and Rosina Lhevinne. Even now at the Moscow Conservatory when we have a youngster who plays very well, we say 'Still, he is not a Josef Lhevinne.' " But surely it is time for today's artists and aspirants to make their own tradition of the piano and of performance in general, rather than spend quite so much effort on imitation and veneration of illustrious predecessors.

10

Horowitz: King of Pianists

VLADIMIR HOROWITZ is the king of pianists. Tickets for the limited number of concerts he chooses to play are sold out as soon as his enthusiastic public is informed; the prices charged are higher than those for any other solo instrumentalist, and rather than play for a mere fee he receives by far the larger part of the box-office proceeds. Of the numerous recordings he has made in the past half-century, most are still available, and big sellers to boot—the German subsidiary of RCA has to this date issued no fewer than twenty of his older LPs in what is grandly called the "Vladimir Horowitz Edition." All his recent live performances, when they have not been issued as regular commercial recordings, are available, for those whose tastes run to such things, on so-called "private tapes."

If he has been greatly successful with a large paying audience, and if he as a pianist has for many years been *primus inter pares* in the estimation of his colleagues, he has not received unanimous critical acceptance; in the past, influential musical opinion-makers as different as Virgil Thomson and B. H. Haggin have found his playing to be full of distortion, distention, and exaggeration. Even by his greatest fans he is mostly seen as a keyboard virtuoso rather than as the musical thinker he obviously must be in order to have sustained his career over these many years in the wide and difficult repertory he has chosen to perform. Still, regardless of the reservations which to some extent swirl about his playing, he is now everywhere recognized as a historical figure, honored and respected even by his former detractors.

As a man, Horowitz enjoys a civilized if enclosed life in his East Side Manhattan townhouse surrounded by the *objets d'art* he collects. His social activities seem largely restricted to an intimate circle of friends and business associates. He has spent a lifetime of close watching over his health, and regardless of his private fears he has until recently impressed outsiders as the embodiment of physical health and vigor. Press accounts in the beginning of 1979, however, told of recent surgery; in any case the sad presumption must be that the career of a man of 75 will one day soon come to a close. Though deeply protective of his privacy, he still has not been above allowing a firm of musical press agents to work on his behalf, and not too many years ago he surprised veteran Horowitz watchers by appearing, the very soul of affability, at a record-signing party sponsored by RCA at Korvette's Fifth Avenue store. He practices regularly, he teaches little if at all; he is content to play his pieces the way he likes when and where he likes to play them. The rest, he is plainly saying, is his business.

Little, in point of fact, is solidly known, apart from vital statistics, about this man who has been both so alone in his success and so successful in being alone. The biographical facts, insofar as they are publicly available, are prosaic, at least by the standards of this dreadfully interesting century. He was born in Kiev in 1904 to Jewish parents of the then-emerging Russian middle class; his first piano teacher was his mother. He graduated from the Kiev Conservatory and the same year made his debut in Kharkov. Though he was more interested in composition than in playing the piano, the Bolshevik Revolution, by depriving his family of its money, forced him to turn toward concert performance. He performed widely in Russia, playing in the 1924–25 season in Leningrad alone about twenty-five recitals, each with a different program. Horowitz went to Germany in the fall of 1925, and in early 1926 played in Berlin a series of three recitals which made a sensation, if not at first a fortune. A triumph in Paris was followed by an American contract from Arthur Judson, then and for many years after the kingmaker of the American musical world.

Horowitz made his American debut—to the wildest audience, and generally favorable critical, acclaim—with the New York Philharmonic under Sir Thomas Beecham in January 1928, playing the Tchaikowsky Concerto on which he was to own a kind of patent. His later association with Arturo Toscanini, which began in 1933, was to provide him both with a wife (he married the conductor's daughter Wanda the same year) and a musical influence which was to be all the stronger because of its closeness to many factors in Horowitz's own musical constitution.

For a period in the late 1930s he retired from concert life, but by the war years he was again giving concerts and making records. After great activity in the 1940s and early 1950s, he retired once more in 1953. It was feared that his departure this time was permanent, but he returned to recording in 1962, and in perhaps the most important event in post–World War II New York musical life, he reappeared in concert at Carnegie Hall in 1965. Since then he has played regularly, if not often, across the country and even in Canada, in addition to giving many New York recitals. In addition to these recitals, he resumed, after a hiatus of 25 years, playing with orchestra; his appearance in January of 1978 with the New York Philharmonic under Eugene Ormandy was an event producing among ticket-buyers the kind of excitement one would expect from a reunion of the Beatles.

Though naturally much is gossiped about Horowitz, little else about his life is firmly documented. As a perhaps happy result, his piano playing is left to explain itself. And fortunately, in searching for that explanation, one is not limited to the happy memories of his many recitals, for his recordings—now numbering about fifty LPs—provide an imperishable documentation of his playing. This documentation is all the more valuable because his playing, perhaps more completely than anyone else's, survives the transition from stage to studio with its essential characteristics undiminished.

Horowitz's recording career began in the same year as his American debut. His first sessions for RCA in Camden, New Jersey, involved several small pieces, among them an arrangement of a Scarlatti sonata, a Chopin mazurka, the Debussy "Serenade to the Doll" (from the *Children's Corner Suite*), and the Dohnányi Capriccio in F Minor. Here may be found in microcosm both Horowitz's distinctive style of playing and one side of his lifelong taste in piano music. The playing is immaculate, tonally crisp, rhythmically tight, and alternates strangely between ferociousness and sentimentality. The repertory is typically Horowitz in its fondness for Scarlatti (though later of course he was to eschew, in line with modern taste, arrangements of this composer in favor of the original), the small pieces of Chopin and Debussy, and minor salon pieces which have ranged from Moszkowski through Dohnányi to Poulenc.

Another and vastly more important side of his art is shown in a 1930 recording of the Rachmaninoff Third Concerto made with Albert Coates and the London Symphony Orchestra. This performance, available today on a "bargain" label, bears profitable comparison with the 1951 remake Horowitz did with Fritz Reiner. The enormously increased power of the recording process itself in an era of tape perhaps unduly exaggerates the difference between the flowing, relatively simple, and affecting though unaffected performance of 1930 and the hard, jewellike, disjunct, and idiosyncratically stressed effort of twenty-one years later. But even when technological change has been taken into account, it is plain that the Horowitz of 1951 was a vastly more self-conscious artist who had mined his past in order to identify and intensify his own most striking traits. And this process, perhaps now marked by exaggeration, can be observed still in operation in the recording of his 1978 Philharmonic–Ormandy performance.

Two recordings made in the mid-1930s display still another, and perhaps the most distinguished, aspect of Horowitz's achievement—his performances of those masterpieces rather delicately perched between the classical and the romantic piano repertory. These records—of the Haydn Sonata No. 52 in E-flat and the Beethoven 32 Variations in C Minor—are remarkable for the evidence they provide of Horowitz's ability to purge his performances of this aristocratic music of the clichéd devices of expressivity which were as common in the 1930s as they unfortunately are now. What Horowitz does with these pieces is to communicate both their structural integrity (deriving from classicism) and the passion issuing from their participation in the rising tide of Romanticism. And the fact that Horowitz has always played all the notes (a phenomenon rarer forty and more years ago than in today's practice-ridden musical environment) hardly hurts the general effect.

But it was a recording of the Liszt B Minor Sonata made in England also in the mid-1930s which was undoubtedly to prove the most influential of all of Horowitz's early performances. The Liszt sonata, which was written in 1852–53, represents a break with the classical tradition of the sonata both in structure and content; though Beethoven had flouted the tradition, in the end he wrote out of the deepest respect for its symmetry and balance. The revolutionary message of Liszt in this work affected no one more than Wagner, who was urged along his own way of musical integration through repetition and alteration of motivic material by Liszt's use here of three themes as the basic material for a piece lasting nearly thirty minutes. But in addition to the architectural significance of Liszt's method, there was also in the sonata much of the scatterbrained personality of Liszt the poet, the piano virtuoso, and the romantic lover. It was this side of Liszt which Horowitz, with his magnificent bag of octaves, chords, arpeggios, and above all his wistful rubati, chose to present. The sonata has never been the same since, and neither have other pianists.

More substantial by far is his 1940 recording, with Toscanini and the NBC Symphony, of the Brahms B-flat Concerto. Listening to this, together with a private-label recording of an actual 1936 concert performance of the Brahms D Minor Concerto with Bruno Walter and the Amsterdam Concertgebouw, one can only conclude that Horowitz, in partnership no less with Walter than with Toscanini, has given to the age of the phonograph its most satisfying and complete realization of these summits of the musical literature.

If the Liszt sonata was the most influential of his early recordings, the 1941 collaboration with Toscanini in the Tchaikowsky B-flat Minor Concerto was not only one of the best-selling 78 RPM classical albums ever made, but was also to provide for seventeen years the standard performance of this most beloved of piano concertos. Even faster, brighter, and more brittle than the recording (with the same principals) made at a 1943 Carnegie Hall War Bond concert, it reigned supreme in its clangor and icy surge until dethroned by the 1958 Van Cliburn post-Moscow-Competition disc. Horowitz could hardly be blamed for the fact that Cliburn's secure complaisance and Southern languor were more in tune with the age of the "thaw" than Horowitz' struggle and flight; in any case, the elder pianist's Tchaikowsky stands as the high water mark of forceful, steely piano playing, with its irresistible suggestion of the pianist as king of the universe.

Toward the end of the 1940s Horowitz turned to Mendelssohn. His performance of the three small "Songs Without Words" remains the definitive statement of these largely ignored cameos; and the present repertory status of Mendelssohn's greatest large-scale piano work, the *Variations sérieuses,* is due to Horowitz's performance of it. Of his expansion of Liszt's transcription of the famous Wedding March from Mendelssohn's *A Midsummer Night's Dream* made during this same period, one can only say that this must have been the kind of piano playing the nineteenth century dreamed of as a complete music in itself. Similarly, his playing of the purely virtuoso Liszt is here as elsewhere without parallel. No one else has managed to take this showily vulgar music, so redolent of the pianist's one-night stands, and cast it in precious metal, thereby rendering a hackneyed *tour de force* such as the Hungarian Rhapsody No. 6 as an elegant, independent musical creation.

A surprising and important aspect of Horowitz's work in the years immediately following the war was his championing of possibly the two most important pieces written for solo piano in our time—the Prokofiev Sonata No. 7 (1942) and the Samuel Barber

Sonata, the only American composition with which he has been associated. The Prokofiev, stemming as it does from that part of the Russian musical tradition which combines forceful contrast and angular melodies, seems to have touched the same chord in Horowitz which was responsible for two brilliant recordings of his augmented version of the Mussorgsky *Pictures at an Exhibition* (1947 and 1951). Here, in addition to the controlled force, energy, and elegance which characterize every note he plays, one finds a special opulence and richness, a quality remarkable for heat rather than warmth.

Some of this quality, much to the work's advantage, informs his performance of the Barber sonata, of which he gave the premiere in 1950. This classic of American music was so fully realized by Horowitz that it remains difficult, more than twenty-five years later and after it has been played as a test piece by hundreds of younger American pianists, to imagine it in a conception other than his. Remarkably for a pianist of his fame, he took the trouble to make both the Barber and the Prokofiev his own; the result is so strong that one can only regret that he never sought—or at least never found—other contemporary works to illuminate.

A recording exists of Horowitz's 1953 recital in Carnegie Hall celebrating the twenty-fifth anniversary of his coming to America. Surprisingly—considering Horowitz's reputation as a purveyor of flash—it contains Schubert's posthumous Sonata in B-flat. During the past fifty years in which it has been widely played, this long, "profound" composition has been considered the property of pianists with minds rather than fingers, of those who think nobly rather than play accurately. It must be admitted that Horowitz's Schubert has little in it of the composer's Vienna, of the dull yet glassy sonority of the pianos of Schubert's day, of the endemic dance rhythm so identified with that time and place.

Perhaps indeed Horowitz's performance of the sonata is not profound, for profundity inevitably implies heaviness—and Horowitz's playing, no matter how loud and furious, is never heavy. Whether he in this case played the true Schubert is certainly open to question; what is not is the penetration of his conception, his dedication to the music, and his ability to preserve the long line of the piece against the temptations it presents to maximize the individual beautiful details of which it has so many.

Around this time Horowitz was also occupied with the music of Beethoven. A year before his retirement from the stage in 1953, he recorded the Emperor Concerto with Fritz Reiner, and in the middle and late 1950s he made two discs of sonatas, one containing the Moonlight and the Waldstein, and the other the Appassionata and the less familiar (because unnamed) Opus 10 No. 3 in D Major. No more than he tried to play a Viennese Schubert, does he present a German Beethoven full of weight, seriousness, and public humility. Horowitz plays Beethoven as virtuoso music, as music written—which indeed it was—by the greatest pianist of his day. And he indulges—perhaps more than is allowable in a time which puts so much stress on puritanism in performance—his fingers and above all his ideas. As a result, in this revered music more than in perhaps any other, Horowitz has been accused of arbitrariness and caprice, of willful injection of his personality into a musical material so important as to make any tampering not only unnecessary but sinful.

During his retirement Horowitz recorded three sonatas by Muzio Clementi, an almost forgotten figure today (save for his piano method, called *Gradus ad Parnassum,* which was popularized in a shortened version by another pianist and writer of exercises, Tausig, and witheringly mocked by Debussy), but in his time a compositional influence on Beethoven, a distinguished pianist, piano maker, and music publisher. It is doubtful that his sonatas will ever become part of the regular repertory, for they seem simultaneously both shocking and stale, always fresh and always old-fashioned. But Horowitz's effort on Clementi's behalf, supported by his elegant playing, is an example of an interest in little-known musical literature all too rare among today's famous instrumentalists.

At this point—the beginning of the 1960s—Horowitz left RCA, his recording company from the beginning of his American ca-

reer, and signed a contract with Columbia;* amid enormous ballyhoo, he once again began busily to record. The resulting discs
(of both new material and of music he had recorded earlier)
showed no falling-off from the past, and only raised the tempera-
ture of the speculation surrounding the question of his possible
return to the platform. In May 1965 the question was answered; a
recital in Carnegie Hall was announced and instantly sold out, as
it could have been ten times over. Horowitz walked out on the
stage hesitantly—it seemed almost fearfully—and proceeded to
demonstrate that as a pianist he had never left the audience's
heart. Columbia recorded the concert, and that recording (with
some few small slips having been corrected) is still available
today. The opening Bach-Busoni C Major Toccata and Fugue
showed the pianist in full control of his monumental powers; if
possible, his performance of this piece seems even stronger
twelve years later on the recording than it did at the concert.
Whatever one's reservations about the propriety of this kind of
transcription, Horowitz justified his playing of it, for he preserved and communicated the counterpoint, the harmony, the
inexorable rhythm, and, above all, the ineffable majesty of Bach
in the original. The Schumann C Major Fantasy which followed
was equally great, for the grand scale of this long piece seems
ideally suited to Horowitz's own sense of structure.

If the first half of this concert testified to his love for the piano's
largest masterpieces, the second half testified as well to the essential continuity of his musical interests. Horowitz was always a
Chopinist, and he has continued to place Chopin at the center of
his pianistic life. Of his many Chopin discs going back to the
beginning of his recording career, all have been powerful technically and personal musically—a rare combination in the playing
of Chopin. Sometimes the sheer force of his fingers and his individual musicality have together seemed to unduly complicate the
texture of Chopin's often fragile music. Of the smaller works, the
strong rhythmic framework of the mazurkas has made them perfect pieces for Horowitz, and both his older as well as his newer

* An aside on the mercurial Horowitz temperament: by the late 1970s he had
returned to RCA, from whom his new recordings are once again available.

recordings of them are unsurpassed. A similar judgment can be made about his performances of three of Chopin's larger pieces, the Barcarolle, the Polonaise in A-flat (Opus 53), and the Andante Spianato. In contrast, the G Minor Ballade which concludes the recording of his 1965 recital seems a shade disorganized to justify inclusion on the highest level of Horowitz's Chopin performances.

Scriabin—whose Sonata No. 9 Horowitz played just after intermission in his 1965 recital—has, as befits a Russian virtuoso, long been an interest of his. During his last retirement from the concert stage, Horowitz devoted a whole record to the works of this composer, including the Sonata No. 3 and 16 preludes; more recently he has made another Scriabin disc as well as one of the music of Rachmaninoff. In these pieces, as in much of the overtly exhibitionistic music he has played throughout his career, the musical content in itself has often seemed unable to bear the weight of Horowitz's great abilities, nor has it always seemed worthy of them.

Quite another story is told by Horowitz's magnificent record of Scarlatti sonatas, which dates from the 1960s. This is classical playing, respecting the music's formal criteria of discipline and order, while at the same time infusing every phrase with the suggestion of freedom and even sensuality. That, as in the case of his recordings of Haydn and early Beethoven, he is capable of effecting such a reconciliation of classicism and romanticism is a true index of the greatness of Horowitz's art; it is a reconciliation that he has fully achieved at his finest moments—and in fifty years these triumphant moments have been many and prolonged.

Upon what, aside from enigmatic genius, is this extraordinary achievement based? Of course, at its foundation lies sheer physical dexterity of an enormous degree. Of all the traditional elements of piano playing—scales, arpeggios, octaves, chords, double notes, and trills—he has well-nigh perfect command. His rhythm is unerring and vital, his memory solid, and his ability to learn and retain numerous compositions great. And on the level of intellect, Horowitz is a brilliant musician, sophisticated in areas other than the piano and well able to make scholarly decisions on vexing musicological questions.

But others—not many, to be sure—have possessed these abilities. What separates Horowitz from everyone else is his characteristic, deeply individual piano sonority. It has been called metallic by those who have not liked it; to his admirers it seems the quintessential sound of a piano. In any case, whatever one's opinion of it, it cannot be forgotten. Its secret would seem to consist in Horowitz's way of controlling a Steinway concert grand of a loudness and brilliance that in anyone else's hands would reduce an audience to a shattered wreck.

The advantages of such a piano—highly different as it is from the usual rich, mellow, and quietly brilliant Steinway—lie not only in its carrying power and easy articulation of rapid passages; still more important is the range of dynamic contrast possible and the resulting differentiation of bass, middle, and treble registers. This differentiation enables the melodic line to be highlighted and the piano's extreme dynamic contrasts to be used without blocking the audibility of the pitches being played.

The resulting piano sound is so powerful and attractive in itself that, as it has been Horowitz's greatest glory, it has at the same time been the aspect of his playing which has more than any other limited his musical acceptance. Once having heard his tone—and it has been captured amazingly well on records—one cannot mistake it for that of any other pianist. Long after the particular pieces he has played have passed from one's mind, his piano tone remains, tending to cover the music and render the individual works more similar in sound and character than they really are.

To blame Horowitz for this, to require of him a more neutral, less distinctive sound—such as was cultivated by other great artists like Artur Schnabel, Edwin Fischer, and Wilhelm Backhaus—is not only to ask that he give up an individual virtue; more than that, it is to ignore the entire historical background out of which he comes, with its idea of the solo performer as the divinely unique interpreter of otherwise dead (because unperformed) musical material. What is involved in this idea is nothing less than the ascendancy of the interpreter over the music. In the case of Horowitz, it is this successful attempt at imposing his personality on the pieces he plays which, in the process of bringing him fame, has also earned him the strictures of critics. For in the past fifty and more years, the intellectual leaders of our musical times have not countenanced such a role for the performers of great music. Instead they have required that the performer reveal the composer, not himself.

At the moment, there are signs that we may well have arrived at the exhaustion of this principle of respectful authenticity; whether this exhaustion signifies the rise of a new performance tradition, a return to an older, more personal tradition, or indeed, the last days of the wide popularity of the music we have loved, is not clear. What is clear is that the music of the great composers of the past has been fully capable of preserving its integrity against what have been seen as either the contributions or the depredations of the most powerful performing personalities. This music is universal in its ability to transcend its origin; even the greatest interpreters, however, speak from and to a particular time and place. A performer such as Vladimir Horowitz is a necessary contemporary representative of the masters whose music he has played, and through his efforts an important pianistic repertory has, for a large and sophisticated public, found its strongest new life and its most relevant expression. As a result, whatever the future of music may bring, his reputation as the finest and most significant pianist of his time is assured.

11

Menuhin: Portrait of a Prodigy

IN APRIL 1929, a twelve-year-old violinist made his debut with the Berlin Philharmonic playing three concertos—Bach, Beethoven, and Brahms—accompanied by Bruno Walter. At the end of the concert, the already immortal Albert Einstein rushed to the artists' room via the stage, embraced the boy, and cried: "Now I know there is a God in heaven!"

The boy was Yehudi Menuhin, and this Berlin performance was by no means his first triumph. Seventeen months before, he had played the Beethoven concerto in New York with Fritz Busch and the New York Symphony. After the concert, the *New York Times* critic, Olin Downes, who had wanted to attend a prizefight at Madison Square Garden that night rather than hear a violin prodigy, found himself drafting a review that in its uncontrolled excitement and enthusiasm seemed too strong to be deserved by any child; the review he finally wrote began with restrained comments about Menuhin's "exceptional musical intelligence and sensitivity," his conveying "very beautifully the poetry of the slow movement," his "refreshing taste and simplicity" in the finale. But then Downes, unable to contain himself, opened up:

It would seem, therefore, that the object ordinarily loathed by reviewers and serious lovers of music—the infant prodigy—is not a myth. . . . It seems ridiculous to say that he showed a mature conception of Beethoven's concerto, but that is the fact. Few violinists of years and experience known to this public have played Beethoven with as true a feeling for his form and content. . . . A boy of eleven [has] proved conclusively his right to be ranked, irrespective of his years, with outstanding interpreters of this music.

Today that boy is a man past sixty, rich in honors, fortune, and musical experience. He continues to play widely, if not as frequently as in the past. Nevertheless, his public performances are guardedly evaluated even by his friends; press comment, though frequently too overawed by the historical ring of his career to urge his retirement, still makes clear that his playing days—at least in concert—are or will soon be over. Yet his records, among them many recent ones of demanding compositions—an authoritative new recording of the Delius concerto recently was issued—continue to sell; and to the available discs of his adult performances are increasingly being added LP reissues of those 78 RPM records which remain documents of the time when he was the infant wonder of the entire musical world.

All this, and the years before his first triumphs as well as the entire period between the beginning and the now inevitable end of his public career, are described by Menuhin in his 1977 memoirs, *Unfinished Journey*. The book is at once painfully pretentious, only intermittently interesting, marred by platitudes and overfine writing, yet withal often profoundly moving and revealing. For what Menuhin illuminates in writing about his life is the extent to which a true prodigy is born old and yet remains a child forever in search of that original maturity. His writing, here as elsewhere, is an only partially witting account of that search, the degree to which it remains unsuccessful, and the miracle of completeness from which it started.

Yehudi Menuhin was born in New York City in 1916, the first child of parents whose intelligence was exceeded only by the strength of their will. Moshe and Marutha (Sher) Menuhin, still alive in the late 1970s at a very old age, were themselves born in Russia, he in the middle of the Jewish Pale of Settlement, and she in the Crimea near Yalta. Because of the pogroms they separately went to Palestine, and then again separately to New York, where they married. Moshe was descended from Hasidic rabbis; after religious and secular studies in Palestine (and attendance at NYU on a mathematics scholarship), he ended up teaching Hebrew school to support his wife and family. His wife, who feels herself a product of Tatar Khans, also worked both before and after her marriage as a Hebrew teacher. Their involvement with Hebrew was totally secular, and in the case of Moshe was accompanied by an antireligious attitude which was later to broaden into a venomous anti-Zionism.

When their son was born he was named Yehudi—the Hebrew word for Jew—as a sign, paradoxically that he was "Everyman, evoking no model and continuing no line." His first years were spent in Elizabeth, New Jersey, where the father found it impossible to get along in the religious atmosphere surrounding the Talmud Torah in which he taught. California—the eternal land of opportunity—beckoned, and Yehudi with his parents (whom he called by the Hebrew words for mother and father, *abba* and *eema*) arrived in San Francisco in 1918, there to begin a quick rise to fame and riches.

The adult Menuhins did not simply give their thoughts and hopes—in the fashion of so many immigrant parents—to Yehudi and to a lesser extent to his younger (and also musically talented) sisters, Hephzibah and Yaltah; these parents devoted their energies entirely to the children, educating, disciplining, and supporting them as if they were already the royal family of music. From the age of two, Yehudi was taken to hear the San Francisco Symphony; it was at one of these performances, when he was three, that he first noticed and was smitten by the concertmaster, Louis Persinger, playing the violin. Persinger—a great violinist, talented pianist, and the most significant American teacher of the violin during the second quarter of this century—was approached, but he refused Yehudi as a student because he had no interest in teaching a beginner. A year marking time with a man who, according to Menuhin, taught him nothing, at least produced the feeling that the violin was no longer a foreign object but rather a natural extension of his body. Then—at five—he again went to Persinger; this time he was accepted, and at his first lesson Persinger played a Bach slow movement for the little boy and his mother. Initiated into sublimity, Yehudi went home drunk on music.

From this point on his progress with the violin was so rapid as to seem effortless; and it was certainly astounding:

Not yet eight years old, I had already learned various "student" concerti . . . , the Bach Sonata in G minor, which had sealed with glory Persinger's first lesson, the Mendelssohn concerto, Lalo's *Symphonie Espagnole,* the first movement of Paganini's Concerto in D major, the Tchaikovsky—wolfing down this huge corpus, hair, nails, and all. . . .

Yehudi had five lessons a week from Persinger. Several years later, when he was on tour, he was to receive a three-hour lesson every day. Though he did not attend school, he was privately tutored, at first by his parents and then by specialists. The education given him lacked science and mathematics, but it was strong in literature and—perhaps because it was obvious that he would travel widely—languages. No heir to a throne could have lived in an environment more orderly, integrated, and efficient; his regimen was of course centered around the violin, but it allowed time even for play with his sisters and with other children who were brought in for just such a purpose.

Menuhin's formal debut, when he was still seven, took place early in 1924; his first orchestral appearance, playing the Lalo with Alfred Hertz and the San Francisco Symphony, occurred the next year, followed closely by his first full-length recital in March 1925, a month before his ninth birthday. Persinger now moved to New York, and Yehudi (accompanied by mother and sisters) followed him there. He made his New York debut at the beginning of 1926 in a concert arranged by his hastily summoned father.

From the time he was seven or eight, Yehudi had wanted to study with a touring violinist he had heard in San Francisco, Georges Enesco, a Rumanian who lived in France. The Menuhins had no money to go to Europe, but fortune, in the guise of a Jewish Maecenas, made it all grandly possible. In Sidney Ehrman, himself an amateur violinist and the husband of an immensely wealthy heiress as well, Yehudi found a patron of extraordinary generosity, friendship, and long-term dedication. Ehrman's approaches to the Menuhins were at first rejected, but after he offered to send the whole family to Europe with Yehudi, the parents gave in, and in 1926 they left America for a year in France. There Yehudi laid siege to Enesco, and before long he had become his pupil and even more his disciple and musical son. Menuhin was later to study some months with the third and last of his major teachers, Adolf Busch—the brother of Fritz Busch, the father-in-law of Rudolf Serkin, and one of the significant musician-violinists of the day—but Enesco's combination of romantic freedom and passionate musical seriousness was the greatest single influence on him. He was to remain Enesco's student, except for the time with Busch, at least until 1936.

Meanwhile the boy's performing career had caught fire. His successes in New York and Berlin were followed by similar triumphs in London and in Leipzig, where he played the Mendelssohn concerto at the 1931 celebration of the 150th anniversary of the founding of the Gewandhaus orchestra. In addition to these appearances on the concert stage, by the middle 1930s, while still in his teens, he had recorded several concerti, all but one of the Bach unaccompanied works, and a variety of sonatas and less substantial salon pieces.

Menuhin spent much of World War II entertaining American and Allied troops in the European and Pacific theaters. As soon as the war was over, he visited Germany to perform for the inmates of the newly liberated concentration camps. Shortly thereafter he found himself campaigning in the United States for the right of the conductor, Wilhelm Furtwängler, then suspected of Nazi sympathies, to perform again. In this, with the help of the pianist Myra Hess, among others, Furtwängler was successful, and later made a series of important recordings with Menuhin, including performances of the Beethoven, Brahms, Mendelssohn, and (second) Bartók concertos.

In recent years, while continuing to play the violin, Menuhin has also turned his attention to conducting, often recording with an orchestra which bears his name. Among the works he has recorded, demonstrating solid musicianship if not a great deal of conductorial excitement, are the symphonies of Schubert (of which only the "Unfinished" is currently available in this country) and the four orchestral suites of Bach. He has directed several festivals, and perhaps dearest to his heart is the Yehudi Menuhin Music School, which he founded in England—where he now lives permanently—in 1963. His school, a place where young musicians from the age of seven may come as boarders to combine grammar- and high-school education with rigorous musical instruction, is an attempt to merge the discipline of the musical training he has witnessed on his visits to the Soviet Union with the personal artistic attention and respect for the individual he himself received as a child. In addition to all this, he has associated himself with a variety of extramusical causes and has as a result become perhaps the most visible of the socially committed musicians of our time.

An evaluation of Yehudi Menuhin must be divided into three parts: the short career of the prodigy; the much longer career of the adult artist; and the influence of the public-spirited citizen he has tried to be. His multitudinous recordings provide the material for a musical evaluation, and his memoirs are a convenient chronicle of his thoughts, pronouncements, and actions on musical as well as other and wider issues.

The tradition of the child prodigy of which Menuhin is a part is an old one, at its highest level limited to a few dazzlingly talented children. Without doubt, the greatest of all musical prodigies was Mozart, whose keyboard performance at eight was described by Johann Christian Bach as beyond "all understanding and imagination"; his early ability at improvisation was astounding and his compositions were remarkable in both quantity and finish. Schubert was also a great composer in his teens; so was Mendelssohn. Liszt was brilliant on the piano as a child, as was Paganini on the violin. Closer to our own time, and restricted almost entirely to the field of performance rather than composition, Josef Hofmann made a sensation at the piano on his 1887 American tour, and coeval with Menuhin's rise were the unhappy prodigy careers of the violinist Ruggiero Ricci and the pianist Ruth Slenczynska.

Of all the performing prodigies of the last century, however, Yehudi Menuhin was the greatest. What marks the playing we can hear on his first recordings (early 1928, when he was twelve) and what must have similarly marked his New York and Berlin debuts, is not simply great ability, unusual promise, and the charming sweetness formerly associated with children. What one hears on these records is fully mature artistry characterized by strong and individual musical personality, rhythmic snap, and complete intellectual integration.

One of these 78 RPM sides—a performance of an anonymous sixteenth-century gaillarde, with Persinger providing a piano accompaniment at once sensitive, restrained, and masterful—goes far to justify the violin as an absolute value, like the human voice, independent of the distinction of the material performed on it. Indeed, Menuhin's adolescent tone, in its pure warmth and high seriousness, itself carries an emotional punch not characteristic of the tone of any other violinist on records. In his early recordings, and frequently in those he made in the 1930s, one hears a transformation of the gut, metal, and wood of the violin into living speech. This is an achievement beyond training and conscious effort, though it must of course be based on them; it is a laying bare of what in the nineteenth century would have been called the very essence of song.

One can hear this miracle accomplished again—if perhaps, due to the large scale of the compositions performed, less completely—in two recordings dating from the next year, 1929. In these Menuhin performs the Bach C major unaccompanied sonata and the Beethoven sonata Opus 12 No. 1 for violin and piano. The Bach in particular would be a superb performance at any age; from a boy of thirteen it is unbelievable. Interestingly, Menuhin was to record it twice later; once in 1934, when he was eighteen, and once in the middle 1970s. The most recent recording is disfigured by a cosmetic coat of reverberation applied by engineers more concerned with making a violin sound like an orchestra than with making it sound like a violin. But the 1934 discs are distinguished not only by the musical intelligence and beauty of tone of the older recording; still more, they present a monumental musical conception, an obvious gain in pure physical strength, and the greater smoothness produced by the use of a superior violin.

If the Bach recording is the high point of the young Menuhin's playing of formally austere music, the Bruch Concerto in G minor, which he recorded in 1931, is a revelation of the profundity contained in a work which is always treated as a mere showpiece. In the Bruch, his singing of the slow movement, in its wisdom and gravity, testifies to what was perceived by many in his audience as divine grace.

Menuhin as a child was quite aware of his extraordinary endowments and the power they conferred upon him. He now writes simply, without any false modesty:

Without qualifications, background, or experience, without knowing adolescent yearning, excitement and disappointment, I could at the age of seven or eight play the *Symphonie Espagnole* almost as well as anyone and better than most.

Menuhin was able to turn this self-knowledge to good use in the accomplishment of his musical—and career—goals. When at the age of ten he received the invitation to make his New York orchestral debut in a Mozart concerto, he "had a reservation: why Mozart, why not Beethoven? To play in Carnegie Hall was to play Beethoven, to arrive was to arrive." The conductor, Fritz Busch, when told of Menuhin's feelings, retorted: *"Man lasst ja auch Jackie Coogan nicht den Hamlet spielen"*—"One doesn't hire Jackie Coogan to play Hamlet." But Menuhin insisted that Busch hear him play the Beethoven, and after he finished the opening passages, he writes, "German endearments came raining down on me. *'Mein lieber Knabe,'* he explained, 'you can play anything with me, anytime, anywhere!' "

Given the physical and psychological problems of growing up, it would have been unusual if this state of perfection had lasted. It did not. In his book Menuhin speaks of the breakup of his violin playing as paralleling the breakup of his first marriage; another and perhaps more profound explanation might reflect on the difficulty an erstwhile child prodigy finds in living without the discipline and support provided by parents and teachers, which is at the same time flattering and so necessary to an immature ego.

But whatever the relationship between his emotional and musical lives, he had, from an early age, recognized the existence of technical problems in his playing. The day after his New York orchestral debut he became aware of involuntary muscular tension in his arms. He could not help realizing increasingly as he grew older that not only his personal life but also his violin playing was "full of holes," his career a destination reached before a proper foundation had been laid.

Perhaps fortunately, Menuhin has been concerned with self-analysis all his life. Applied to the violin, the concern to understand and exert conscious control has led him to books, teachers, and in the 1950s to the practice of yoga as a means of relaxing what must have been otherwise ungovernable tension. This involvement with yoga began during a 1951 trip to the Orient, and in India he went so far as to engage a guru, who for fifteen years thereafter came to Europe every summer to guide Menuhin's exercises. A predictable corollary to his belief in the value of yoga is a dedication to an almost completely vegetarian diet and in particular a total avoidance of white sugar and white flour. He finds that this new way of life has deepened his control over the violin beyond what he knew as a child; it is perhaps enough that it has enabled him to continue performing at times when he must have been close to despair.

Be all that as it may, the evidence of his playing difficulties can be heard on the many recordings he has made in his adult life. They are most noticeable, as might be expected, in new recordings of works also done earlier. Such is the case, for instance, with his recent Bruch Concerto in G Minor, which he had played so marvelously at fifteen. Comparing the newer recording to the older, one is conscious of a technical stiffness, a kind of clumsiness in getting around the violin, and above all a certain thinning and tightening of his once rich and seemingly easily produced tone. On the other hand, while there can be no doubt of this mechanical decline, the newer recording is redeemed by the nobility and penetration of his conception of the work, qualities lacking today among his younger colleagues. Much the same could be said of his two recordings of the unaccountably neglected Elgar concerto, the first made in 1932 (with the composer conducting) and the second in the middle 1960s.

But Menuhin has not, in the fashion of so many youthful successes, spent his life in an attempt merely to repeat his first triumphs; his repertory is vast and adventurous. He has recorded all the major works for violin and orchestra—with the exception, it seems, of the Sibelius and Tchaikowsky concertos—and several for the viola in addition. He has not shied away from the difficult (and still knotty for the audience) works of Bartók, and he has recently recorded the concerto of Alban Berg with Pierre Boulez. Contenting himself neither with already existing masterworks nor with the minor romantic pieces obligatory for virtuoso violinists, he has commissioned works from such famous composers as Bartók and Ernest Bloch, and from lesser-known writers as well. Nor has he restricted himself to the performance of what is normally accepted as serious, "classical" music; successfully appealing to younger audiences, he has in concert and on records attempted to combine Western instrumental performance with Indian artists and their music, and he has recorded, in the form of duets, renditions of 1930s popular songs with the famous jazz violinist Stephane Grappelli.

It is likely that some of the same motives and energies which made possible and encouraged his exploration of the violin repertory also turned his attention to social and political issues. In addition to his efforts after World War II on behalf of Furtwängler, Menuhin was early active in arranging for Soviet artists to play in the United States, and he was a vocal supporter of Ros-

tropovich—and Solzhenitsyn—in their battles with Soviet of-
ficialdom, battles which to a limited extent Menuhin shared during his 1969–75 term as president of the International Music
Council (an offshoot of UNESCO). Similarly, though he had for
many years owned a house in Greece, he made public his unwillingness to return to Greece during the Colonels' regime, just as
he would not, for a time after 1956, visit Hungary.

But of all Menuhin's positions on nonmusical matters, it has
been his views and actions in relation to his fellow Jews, and specifically to the state of Israel, which have provoked the most discussion. Already in 1947, on one of his early postwar trips to Germany, he was accused, at a Displaced Persons camp, of being a
little too quick in his willingness to forgive the Germans their
crimes. In defending himself, he writes that he believed

insistence on vengeance, excluding all other response, was, however understandable, a weakness. Patriotism cannot be enough if it puts beyond
consideration most of the human race. I too was a creature of my experiences, and they had shown me my fellow man the world over, even in
Germany.

This statement, both in the burden of tolerance it places on
Jews and in its demand that they resist what he sees as their own
tendencies toward parochialism and exclusionism, is very revealing of Menuhin's idea of what it means to be a Jew. He is obviously proud to be a Jew himself, at least as far as that designa-
tion refers to his ancestors. And yet, with that pride goes a
marked residue of the opinions of his father, who made no secret
of his negative feelings both about the Jewish religion and about
Zionism.

Yehudi himself cannot be held responsible for his father's prej-
udices, but there is evident in his memoirs a profound unease on
matters Jewish. It is plain that he regards Israel and the Jewish
people with a certain rueful affection, but it is also plain that for
him all nationalisms—not least among them the Jewish variety—
are oppressive and stifling, blocking the way to that internationalism which is the goal of so many who aspire to decency. He

has played many times in Israel and even helped to raise money for charitable organizations there, but at the same time he cannot forbear lecturing Zionists and their sympathizers on their duties toward the Palestinians and their Arab brothers. He is an advocate of Middle Eastern confederation and one suspects that, without fully realizing the consequences, he would welcome the eventual integration of Israel into the surrounding milieu and its disappearance in its present form as a distinctively Jewish state.

Controversial as Menuhin's attitudes toward things Jewish may be, they are entirely consistent with his general stance on world affairs. And this stance, in its pretension to being above ideological struggle, in its assumption of neutrality in the service of the brotherhood of man, in its hope for a new society combining the best features of the socialist and democratic worlds, in its reliance on passive resistance to one's friends and graceful compromise with one's enemies, falls very much within the accepted canon of liberal opinion. If his views have not found acceptance everywhere, from his comfortable position in the center of contemporary morality he can easily enough class the objectors as unconverted souls with whom an extra effort is required.

It is difficult not to see this emphasis on universalism and internationalism, which is so apparent in Menuhin's nonmusical public life, as deeply related to, and indeed coming out of, his great performing career. For it is an expression of the logic immanent in such an activity as playing the violin for ever larger and—one hopes—ever more appreciative audiences. A performer does not perform for himself, and still less does he perform for the composer or for some abstract idea of music itself. He performs for people, and the fewer who are *a priori* excluded from his sway, the better. A composer, as an original creator, cannot avoid taking sides and thereby making opponents as he makes adherents; a performer must try to satisfy all audiences and all musics. Thus, performers are perhaps even more tempted than most other people to serve the regnant political, social, and cultural ideas of their day.

Yehudi Menuhin is not to be condemned for such service. But

neither is he to be credited—as he so often is—with extraordinary fidelity to the duties of human leadership. It is not as a leader of mankind that he is significant; it is as a violinist and exponent of a great musical literature that he has made his mark, first in a childhood of genius and then in an adult life of solid if less glamorous and overwhelming artistic accomplishment.

The Performer's Predicament

IN ORDER to understand the situation of performing musicians today, it is necessary to realize that there is now, to a historically unparalleled extent, no relationship between the music famous artists perform and the music serious composers are writing. The evidence from concert programs and the box office is ubiquitous. A performer's career can no longer be advanced, but rather only harmed, by any association with new music. Such new music as is programmed is played either by musicians at the second level of public renown or—and then only occasionally—by stars making a quick descent into charity. No matter by whom it is performed, the new music is hastily learned and quickly forgotten.

Even that doughty champion of the avant-garde, Pierre Boulez, conducted a largely conventional repertory of music by dead composers during his years at the New York Philharmonic; and for all that, he left his post with a dissatisfied audience which, despite his efforts to please them, saw him as what some members of his own orchestra have called "Twentieth-century limited." And it is plain that the appointment as Boulez's successor of Zubin Mehta, a "name" long connected with the imposition of conductorial personality on widely accepted music, was fresh proof of the primacy in today's music business of the performer over the contemporary composer.

It is paradoxical, however, that notwithstanding their present centrality, there seem today to be fewer famous performers and certainly fewer interesting ones than at any time in memory or than can be found in accounts of our musical past. Several examples in support of this generalization come immediately to mind. Thus, in order to snare a famous conductor, orchestras are increasingly required to agree to his retaining his previous post and therefore holding two positions at the same time; great opera companies are obliged, in order to keep their reputation for high-quality singing, to engage the same circuit-riding stars as appear at every other major house instead of being able to develop and keep their own regulars in lead roles; the solo recital, save for those given by a handful of artists, is becoming increasingly unsalable.

In line with this situation, the prevailing tone of criticism of today's performers, as may be seen from a cursory reading of the daily New York press, is marked by that combination of pedantry and caprice which characterizes the intellectual journalism of the bored. This generation of music lovers, furthermore, has developed a specific vocabulary to describe the performers they hear: terms such as streamlined, efficient, analytical, objective, up-to-date, and modern in themselves evoke the loss of interest by the musical public in contemporary performers. Pockets of enthusiasm do exist, but they seem more often than not limited to a few conductors and singers who are not considered musically very serious or to those stray instrumentalists whose careers, as with Van Cliburn and Mstislav Rostropovich, intersect with the major currents of twentieth-century political life.

Why should there be, at a time of such concentration on performers, so few really significant ones? Many reasons have been suggested, from poor education in music schools to the hardships of jet-age travel on the artists most in demand. But perhaps the most important cause of this dearth of performers is generally overlooked, partly out of conventional piety and partly also out of the very real difficulty of proposing a solution. I refer to that same state of affairs which is responsible in the first place for today's abnormal emphasis on performers at the expense of composers—the absence in our musical life of a viable new music and the resulting severance of the historical link between contemporary composition and contemporary performance.

The present situation is relatively new, for even in the recent past composition and performance were closely connected. At least until World War I, for example, the leading composers of the day were often themselves the greatest executants. As is widely known, Bach was a virtuoso performer of his own keyboard works; so were Beethoven and Chopin. Liszt, in addition to being an unsurpassed performer of his own pieces, was legendary for his performances as pianist and conductor of music by others as well. Wagner was famous as a conductor of Beethoven. In this century, Gustav Mahler was, until his death, better known as a conductor than as a composer. Even the greatest purely instrumental figure of the nineteenth century, Paganini, played his own music, much of which has remained in the violin repertory (and some in the piano repertory as well, due to Liszt's transcriptions) to this day. Closer to our time, Richard Strauss was a revered conductor of a wide repertory, including his own music. The achievement of Sergei Rachmaninoff as a pianist was and is widely recognized, but at least two other major twentieth-century composers, Béla Bartók and Sergei Prokofiev, were also active and phenomenally gifted pianists.

Even performing musicians who were not composers—virtuoso instrumentalists and singers—played the new music then being written as a matter of course, because the audience demanded it. The last three-quarters of the nineteenth century, for instance, were marked by a popular rage for the latest products of serious musical culture, and musicians hastened to satisfy the public by, if necessary, transcribing the latest hits for every barely possible instrument and combination of instruments. In this way, long before the piano-roll and the phonograph, contemporary music was almost instantly propagated along with the reputation of the performer.

But now, no longer able to exercise his traditional artistic function of presenting new music to an expectant audience, the performer has had his attention turned of necessity to a music already long since accepted into the museum of culture. As if in response to the decline of new music, this old repertory, which stretches from way before Bach to Strauss and Puccini, has been dramatically rediscovered, expanded, and revitalized. The process of giving new life to old music is not of course unique to our own time; it began in the nineteenth century, with Mendelssohn's revival of Bach, Wagner's championing of Beethoven, and Anton Rubinstein's later historical piano recitals. But it was not until our century that accurate texts of the great classical masters (Bach, Beethoven, Schubert, Brahms) were widely disseminated. And of major importance to today's generation of musicians, because of the present impossibility of refreshing the old music with insights gained from successful exhibition of the new, the performance of this great body of work has come under the universal sway of the two leading dogmas of musical interpretation—historical authenticity and exactitude.

The dogma of authenticity has strangely taken two different forms as it has been applied to the two different kinds of music making up the established repertory—the music written up to and including the time of Beethoven and Schubert, and the music, usually styled "Romantic," written from the time of Schumann to World War I. For the older repertory, "authenticity" has involved not only editions purged of inaccuracy and editorial emendations but also, in the music of Bach and his predecessors, a return to original instrumentation and ornamentation.

The effect of this return to the text may be seen clearly in the enormous contributions of three artists who flourished most gloriously in the period between the two world wars—the pianist Artur Schnabel in Beethoven and Schubert, the harpsichordist Wanda Landowska in Bach, and the conductor Arturo Toscanini in Beethoven. What was so important about the accomplishments of these artists is not simply that (as in the case of Schnabel and Landowska) they were willing to explore less known repertory, or (as in the case of Toscanini), to proclaim a new identity of the performer with the greatest music. Nor did their importance lie either in their undoubted technical abilities or in their openly proclaimed devout commitment to music. The monumental success of these artists lay in their ability to convince a large and sophisticated audience that having been cleansed of the errors of the past, the music was now being presented to them for the first time new from the mint, resplendent in the purity of the composer's intentions, and untouched by the hands of adulterators.

No longer was the music of the past to be at the mercy of egotistic romanticizing interpreters with their exhibitionist distortions. Indeed, in the 1920s it had begun to seem intolerable to the musically sophisticated that performers existed in order to express themselves. Fully consistent with the modernist revolt against the glorification of the artist's personality, a demand arose for presentation of the music of the greatest composers as it really was written, with performers serving as no more than a transparent medium.

Here is the significance of Landowska's oft-quoted remark to a colleague: "You play Bach your way, I will play him his way." Schnabel's biographer, César Saerchinger, put it less wittily but even more religiously in his description of the rule governing Schnabel's edition, done in the 1920s, of the Beethoven piano sonatas: "Strict adherence to the composer's will as expressed in the original text was at all times his supreme command."

This principle of obedience, which has given birth to the idea of an objective interpretation, has been expressed in perhaps its most extreme form by the conductor Eugene Ormandy:

The pertinent problem of musical interpretation has been happily epitomized in an observation made by Arturo Toscanini. . . . The maestro listened with me to the broadcast of an orchestral performance. He sighed and quoted a remark that the Italian composer Arrigo Boito once made to him: "Blessed are the arts that do not need interpreters. They cannot be poisoned by histrionic mountebanks as is too often the case with the divine art of music."

Ormandy goes on to quote Verdi:

As to conductors' inspiration and as to creative activity in every performance, that is a principle which inevitably leads to the baroque and untrue. . . . No, I want only one single creator, and I shall be satisfied if they perform simply and exactly what he [the composer] has written. . . . I deny that either singers or conductors can "create" or work creatively.

After all this, it comes as a shock to hear the recordings of Beethoven and Schubert sonatas by Schnabel, of Bach on the harpsichord and Mozart on the piano by Landowska, of Beethoven symphonies and Verdi operas by Toscanini. In listening to them one searches in vain for evidence of that divine humility, of that extinction of the performer's ego which the ideology had promised. One finds numberless musical virtues—every blessing of individuality, excitement, and original creativity which the hated romantics had preached—but of fulfillment of the ideology, of total submission to the composer's *ipsissima verba*, very little. One need only mention Schnabel's softened melodic contours, as well as his freely changing tempi, fluctuating widely without direction from Beethoven's and Schubert's texts; Landowska's massive rubati and exaggeration of scale through imaginative use of romantic tone-colors and doublings; Toscanini's actual rescoring—even in the sacred Ninth Symphony—of Beethoven's orchestration for greater acoustic effect.

Yet for our generation of serious musicians, the ideology has become regnant. They use the best, most scholarly editions, they listen to the most "correct" performers on records, and they use all the tools of historical criticism to vitiate and destroy each other's—and their own—instinctive musical conceptions. This abdication of personality and individual musical difference increasingly results in note-spinning and loss of musical effect not only upon the audience but upon the future work of the performer himself.

If the application of historical authenticity to the great works of the pre-Romantic tradition has involved a return to the text, and a rejection of older performance tradition, the performance of romantic music, in addition to textual accuracy, has produced a return to the tradition of old performances, to the practices of those virtuosos in whose hands alone the music is felt to have achieved full existence. This attitude toward past performances has arisen as a partial component of the so-called romantic revival, and to some extent is a reaction against the excesses and intellectual pretensions of the objective school of interpretation with its reverence for scholarship and high art.

Where the likes of Schnabel, Landowska, and Toscanini execrated the traditions they inherited as the repository of mannerism, artificial style, and literal error, today's interpreters of Chopin, Liszt, and Tchaikowsky generally extol the performers—Josef Hofmann, Sergei Rachmaninoff, and Fritz Kreisler, to name only three of the greatest—with whom romantic music has been associated. Technical instrumental considerations, singing tone on the piano, vibrato and staccato on the violin join quasi-scriptural discussions as to the beauties of certain mannered rhythmical distortions. These rhythmical distortions, as well as their accompanying skewings of the notated melodic line, become virtues to be undeviatingly imitated.

Among conductors, immersed now in a competitive battle to produce yet more splayed and fragrant renditions of Bruckner and Mahler (perhaps to make up for the paralyzed though cleansed Mozart and Beethoven they present), the same interpretative goals obtain. Here Wilhelm Furtwängler, with his appearance of visionary penetration into the composer's very soul, is the model. And if the resulting interpretations can be spiced up with some of the physical gyrations of Leonard Bernstein and the relentless propulsion and extreme dynamic contrasts of Sir Georg Solti, so much the better.

It is significant that what is being looked to as a musical ideal is in no sense the real virtue of any of these performers. For the elegance and restraint of Hofmann and Kreisler, the icy brilliance of Rachmaninoff, the profundity and unfailing nobility of Furtwängler (and of course the freedom of Bernstein and the tautness of Solti) are scarcely imitable. What can be and is imitated are the superficial manifestations, the minor though showy defects and eccentricities, which accompany all stirring and original art.

The second triumphant dogma of our time, exactitude, follows quite naturally from the fact that attempts at authenticity, at the reproduction either of text or performance, are essentially imitative. It is a requirement of all imitation that it resemble the model as closely as possible. That which the performer does, he must do exactly. Wrong notes, rhythms, phrasings, dynamics, and instruments cannot be seen as mere accidents or only well-intentioned mistakes; they represent *error* and must be uprooted. And so we have today's cult of musical cleanliness, in which note-accuracy is the supreme good. But unfortunately, as performances conceived and evaluated in these terms become better, they become more indistinguishable. It is a sad fact of today's musical life that artists can be told apart only by their characteristic weaknesses, not by their unique and individual strengths.

It cannot be too highly stressed that the chief problem of musical performance today is these various modes of slavish orientation to the past. Performers by themselves can do nothing about the current state of new music and its absence from musical life. But performers do have some control over the way they do their own work. It is possible, for instance, to do something about the present dependence young artists have on the great number of old performers who as teachers are becoming increasingly institutionalized at the highest levels of our music schools, upon phonograph records as the repository of performing virtue, and upon an academically trained critical press all too ready to apply to live performance the standards of graduate-school musicology.

The solution to the problem does not lie in discarding the past as useless, in ignoring what composers have actually written, or in disregarding what past performers have found out and made available concerning the music to which they have devoted their lives. The solution lies in elements too refined, too complex, and above all too *musical* to be notated symbolically, taken off a recording, or learned in a journalistic account of past heroes. The vital elements of a performance can only come from the direct, unmediated relationship of the performer to the music, a relationship of course often affected but not finally determined by training, scholarship, or convention. Until performers once again learn to enter free of fear and false respect into such a relationship with the music they play, the situation is unlikely to improve.

13

In the Matter
of Interpretation

IN REFERRING over and over again to the piano, I am not
merely displaying a bias toward my own instrument. The piano
remains by all odds our most popular serious musical instrument.
Not only is a piano in the house—not to mention piano lessons for
the children—even today a mark of social advancement, but at
the level of public fame, major solo careers modeled on those of
the past are still being made, if in smaller numbers. Once having
made those careers, the lucky performers last longer on the stage
than their string and vocal colleagues, if not as long as this
century's remarkable breed of orchestral and operatic conductors. This evidence, along with the existence of a large body of
master-works written for the piano and its immediate forebears
and going back before Beethoven to Mozart and Haydn, makes it
easy to think the piano has always been with us and, as a natural
corollary, will always be so.

Since this view of the piano's eternality is so widely held (even
in the face of the fact that both the piano and the solo recital in
their present form date only from the last half of the nineteenth
century) one can only welcome the opportunity two recent
books* provide for us to examine the current state of affairs in the
piano world. Such an opportunity is all the more interesting because these books, and their authors, have different approaches

*Alfred Brendel, *Musical Thoughts and Afterthoughts*, Princeton University Press; Reginald R. Gerig, *Famous Pianists and Their Techniques*, Luce.

and indeed different subjects; the well-known Austrian pianist Alfred Brendel is concerned with great music and its intellectual and emotional communication, while Reginald Gerig is a happy example of a type so necessary to the health of pianistic culture—a man with an insatiable curiosity about what makes the fingers go.

Mr. Brendel, whose career has recently seemed to take on a new dimension of international renown and activity, begins his book with an article dating from 1966 and written to mark the completion of his recording of Beethoven's piano works. Here he discusses the conditions under which the recording was made, the differences between Beethoven's piano and ours, and many of the pieces themselves. He has some wise things to say about texts and editions, and is to be commended for taking a strong position against those performances whose primary goal is historical exactitude.

In his immediately following comments on this article—one of the "afterthoughts" of his book's title—he expands his remarks on the tasks of the interpreter to treat in enlightening detail Beethoven's indications for dynamics, expression, accentuation, pedal, and modifications of tempo. The next, and last, of his three pieces on Beethoven is a consideration of the relationship in his sonatas between their psychological content and the formal means which express that content. He defines the sonatas' content as "a drama in which the character of the principal theme predominates." This predominance is conveyed by a process which Brendel calls foreshortening—the melodic, motivic, harmonic, and rhythmic condensation and tightening of the musical material.

The second section of Brendel's book is concerned with Schubert's piano sonatas and their defense against charges that the composer's style did not develop, that his sonatas are failed copies of Beethoven lacking the stronger passions, and are finally unpianistic. It comes as no surprise that, to Brendel, Schubert's greatness is equal to, if different from that of Beethoven. The difference lies in the fact that compared to Beethoven the architect, Schubert composed like a sleepwalker. In Beethoven's sonatas we never lose our bearings; they justify themselves at all times. Schubert's sonatas happen. There is something disarmingly naïve in the way they happen.

If Schubert has been neglected, for Brendel there are many reasons; chief among them are his lack of virtuoso self-confidence, the lack of performance and publication during his lifetime, his initial reputation as a (mere) songwriter, both the classicism of music lovers (their preference for Beethoven and Mendelssohn) and their Romanticism (their distrust of Schubert's happy use of classical forms), his uncomfortable demands upon performers, and finally the desire of the Viennese public for the easygoing Rossini and Donizetti. That these many reasons may strike a reader as often contradictory seriously diminishes neither their individual suggestiveness for performers nor their interest for music lovers who feel a need to place their love for Schubert in some kind of intellectual context.

The writings on Liszt which follow are an attempt—successful only, one suspects, with the already converted—to reclaim that composer and pianistic idol for serious music. Liszt's work, Brendel finds,

faithfully and fatally mirrors the character of its interpreter. When his works give the impression of being hollow, superficial, and pretentious, the fault lies usually with the performer, occasionally with the (prejudiced) listener, and only very rarely with Liszt himself.

On this view, Liszt both in composition and performance was a phenomenon of expressiveness rather than virtuosity, a great revolutionary who because he earlier than anyone else saw the future of musical harmony has been defended by such modern figures as Busoni and Bartók. An indication of Brendel's willingness to challenge the until recently accepted image of Liszt as an aesthetic charlatan is his championing of the composer's monumental Variations on a Theme of Bach (using a basso continuo from the first movement of the cantata *Weinen, Klagen, Sorgen, Zagen*). Though such a respected musical figure as the late Pierre

Monteux saw this work as one of the greatest achievements in variation writing since the famous Chaconne of Bach, it remains unplayable, on grounds of good taste, in polite intellectual society; one wishes Brendel luck in his fight.

The remainder of the book includes three short sections on Busoni, two on Brendel's revered teacher, Edwin Fischer, and one on the problems a concert pianist has with the pianos available for his use. His writings about Busoni's music leave one interested, perhaps more to read about that enigmatic character than to hear his music. His writings about Edwin Fischer will help to keep alive the name of an artist whose many recordings of Bach, Mozart, Schubert, Beethoven, and Brahms have received less public attention than those of his contemporary Artur Schnabel as documents of the performance style regnant in Germany and Austria in the 1920s and 1930s. His complaints about pianos will be immediately understood and sympathized with by his colleagues; his requirements for satisfactory instruments are sensible and practical, as is his suggestion that pianists learn something about the inner mechanical workings of the instrument to which they devote their lives.

But for all the valuable facts and ideas contained in this book about the composers and their music—and piano performance as well—it is plain that the significance of Brendel's literary efforts is the same as his reason for writing at all: to justify and perhaps even expand the individual role permitted to an interpreter by our present guardians of musical virtue. He makes clear, for instance, the insurmountable difficulties which lie in the way of the perfect recapture of original performance styles; he writes succinctly and without regret "we have to resign ourselves to the fact that whenever we hear Beethoven on a present-day instrument, we are listening to a sort of transcription." For him the interpreter should not only try to understand the intentions of the composer—intentions which in any case can only partially be understood from the musical notes and markings in even the most accurate and detailed text—but also "seek to give each work the strongest possible effect." He frankly calls the "notion that an interpreter can simply switch off his personal feelings and instead receive those of the composer 'from above' " a "fable."

Though Brendel is very much a child of our intellectual times in his frequent disclaimers of any desire to distort what the composer has written, he realizes that the authenticity and the strong effect after which he aims may not always result one from the other. It is precisely because Brendel, in addition to his high pianistic skills and his dedication to the music he plays, is so conscious of himself and of his own role in his work that he may be counted as a fruitful force in bringing new life to music which may have begun to seem to many both overplayed and overfamiliar.

If Alfred Brendel has resolutely taken the musical high road, some may feel Reginald Gerig, by writing at such length about piano technique, has taken a lower one. In point of fact, his book does more than discuss the famous pianists and their technique promised in the book's title. It is also a potted history of keyboard instruments and the music written for them from the time of Rameau and Couperin and even earlier; in addition it is greatly concerned, especially in its coverage of the last century (which properly takes up more than half of the book) with famous theorists and their technical systems.

Much of the contents of Gerig's book is composed of lengthy excerpts from fairly well-known (as well as some less standard) how-to-do-it manuals. To these extended passages he adds his own commentary, beginning by stating his own preference for a "natural" piano technique, one based upon "those laws of nature . . . concerned with physiological movement and muscular coordination." Great pianists, he finds, discovered and used these laws often by instinct; those not so gifted have often fallen prey to arbitrary systems "contrary to natural law and distorted in perspective."

Gerig describes the early clavier approaches recommended by the seventeenth-century Italian and English schools, in addition to the advice of Rameau and Couperin. He calls this knowledge valuable for pianists who by studying the harpsichord and the clavichord will "discipline their touch . . . [and] sharpen their listening powers." He discusses the work of C. P. E. Bach and quotes at length from his *Essay on the True Art of Playing Keyboard Instruments* (1753 and 1762). For Gerig, the essence of touch used on those keyboard instruments which antedate our modern piano was close finger action with minimum involvement of the arm, and it was this approach which underlay the technique used to play the new and quickly popular piano.

Gerig notes that the early great practitioners of the piano—Mozart, Clementi, Cramer, and Hummel—were still tied to the old finger technique, though legato playing, not only in melodic passages, was becoming ever more important; still it was Beethoven who as the first modern pianist used a technique developed from the piano itself and involving the whole body. Beethoven's reliance on always more powerful pianos, joined with the expressive demands of his music, was at odds with older traditions of elegance and restraint; it was also ironically at odds with the lasting influence of his devoted pupil Czerny, who through his thousands upon thousands of finger exercises led generations of piano students in the direction of mechanical facility achieved through rigidity and tension.

But the pace of pianistic advancement was now accelerating not only with the demands for melodic playing, power, and even greater dexterity in the new music of Chopin, Schumann, Brahms, and Liszt—all composers whose opinions on piano playing are fully described and quoted here; a parallel development was the proliferation of methods designed not to teach the piano to would-be virtuosos but rather to instruct a mass playing public.

Gerig is very informative on one such commercially successful attempt, an appliance called the Chiroplast. This device, later recommended by Liszt, was a rigid framework through which the hands were inserted in such a way as to guarantee the proper position and movement of the fingers, hands, and arms at the piano. The significance of this and of the other mechanical aids which followed was not simply the flamboyant demonstration it provides of the general reduction of genius to method which is characteristic of art and science in modern times; it seems to this writer that the use of the Chiroplast and its children aided piano playing no less efficiently, if perhaps less musically than the piano teachers of the day. For what the appliances and the teachers had in common was the instruction of students by appearance and imitation, by caring how the body, arms, hands and fingers *looked* rather than by how the proper muscle movement and sensations might be felt and directed by the student. It was beginning to be obvious then that a more rational technique could only be based upon an understanding of the physical reality beyond deceptive appearances.

Great progress was to be made in the last half of the century by a number of teachers (rather then great pianists) beginning with Ludwig Deppe (1828–90), best known in the account of his work given by the American Amy Fay in her still fascinating *Music-Study in Germany* (1880). From this point on, Gerig's book becomes more than a collection of fine phrases about graceful posture and platitudes about elegant execution. Deppe, whose high importance the author rightly estimates, had the great virtue of approaching the piano on the basis of what the muscles and joints seemingly not directly involved—those of the arm and body supporting the fingers and hand—do in order to produce the desired sounds. He emphasized the movement of the arm in playing, with chords to be played with the arm's controlled free-falling weight. In this he was followed to the point of exaggeration and distortion by the theorists of the weight-and-relaxation school (wittily if inaccurately characterized by a wag as the pupil waiting while the teacher relaxes) and its leader, Rudolf Maria Breithaupt (1873–1945). Gerig, though he properly sees the school of Breithaupt with its rejection of control and tension as a needed correction to the preceding high-finger school and the resulting frequent digital paralysis, is also surely correct in opposing the idea that falling weight alone can play the piano.

Gerig suggests, as he approaches the present, that a proper intellectual and practical basis for piano technique may be found in the scientific researches of the American Otto Ortmann and their practical application and extension by Arnold Schultz in his *Riddle of the Pianist's Finger* (1936). Schultz, building upon Tobias Matthay (the teacher of Myra Hess) as well as upon Ortmann, provided a system based both upon necessary muscular relaxation and active finger coordination. It is remarkable that the most valuable part of Gerig's book comes to an effective end with an account of the work of these two Americans; will a future edition continue, now that the piano has become a rage in the Orient, with a description of Japanese and Korean theorists?

As it stands, Gerig's book would have benefited from a consideration of the technical approach of such recent important teachers of successful soloists as Sascha Gorodnitzki, Adele Marcus, and Rosina Lhevinne in New York, as well as Ilona Kabos in London; the brief description—relegated to an extended footnote—of the work of one such teacher, Isabelle Vengerova (the teacher of Leonard Bernstein and Lukas Foss among many others), only mentions some general precepts without discussing the peculiar atmosphere of terror and intimidation which accompanied so much of her teaching and that of an assistant as well.

It is regrettable that there is in this book no real consideration of the technical methods employed by the greatest pianists of the century, among them Hofmann, Rachmaninoff, Horowitz, and Artur Rubinstein. Though the approach of Vladimir Horowitz in particular seems deeply idiosyncratic, many younger pianists have none the less made rigorous attempts to imitate him; an analysis by Gerig of the reality underneath what they thought they were copying would have been welcome.

A deeper question about this book—one hesitates to call it a shortcoming, because it is unclear that anyone could, given such a subject, have done otherwise than Gerig—lies in its entire orientation toward a great musical past, a past of composition and pianism against which the present seems meagre and derivative. Gerig does discuss the pianistic novelties of Cowell and Cage and the double keyboard piano of Emanuel Moór, but it is plain that his heart and his mind both lie with the performance of the extraordinary body of music written in the nineteenth century. It is melancholy to observe that Gerig can quote not only without disapproval but also without discussion the following passage in a letter written him in 1967 by Professor A. A. Nikolaev, pro-rector of the Moscow Conservatory:

> In our program of examinations, we include compositions bringing out a vast technical ability of a young musician. Frequently students perform études by Chopin, Liszt, Rachmaninoff, Scriabin, Debussy and other contemporary composers.

And as it is with Gerig and Professor Nikolaev, so it is with the world; the most important and influential piano works of the last sixty years, those of Schoenberg and Messiaen (unmentioned, significantly in this book) have ultimately won few listeners and fewer performers.

As a result, it seems that what Gerig means by a "natural piano technique" is one which, in its constant emphasis on cantabile legato, and sonorous tone, uses the body in such a way as to make the great masterpieces of the past sound the way we know they ought to sound—a knowledge based not upon contemporary creativity but rather upon our memory, largely inherited or the result of avid listening to recordings, of dead performances.

Though Gerig early quotes Josef Hofmann's statement that technique "is a chest of tools from which the skilled artisan draws what he needs at the right time for the right purpose" his book is testimony to a fact which he only partially takes into account—that technique is anything but artistically neutral. He does make well the case for the relationship between musical playing and a musically based mechanical approach; he does not consider the extent to which a technical approach, because it grew out of older artistic demands and tastes, can imprison the art it attempts to convey, and close off a fresh look at its undiscovered possibilities.

This is a fault of which Alfred Brendel in his consideration of interpretation is more free than is Gerig in his consideration of technique; nonetheless, both authors seem so concerned with a past art and its execution that one misses any suggestion that the piano has a future not fully contained and proclaimed in its past.

Indeed, they have little choice, for there is no longer any widely viable new music being written for the piano, and no longer, for the first time in the history of the instrument, are there great pianists who are also great composers. The effect of this lack of new raw material on pianists and audiences, and upon the very act of playing the piano, has been the freezing of the repertory as well as the institutionalizing of interpretive conceptions. It is this sorry state of affairs which explains the finally recherché character of Gerig's book, and the faint tone of embattled defensiveness which so often marks Brendel's. They, as many artists and teachers today, are doing their talented best; it is hardly anyone's fault alone that present efforts seem insufficient reasonably to predict a future consistent with the piano's past glories.

14

Does Performance Matter?

IN THE PRECEDING two chapters I discussed the problem of the communication of music from the standpoint of the performer. In this chapter I propose to look at the problem from the standpoint of the music. It is, of course, a commonplace idea that performance is of great importance in the communication of serious music. In a sense, it is easy to see why this should be so; for most people, music can only be heard when it is performed. But the value attributed nowadays to performance goes beyond this practical consideration. Indeed, there can be little doubt that we live in a musical age which exalts the performer, renders him fame and fortune far in excess of what is granted to living composers, and even confers upon a lucky few a measure of immortality through the medium of recording.

As a pianist, I have spent much of my own musical life in an atmosphere carefully structured to produce active believers in this cult of performance. I was trained mostly by Russian teachers, ending with three years of lessons from the queen of Juilliard piano teachers, Rosina Lhevinne, who died in 1976 at the age of ninety-six. From her and from my previous teachers I received a rigorously strict education in the way the piano was played in Russia even before the turn of the century; viewers of the recent films on the Kirov ballet school and on Russian gymnasts will have some idea of what this training was like in spirit even if not in specific content.

More was involved than simply learning how to master the piano mechanically. What to do with every piece—which of the innumerable technical and musical options to employ—was a matter of equal importance. How seriously such details were taken for their effect on the final result may be seen from a tense exchange I had with Mme. Lhevinne during one of my lessons in the early 1960s. I was playing for her the Emperor Concerto of Beethoven, a work which I was to perform the following week with a minor orchestra in California. As I started to play the opening cadenza, she immediately objected that I was using the damper pedal—the mechanism on the piano, operated with the right foot, which sustains the sounds after the fingers have released the keys—much too much. When I demurred, she said: "But last night you went to hear Richter: didn't you hear how *he* used the pedal?" When I answered that the famous Soviet pianist's pedaling was the one aspect of his playing I disliked, Mme. Lhevinne softly answered, after a pregnant and hostile pause: "I only wish for you the same success."

Every detail, then, was of major importance to the performance as a whole. I myself accepted this general proposition in evaluating both my own work and the work of others. And so, it seemed, did everyone else. Thus, whenever I went before the public I found, as does every performer, that I was critically judged in terms of how well I had satisfied the finely detailed standards of each reviewer, standards which were based upon the most careful discrimination of difference. The problem was that these differences themselves differed very widely from reviewer to reviewer.

There was one school of performance which tried to solve the problem of difference with a single intellectual stroke. This was the school of historical authenticity, preeminently associated among pianists with the name of Artur Schnabel. To Schnabel and his followers, the right way to perform a piece of music was not the way decided by the performer (or by his teachers!); the right way—and the only way—had been decided by the composer in the very process of writing his piece. For proponents of this position, there was no longer any discussion of Rubinstein's tone versus Horowitz's, of Hofmann's staccato versus Rosenthal's or even Rachmaninoff's Chopin versus Cortot's. For these fundamentalists, the question was not how an artist expressed himself through his own interpretation, but whether he expressed the music through fidelity to the composer's intention.

In practical terms, this meant playing fully, no more and no less, what was notated in the best possible edition of the music, and the subordination of the performer to the music. Yet even this attitude of fidelity to the text (called *texttreue* in German) turned out to be only another means of identifying differences and assigning importance to them. That these differences were seen as involving authenticity rather than virtuosity and self-expression hardly meant that they no longer counted: indeed, from this point of view, the music depended even more heavily on performance (the "right" performance) than ever before.

For a long time now I have been nagged by doubts about the cult of performance, but it is only since I began listening to many more performances than I once had occasion to do, and to listen to them, as a critic, in quite a new way, that these doubts have begun to crystallize. For example, once, in preparation for an article on Wagner's *Ring*, I listened with score at least once to nine different complete performances of the entire cycle—approximately 135 hours of music—as well as to most of the recorded performances of one or another part. As I listened, the music remained beautiful, but to my surprise the specific performances seemed to count less. Except for some miserable singing on one set of recordings, and the intrusion of English on another, all the versions were more than adequate to allow for the deepest musical pleasure; but beyond that, the highly talented individuals involved tended to become increasingly vague in my mind as compared with the power of the music itself. The differences in performance—here faster, there slower; here louder, there softer; here a singer with a better voice, there a singer with a more passionate characterization—were essentially nugatory.

It was the same with recording quality and technique. The relative range of quality in those recordings was wide, an under-

standable product of their varied ages and the original purpose
for which they were made. But a very few minutes of listening to
each recording was enough to accustom me to its technological
level. Here as elsewhere, as my catalogue of differences length-
ened, my assessment of their importance became weaker. The
music still came through, and the music was what mattered the
most.

But this was opera. What about other kinds of music? Would
the same conclusion emerge from a similarly concentrated exposure to many different performances of, say, symphonic
works? In an effort to answer the question, I chose for consideration perhaps the most widely played instrumental music—and
some of the most beautiful and influential as well—ever written:
the nine Beethoven symphonies.

The current Schwann catalogues list 20 versions of the complete set; more are available in better record stores from European companies which have not chosen to have them widely distributed here, and still others have been made and are now
discontinued, awaiting repackaging and reissuing at lower prices.
In addition to all this, there are countless recordings of individual
symphonies by every major conductor and many others little
known or even ignored.

Out of this embarrassment of riches I have listened to ten
complete sets: one each by (in alphabetical order) Ernest Ansermet, Bernard Haitink, Otto Klemperer, Erich Leinsdorf, Willem
Mengelberg, George Szell, Arturo Toscanini, and Bruno
Walter—and two by Herbert von Karajan. I have also listened
to individual symphonies performed, sometimes more than once,
by Pierre Boulez, Colin Davis, Wilhelm Furtwängler, Jascha
Horenstein, Karajan, Erich Kleiber, Klemperer, Pierre Monteux, Arthur Nikisch, Fritz Reiner, Victor De Sabata, Hermann
Scherchen, Leopold Stokowski, Toscanini, Walter, and Felix
Weingartner.

All these recordings are well known, and some of them are
famous. They have been exhaustively and repeatedly described
by highly competent critics both in contemporary reviews and

later in fully annotated articles and discographies. Though there is always some, and occasionally a great deal of, disagreement among these evaluations, a consensus about each conductor's work tends to emerge with which it would be difficult to quarrel. Toscanini's records are fast, bright, tense, and often exciting; Mengelberg's are wayward, arbitrary, distorted, and provocative; Klemperer's are serious, humorless, heavy, and "profound"; Szell is vital, interesting, somewhat plain, and concerned with getting the best possible playing from his orchestra; Karajan is brilliant, a bit slick, and strangely moving in his icy control. And so it goes.

Among the performances of single symphonies, Boulez in the Fifth sounds remarkably uncommitted either to the music or to the tradition which has grown around it; Furtwängler unconsciously tears the music apart and therefore sometimes achieves effects of the utmost plasticity; Scherchen takes some unusually fast tempi in the *Eroica;* Weingartner offers a curious combination of unmannered conceptions with lush orchestral executions. And so on.

The differences, then, are certainly there in the large. And they are also present in detail, as I discovered by selecting two passages—one in the First Symphony and the other in the Seventh—which pose two distinct kinds of problems in performance: one in the conductor's fidelity to the text, and the other in the level of orchestral playing which he is able to elicit.

The passage in the First Symphony is the second theme of the first movement. Here the problem for the conductor is to find a tempo which will both accommodate the tranquil opening of the theme and its weightier and more outspoken continuation, and at the same time not be so different from the pace of the rather skittish first theme as to lose the possibility of overall integration.

Of the recordings I have listened to of this section—fourteen in all—the greatest contrast is between Mengelberg and Leinsdorf. Mengelberg, though he does not take a slower tempo to begin the second theme, adds a *ritenuto*—an immediate slowing down—to the bars introducing the weightier music that follows. Not content with that slackening, he concludes the phrase with an enormous *ritardando*—a gradual slowing—on the *fortissimo* chords which introduce the return to either the semiobligatory repeat or, after the repeat has been played, to the development section of the movement. But Leinsdorf, possibly the most textually observant of the conductors I heard here, will have none of this alteration of tempo. Since the score indicates no change in this particular section, Leinsdorf plays it in the very fast *allegro con brio* tempo which Beethoven prescribes for the main body of the movement.

Of the other conductors, both Klemperer and Haitink are as rigid as Leinsdorf, but in a slower overall tempo. Haitink goes along at a middle-of-the-road pace while Klemperer chooses a tempo so slow as to give a ponderous and dour impression. Szell, Monteux, and the two Toscanini versions are, in ascending order, slightly more flexible rhythmically, though always within a strict classical framework. Karajan in both his later recordings shows a greater willingness to take liberties, but these are pale compared to Mengelberg's. Walter and Furtwängler, though they bear some resemblance to Mengelberg in their perception of the demands of the music, are carefully discreet in their deviations from a single tempo.

Do these differences in performance make any difference to the experience of listening to the music? I cannot see that they do to any significant extent. Even Mengelberg, though his recordings are currently the subject of attacks in the musical press for what is considered their interpretative license, hardly seems to be doing more than underlining what Beethoven wrote.

The opening of the last movement of the Seventh Symphony presents difficulties not so much of musical interpretation as of execution. Chief among these at the start are the articulation of winds and brasses in the repeated notes and the clarity of the first violins in several short scalic patterns. Coming slightly later are the fast dotted rhythms for the strings and the rapid two-note phrases in the first violins. In both passages, not only clarity but good tone is the goal.

Of the fifteen versions I listened to, the Cleveland Orchestra under Szell undoubtedly surmounts the problems of these passages better than any other group; the Orchestre de la Suisse Romande under Ansermet is the poorest performer. Both in clarity and tone quality alike, all the other orchestras—including such legendary groups as the Boston Symphony (Leinsdorf), the Concertgebouw of Amsterdam (Mengelberg), the 1937 New York Philharmonic (Toscanini), the NBC Symphony (Toscanini), and the Berlin (Karajan) and Vienna (Furtwängler and Karajan) Philharmonics—fall in between.

Nevertheless, despite these perceptible differences, all in all the better performances are only marginally clearer, cleaner, and of more pleasing sound than the lesser efforts. And in any case, no orchestra, including the Cleveland, plays the passage perfectly, and no orchestra, including the Suisse Romande, plays it so badly as to interfere to any serious degree with the music. All the performances I heard adequately communicate the structure of the music and its emotional power.

Of course it may be that this is so only because the average level of artistic achievement on these records is very high. Yet there are grounds for thinking that even differences vastly greater than those which are present in these Beethoven recordings matter only marginally. Two kinds of evidence, admittedly speculative, may be adduced here. The first concerns what may be reasonably suspected about the early performances of what we now accept as the great masterworks, and the second involves the curious phenomenon of transcriptions.

Anyone who has had anything to do with the performance of new music knows just how tacky most of these renditions actually are, and how approximate is the fulfillment of the composer's notes and performance directions. I wish I could say that I am talking here only about subtle matters, but in fact veterans of such performances know in their hearts that survival often must replace fidelity as a goal in this kind of work. While modern music is indeed hard to perform, there is no reason to suppose that it is harder for us than the new music of the nineteenth century was for the performers who first had to play it. Certainly composers, then as now, complained bitterly about the performances they were accorded. It would therefore seem likely that such works as the Beethoven symphonies were themselves mangled on the concert stage early in their lives, subject as they must have been to lassitude, perversion, and simple incompetence. And yet the masterpieces established themselves—to the point that present-day performers are often accused of *lèse majesté* if they fail to play them to the highest possible standards.

The scandal about transcriptions has now mostly died down; not because they have been accepted, but rather because they have been driven out of existence in polite society. So completely have they vanished from orchestra programs and the repertories of refined instrumentalists, that it is easy to forget how much the most famous music in the Western tradition owes to its being thus retailed. In the nineteenth century, in the absence of recordings and of today's many concerts, orchestral and chamber compositions were circulated in transcription designed for amateur four-hand piano performance in the home. Professional soloists also made a practice of playing transcriptions of operatic and even orchestral excerpts. All this helped to keep the music alive. In more recent times, Bach's popularity owes much to the inflated and often bombastic transcriptions made by and for Leopold Stokowski and other famous conductors of modern orchestras. (Something of this practice continues to exist, though outside the world of serious music: electronic, "synthesized" performances of both Bach and Debussy have become bestsellers in the pop market.) In short, the music has survived, and indeed prevailed over, even the most vulgar distortions of performance.

Another example of the power of great music to survive inadequate performance may be seen in the remarkable recording of the Beethoven Fifth made by Arthur Nikisch with the Berlin Philharmonic in 1913. In this performance, because of the inability of the primitive acoustic recording process to capture sufficient sound from the strings, brass and wind instruments were used to add volume. Yet what emerges from the record is the symphony itself. It is not the work played by an orchestra in a live concert, not a modern recording, but it is, simply and powerfully, the very core of what Beethoven created.

No one, surely, would argue for the positive virtue of stone-age recording processes or incompetent performances. But recording techniques have long since ceased to be a problem, and even competence is becoming less and less of an issue. There was a time when a performer could either get through a piece—playing as many of the notes as correctly as possible, as audibly as possible, and as musically as possible—or he could not. Records have changed all that. Since the late 1940s, magnetic tape has enabled each note, if necessary, to be recorded separately and then, thanks to the miracle of inaudible splices, assembled into a "whole" performance. When this convenience is added to the electronic manipulation of sound level, tone color, and room ambience, the very possibility of incompetence in the old sense disappears. The weak sound strong, the old young, the dull bright, and the sloppy precise.

Thus, on records, technically excellent performances have become as routine as they are—and always have been—rare in the concert hall. Perhaps it is this above all which has made performance, in spite of its present position in musical life, seem so much less consequential than it did once upon a time.

Part Three

THE SCENE

NO MORE THAN ARTISTS, members of the audience hardly make up their minds by themselves. The relationship between a listener and a composer, between a listener and a performer, is not quite one-to-one. Forces other than purely musical ones go into the making of taste. In music as in other forms of art, wider intellectual currents and commercial factors alike influence the evolution of public preferences and creative decisions. The role of intellectuals outside music in forming the aesthetic climate is in many ways an unexplored chapter in contemporary musical life.

A significant example of this role in the past is provided by the hitherto largely unknown musical writings of the poet and would-be politician Ezra Pound; this ambitious autodidact provided in his own arbitrary likes and dislikes a significant example of the early-twentieth-century modernist rejection of the romantic era.

Another crucial influence on the formation of musical taste has been the development of sound recording. Not only has this industry made the masterpieces of both composition and performance widely and cheaply available; in the very process of creating a consistant level of performance unapproachable in the concert hall, it has elevated the established repertory and the received fashion of its execution to the status of enshrined institutions. And as if to show its power to make something out of nothing, the recording industry is even able on occasion, as in the case of the former child prodigy Ervin Nyiregyházi, to attempt the creation of a career out of the wreckage of a life.

Another commercial factor operating on music since World War II has been the rise of contests as the principal means of choosing performers for the concert stage. This development deserves scrutiny as much for the motives of the contests' sponsors as for the value of the contest selections themselves. And finally the way all of the many factors mentioned in these pages come together to constitute our musical world deserves discussion from a standpoint not overly influenced by either the naïve optimism of music lovers or the professional optimism of the beneficiaries of the *status quo*.

15

The Rise of
Modernist Taste:
Ezra Pound

EZRA POUND was a self-appointed expert in all manner of nonpoetic subjects he found interesting. For Gertrude Stein he was a tiresome village explainer; Max Beerbohm gleefully quoted Pound's father as saying with beaming parental pride, "That kid knows *everything!*"

Pound was better known for his presumptions in some areas than in others. In economics he devoted much time and print to his obsessions with the sin of usury and the nostrum of Social Credit, and in politics he parlayed his sympathy for Mussolini and Fascism into a United States visit in 1939 to explain the world to a motley group of American politicians. For all these pretensions he paid a large personal price, when his wartime propaganda broadcasts for Italian radio resulted in an indictment for treason and thirteen years of subsequent confinement in a Washington D.C. insane asylum.

Some of Pound's expert interests may be considered, however, rather more benign. In an intellectual age which likes to attempt separation of art and life, disastrous consequences—either for society or for the poet himself—are not often claimed for Pound's aesthetic tastes and attitudes. Deeply interested in painting and sculpture, for example, he was associated with Wyndham Lewis in the Vorticist movement and also published in 1916 a memoir of the short-lived French artist Henri Gaudier-Brzeska.

But the nonliterary field which most occupied Pound was music. He did not come from a particularly musical background, and does not seem to have had any serious musical training either. Nonetheless, his mother did play the piano and the organ, and the family on occasion gathered around the keyboard for sessions of music-making in which young Ezra—according to William Carlos Williams—"couldn't even carry a tune."

*Ezra Pound and Music** is the first of two volumes on Pound and music planned by its editor, the Canadian composer and author R. Murray Schafer. In his preface, Schafer states that the second volume will be concerned with Pound's efforts to realize his theoretical positions in actual music; the first volume presents all the poet's writings on music, interlarded with a running commentary by the editor. In addition, Schafer has provided both a longish introduction containing many examples of the influence of music on Pound's poetry, and at the end of the book a helpful set of short biographies of the now-frequently-forgotten musical personages mentioned therein.

Pound's activities in music undoubtedly received a powerful thrust from his poetic concern with Provençal verse. He looked with nostalgia and even envy at the troubadours and what he saw as their fusion of words and music. He saw the development of poetry as having gone away from that union, and he thought the development harmful. In the then contemporary world of English poetry of the early twentieth century, he found a relation between the new metrical freedom of *vers libre* and rhythmical irregularities in music; in support of *vers libre* he quoted Couperin's observation from *L'Art de toucher le clavecin* (1717): "We write differently from what we play."

His musical writings may be said to have begun with a 1912 article for A. R. Orage's weekly *The New Age* on the relation of po-

* R. Murray Schafer (Editor), *Ezra Pound and Music: The Complete Criticism*, New Directions.

etry and music. The same year he collaborated with the pianist Walter Morse Rummel on a collection of troubadour songs, providing translations and searching for some of the original music. About 1914 he met Arnold Dolmetsch, the author of a significant twentieth-century manual on early music performance, *The Interpretation of the Music of the XVIIth and XVIIIth Centuries* (1915). From Dolmetsch he obtained a clavichord, about which he remarked, "So here I am with a clavichord beside me, which I can't afford, and can't reasonably play on."

Pound wrote a long article on Dolmetsch for *The New Age* the next year which set the content—if not quite the acerbic tone—of the criticism he was to begin writing for that magazine two years later. His decision to be a music critic was in all likelihood not only the result of his musical interests but also of a pressing need to earn a living. From 1917 to the end of 1920, he reviewed London concerts under the pseudonym of "William Atheling." As was his habit, he took his work seriously, attending hundreds of recitals in London's smaller halls—Bechstein (later Wigmore), Aeolian, and occasionally Steinway. The small amount of time he appears to have spent going to orchestral concerts and operas, though it accorded with Pound's preference for individual and small-group efforts rather than large agglomerations, may also have been influenced by the greater difficulty, then as now, of getting free press tickets for highly successful mass attractions.

There is no point in laboring Pound's formal incompetence. He was aware of it himself and often wrote regretfully about his technical lacunae. But because the self-awareness of his shortcomings did not pass over into any feelings of critical incapacity, it is necessary to mention how lacking his writing is in details about the performances he reviewed; he does not ever remark that a performer played wrong notes. He does not seem to have realized that comprehensive criticism, just as in poetry, can be written in music only on the basis of the same intellectual equipment—even if not the same artistic skill—as was required to carry out the creative task in the first place.

Instead Pound depends upon describing his own emotional reactions to what he was hearing, in terms which he might expect would rouse similar feelings in the reader. Thus a not untypical short review reads in its entirety,

PHILHARMONIC QUARTET (Aeolian) good firm quartet, no need of any special superlatives to describe them. First movement Schumann F major, Op. 41, 2, probably as good a piece of work, or better for its time than the Ravel [Quartet], possibly, even, more inventiveness. Languishes in Andante, Scherzo rather vacuous, Finale improves.

In the many long reviews, Pound was at his most fascinating in discussing pianists and singers. The piano—or PYE-ano as he liked to call it—was his *bête noire*. He disliked its sound, preferring the tone of earlier, plucked instruments; he wondered whether the opening of the piano part of the Beethoven Kreutzer Sonata would have sounded better on the harpsichord. Piano concertos he disliked—among them those by MacDowell and Grieg—though he had sympathy for the solo music of Chopin. He was quick to see the excellence of the then young Artur Rubinstein, but in a perverse judgment found his Chopin "despicable" and his Bach "magnificent" for its contrapuntal mastery.

Toward singers Pound was often vastly more enthusiastic. Those who most claimed his attention were the more serious artists, such as the tenors Vladimir Rosing and Yves Tinayre. Not only did he devote a great deal of attention here as elsewhere to repertory—in the case of Rosing and Tinayre, the Russian and early music respectively—but often he stopped to examine repertory and performance in terms of textual values. Though Pound was scornful of the English practice during and after the First World War of singing German lieder in other languages, it is curious that in the many places in this book where he discusses the attempts made to set words to music he nowhere mentions the late Romantic composer Hugo Wolf, who perhaps more than anyone else in the two centuries before ours thought deeply and successfully about the problem. One can also wonder at Schafer's failure to point out this surprising omission.

In all of his critical writing, Pound seems most to have been concerned with rhythm. Here he liked discrete sharp-edged blocks of sound, marked by clear outlines, with "the *beat* . . . a knife-edge and *not* the surface of a rolling-pin." He preferred long-term effects achieved by continuity of the (right) tempo to the frequent slackening and quickening of the movement associated with the vagaries of Romantic interpretation.

While Pound advocated such modern and less personal rhythm in the performance of familiar music of the nineteenth century which he disliked—he referred to Schubert's B-flat Trio as "weeping camembert"—the obvious applicability of such straightforward pacing was to the more linear and less harmonically dense pre-Romantic literature as well as the modern music just then beginning to be written. He called what he liked "pattern music," and in his memoir of Gaudier-Brzeska he wrote: "Music was vorticist in the Bach-Mozart period, before it went off into romance and sentiment and description." The music he most enjoyed, composed even earlier, had "tones clear as brown amber" and according to someone Pound quotes (probably Dolmetsch) was "beautiful even if you play it wrong." For Pound this music was cool and structured, "certain main forms filled in with certain decorations."

Against this ideal Pound contrasted impressionism, music he found "like a drug," which "starts with being emotion or impression and then becomes only approximately music." This was the end of the road he thought, reached by Wagner and Scriabin; the epitome of music's fate was Beethoven, "the symbol of the suffering or decadence of the European ear, and the general triumph of loudness."

As Schafer points out, Pound does not seem to have heard during his work as a music critic many of the important works written around the second decade of the century. Schoenberg is never mentioned, and Stravinsky may have been played only once in his hearing. In English music he was contemptuous of recent native composers—Bax, Bowen, Bridge, Davies, Elgar, and Ireland—and their patriotic boosters; he much preferred the revival of Hebridean folk music by Marjory Kennedy-Fraser and her daughter Patuffa.

Pound's move to Paris at the end of 1920 marked a shift in his musical activities from journalistic scrutiny to personal involvement as composer and theorist. While still in London he had conceived the idea of an operatic setting of Villon's poem *Le Testament*, and in 1921 as soon as he was established in Paris he set about writing the music. For this task he needed technical help, at first from the English pianist Agnes Bedford, to whom he dictated the first sketches of the opera.

Though a fuller evaluation of Pound's creative work in music—chiefly his opera—might well await Schafer's second volume, it can still be said that listening to *Le Testament de Villon*, now available in an American recording, is dismaying. Such a hearing does nothing to justify Hugh Kenner's comment that "His musical sense, untrained, was of four-dimensional sureness." On the contrary, the opera, with its attempt at a neo-troubadour style along with the use of exotic instruments, makes an impression of vocal monotony and fife-and-drum orchestration. Some of the arrogance which underlay Pound's attempts at composition deserves citation here, if only for the light thrown on the way he approached listening to the music of others:

Sat through the *Pelléas* the other evening and am encouraged—encouraged to tear up the whole bloomin' era of harmony and do the thing if necessary on two tins and wash-board. Anything rather than that mush of hysteria, Scandinavia strained through Belgium plus French Schwärmerei. Probably just as well I have to make this first swash without any instruments at hand. Very much encouraged by the *Pelléas*, ignorance having no further terrors if that DAMN thing is the result of what is called musical knowledge.

Another significant musical interest of the Paris years was Pound's espousal of George Antheil, a young American composer and the self-confessed "Bad Boy of Music," who also served the poet as an orchestrator during the completion of the Villon opera.

Antheil's *Ballet Méchanique* (performed at its 1926 Paris premiere by eight grand pianos, percussion, electric bells, and two
airplane motors with their propellers) was one of the chief artistic
scandals of the 1920s. At this time Pound heard in Antheil's
music "a world of steel bars, not of old stone and ivy"; in contrast,
Stravinsky seemed only "a comfort, but one could not definitely
say that his composition was the new music."

As a result, when Pound published his major theoretical statement on music in 1924 he included an appreciation of Antheil
from which the preceding comment on Stravinsky has been
quoted. The resulting book, *Antheil and the Treatise on Harmony,* has led a fitful life, last being reprinted (prior to its appearance in the present volume) in the United States a decade ago
with an introduction by the American art-song writer and pi-
caresque diarist Ned Rorem. The section on Antheil was of little
permanent interest as Pound tacitly recognized when he allowed
the *Treatise on Harmony* to be reprinted by itself in England in
1962.

Extravagant claims have been made for Pound's achievement
as a harmonic theorist. Schafer ranks Pound's work with that of
Schoenberg and Heinrich Schenker as the only contributions "to
the science of harmony in our century." It is not that Schafer, in
making this extraordinary judgment, is unaware of Pound's musical inadequacies and superficialities; he often throughout his
commentary calls explicit attention to them. But he always manages to find the saving remnant. Thus, in discussing the *Treatise
on Harmony,* he remarks that though Pound has here written "a
scramble of jottings on a subject about which he could be expected to have only the vaguest notions . . . they are the *right*
notions. . . ."

His prime notion in this area Pound states as a law:

A SOUND OF ANY PITCH, OR ANY COMBINATION OF SUCH
SOUNDS, MAY BE FOLLOWED BY A SOUND OF ANY OTHER
PITCH, OR ANY COMBINATION OF SUCH SOUNDS, providing
the time interval between them is properly gauged; and this is true for
ANY SERIES OF SOUNDS, CHORDS OR ARPEGGIOS.

Remarkable man, to have had as late as 1924 such clear and simple ideas about harmony. Unfortunately such clarity and simplicity was no more than a product of Pound's lack of technical musical knowledge; his ignorance enabled him to think he was writing about harmony when in point of fact he was writing about rhythm. For while it is undoubtedly true that to some extent all the constituent elements of music—among them pitch, harmony, rhythm, duration, timbre, and tempo—are able to influence and even alter one another, they retain their own existence both as objects of study and of perception. By turning harmony into the rhythm about which in his poetry he knew a great deal, Pound was able to bypass consonance and dissonance, the traditional (and current!) material of harmony, about which he knew nothing. That he was able to do so with such bravado is enough to render his work of interest as an example of the assertion of ego.

In 1924 Pound left France for Italy, where he was to live until arrested twenty years later by his victorious countrymen. But his musical activities continued abroad. In 1926 *Le Testament* was performed for the first time, in excerpted form, at the Salle Pleyel; in 1931 the complete opera was broadcast by the BBC. In Paris one of the singers was Pound's favorite Yves Tinayre, and the violinist was Olga Rudge, an American artist whom Pound had also heard during his days as a music critic; Miss Rudge had given birth a year earlier to Pound's daughter Mary, and was to be—along with Pound's wife Dorothy—his lifelong companion.

A new phase of his musical life began in 1933, with the start of a small but choice concert series in Rapallo, where he now lived. In this resort town Pound thought music could be presented during the "Fascist 'Era Nuova'" free from the "noose of international finance." The concerts featured Miss Rudge and local musicians, with the collaboration of the German pianist Gerhart Münch and the frequent visits of such esteemed guests as the Gertler and Hungarian String Quartets, and took place until the Second World War.

Organized and publicized by Pound, the concerts were marked by a strong didactic emphasis on blocks of music—concentration on individual composers, and their contrasting with others both similar and different. In this way a then unfamiliar repertory, such as the keyboard works of Bach, the Mozart sonatas for piano and violin, and early English and Italian music, was presented along with Debussy, Ravel, and such moderns as Bartók, Honegger, Serly, and Stravinsky as well; the emphasis throughout was on the music performed, not on the star performing personalities of the international concert world. A corollary to these concerts was the work undertaken by Miss Rudge, with Pound's help, to find, make available, and perform the work of Vivaldi, whom Pound increasingly saw as on the level of Bach.

Pound seems to have been little musically active during the war, and afterwards the insane asylum was hardly the place for many musical experiences. Once released, he was content, in this area as in others, to rake over the past, talking about musicians in the *Cantos,* attending a performance of the Villon opera at Spoleto in 1965, and discussing his work with the writers and followers who came to see him. Evidence of this life in the past diminished with the descent into silence which he underwent—whether as a result of conscious choice or of senility is not clear—in the years before his death in 1972.

Given the ephemeral nature of most music criticism, what is there—in addition to Pound's reputation as a poet—to justify this long and expensive book? It seems plain that such justification cannot be found in any influence Pound had on music or musicians. His criticism was little read by professionals as it was appearing, and has been even less read since that time; his opera remains essentially unknown to the present day. There has been no rush of composers to set Pound's poetry to music. In this area Pound's avowed demand—"Premier principe—RIEN that interferes with the words, or with the utmost possible clarity of impact of words on audience"—could hardly have been expected to attract the interest of composers with traditionally high opinions about the importance of music.

The influence of music on Pound, obviously, is a vastly more considerable question. There always were many musical references in his poetry, and one of the *Cantos* in particular—number LXXV—is little more than a reproduction of the violin part from Münch's reconstruction of the lute version by Francesco da Milano of the Janequin *Chant des Oiseaux*, as it was played many times at Rapallo. Schafer's introduction, in its application of concrete musical terms—legato and staccato phrasing, rests, antiphony and especially fugue—to Pound's poetic procedures, might well seem to musicians to run the risk of confusing literal with metaphorical meaning; there is an important sense in which talking about "The Music in Pound's Poetry" (Schafer's subtitle for the introduction) is as much or as little meaningful as discussing the poetry in Beethoven's music. But Pound himself often disregarded his own advice not to talk about one art in terms of another, and in any case there can be little doubt Pound gained both metrical freedom and an idea of precision of language and image from what he knew of music. In a wider sense, music meant to Pound one of the constituent elements of the civilization out of which he wrote and which he had definite ideas for saving.

It is impossible not to admire Pound's style. By turns acid, contemptuous, opinionated, witty, and tender, his words and the way he uses them are unfailingly interesting. Whatever the specific intellectual merits of particular passages, when we read him about music we are always aware of Pound the man, Pound the crank, Pound the suffering witness—but always Pound alive. And as is true with so many literary products of our age, perhaps the highest compliment that can be paid this book is to say that it is continuously captivating as autobiography.

But for those deeply interested in music, a further and greater interest inheres in Pound's musical writings. This book is significant as evidence of a new musical taste—in this case not simply the taste of a great but deeply flawed mind, but more importantly that of an entire intellectual generation. At the time Pound began to write about music there was a widespread feeling among the musical avant-garde and their supporters, in tune with wider intellectual trends, that it was time to liquidate the massive and suffocating presence of the nineteenth century.

To replace the Romantic century presented special problems—indeed so far as the general musical public is concerned, such a replacement has not yet proven possible. For music was then the summit of the arts and the century itself was perhaps the leading musical epoch of history. The key to destroying its hegemony was to attack in the name both of the old and the new, of the music before Beethoven and after Wagner and his followers. Among composers no better example of this phenomenon can be found than Stravinsky, with his barbaric and shocking *Rite of Spring* (1911–13) and his shift several years later to neoclassicism. Among more aware performers, the same developments can be observed in the work of Pound's friend, Arnold Dolmetsch, to revive early music; on a more commercial level, from this time can be dated the career of the harpsichord virtuoso Wanda Landowska and her revival of the music of Bach, Scarlatti, Couperin, and Rameau. Other enlightened performers, oriented toward the new, became involved with such ventures as Arnold Schoenberg's Society for the Private Performance of Music (1918), and its numerous semipublic successors.

It is remarkable how Pound, from his first writings on music, so fully caught this mood. In literature and art his famous phrase in *Hugh Selwyn Mauberley* (1919) about the war as having been fought for a "botched civilization" is no more than a completion of his remark in 1918 about Gaudier-Brzeska: "only those shut in the blind alley which culminates in the Victorian period have failed to do [him] justice." More provocatively than Paul Rosenfeld and Carl Van Vechten—two American modernist critics of the day—he rejected close to all of what he called in 1938 the "slop of the damned XIX century." It surely is not going too far to see in this rejection a relation to his political and economic views; not only did he not like the music of the bourgeois century, he did not like either the bourgeois philosophy or the economic system which underlay that music.

More than that, it is possible to see in Pound's enthusiasm for both the order of Vivaldi and the provocations of George Antheil a reflection of the twentieth-century intellectual fascination with authoritarian solutions achieved within a framework of revolutionary politics. That he should have reached this remarkable integration of his life, his art, and his times in such a squalid cause is evidence enough of how closely he resembles that other artist and universal expert, Richard Wagner, in remaining always seductive and finally unassimilable.

16

Both Sides of
the Record

IT IS REMARKABLE—considering that sound recording
was invented by an American—that even in the United States its
hundredth birthday has produced so little of original historical
value for either the music lover or the serious collector. Magazine features, breezy newspaper articles, a publicity packet from
the Recording Industry Association of America: such would seem
to be the response to this important anniversary of an invention
whose sound can scarcely be escaped the world over.

One should therefore be grateful for Roland Gelatt's *The Fabulous Phonograph* (first published in 1955, initially revised in 1965,
and most recently issued in 1977). It must be said at the outset
that despite all reservations his book remains the best available
popular history of the phonograph; compared with Read and
Welch's crotchety and over detailed *From Tin Foil to Stereo*
(1959; second edition 1976) and Schicke's thin *Revolution in
Sound* (1974), Gelatt's work is informative without being obses-
sive, readable without being superficial, and reasonably inclusive
without any pretense to completeness. He has chosen to write
his book in a style characteristic of the best light social history, a
style familiar to readers of Frederick Lewis Allen's accounts of
American life in the 1920s and 1930s. The hallmark of this style—
making perhaps no easier the communication of history on either
a scholarly or tragic level—is its courting of the reader through a
slightly distant and half-amused recounting of the foibles, blun-

ders, and cupidity of great men who were never quite able to see the pot of gold so obviously lying at their feet.

There can be little doubt that the titans of this story were flawed. Beginning with the great Edison himself, the past of the phonograph is replete with confusion, error, and obstinacy only partially redeemed by flashes of inventive genius and pure luck. The phonograph was waiting to be invented in 1877, when Edison in the midst of his work on the harmonic telegraph first converted the theory of a possible phonograph into a crudely working model. Though almost from the start of his work on sound reproduction he had conceived the idea of using a flat disc as the repository of the necessary grooves, he instead decided to concentrate upon the unwieldy and fragile cylinder; with stubbornness worthy of a better cause, Edison did not introduce his version of the disc until 1913, and indeed continued to produce cylinders for a dwindling market until his company left the production of recordings for entertainment in 1929.

Edison's early patents were soon challenged in the United States by two Englishmen, Chichester Bell (the cousin of Alexander Graham Bell, the inventor of the telephone) and Charles Sumner Tainter. The patent they received involved the substitution of wax-coated cardboard for the tinfoil with which Edison had covered his cylinder. Shortly thereafter, in 1887, a German immigrant named Emile Berliner applied for a patent on his invention of a lateral-cut (as opposed to the vertical groove cut of both the Edison and the Bell-Tainter cylinder) flat-disc machine.

Three devices now existed for recording sound: the two closely related cylinder systems—the Edison phonograph and the Bell-Tainter graphophone—and the louder but coarse-sounding Berliner gramophone. The stage was thus set for years of patent wars, commercial piracy, uneasy and short-lived truces, and final centralization of the recording business after 1902 into two giant holders of patents—the Victor Talking Machine Company and the Columbia Graphophone Company.

Following Edison's original invention, the cylinder phonograph had been used for business purposes (as a dictaphone machine in offices) and for amusement (as a penny arcade attraction). Its business use soon failed, thanks to the resistance of mostly male office-workers worried about the effects of mechanical competition, as well as the imperfect operating condition of the machines themselves; its amusement function depended upon the reproduction not of fine music but rather of whistlers, comedy acts, and brass bands. But with the coming of the Berliner disc and the cheap and reliable spring-wound motor invented for it by Eldridge Johnson, the finally generically named phonograph (except in Britain, where it has been usually called in this century the gramophone) began its career as a documenter of music, at first vocal and operatic, but increasingly instrumental and orchestral as well.

Gelatt is particularly strong in his description of how important Europe rather than the United States was in the musical-commercial development of the recording industry. For though the phonograph was largely an American product, its enduring early recordings were from the beginning totally European in music and almost so in performers. Moreover, it was the European audience for great music which both inspired and supported the most successful merchandising idea in record history—the HMV Red Label (copied in America by Victor under the name Red Seal) celebrity artist series; and this stable market later resisted the blandishments of radio, continuing to buy recordings of classical music even during the worst of the Depression.

It was of course not only Caruso, beginning with his first recordings in 1900, who made the phonograph into what Gelatt has nicely called a "musical instrument." By the First World War almost every great voice of the first years of the century was available on records; what is often forgotten especially in America is that by the end of the acoustic era in 1925—by acoustic is meant the use of the sound waves themselves, without electrical amplification, to provide the sole mechanical force required to incise the original disc—all nine Beethoven symphonies had been recorded, some of them more than once. Among other recordings available were works of Mahler and Bruckner, quartets by

Brahms, Mozart, and Beethoven (the opus 131!), and even a tone poem of Strauss—*Also sprach Zarathustra.*

Though the acoustic process was finally able to produce tolerable results (and although Edison had supposedly proved, in so-called "tone-tests," that an audience could not tell the difference between the live performance of an artist and the Edison recording of that performance when both followed each other on a darkened stage) it could hardly be doubted that recordings, especially of the orchestra and the piano, were only pale and distorted imitations of the sonic reality. The coming of radio in the 1920s provided millions, especially in America, not only with free music but also with better reproduction of that music than they could get from the contemporary phonograph. The obvious answer was to apply the concepts of electricity not only to the transmission of music through the air but also to its recording.

By 1925 this had been done, with most of the public credit for the achievement going to the work of the Americans Harrison and Maxfield at the Bell Laboratories. The executives at Victor were at first loath to go to the new electrical process, for it smacked to them of their hated competitor, radio. But sagging sales left Victor no other option, and by the end of 1925 electrical recording had triumphed.

Now began what in retrospect must seem like the golden age of both recording and of those collectors affluent or thrifty enough to afford the then expensive discs. Not only were there to be available up-to-date recordings of all the great symphonic masterpieces, famous passages and extended excerpts from opera, and short pieces *ad infinitum,* but also for the first time the complete Beethoven piano sonatas (in an integral performance by Artur Schnabel), albums of songs by Brahms and Wolf, and perhaps more surprisingly the Edwin Fischer recording on the piano of the whole *Well-Tempered Clavier* of Bach as well as four complete operas of Mozart—*Le Nozze di Figaro, Don Giovanni,* and *Così fan tutte* from Glyndebourne, and *Die Zauberflöte* from Berlin. If contemporary music was still largely ignored by the great recording companies, of whom EMI (now comprising both HMV and English Columbia, with reciprocal repressing rights which lasted until the 1950s from the less-active Victor and Columbia in the United States) was the unquestioned leader, a more than impressive start had been made toward the recording of the late-eighteenth as well as the entire nineteenth-century literature.

The Second World War, though it entailed diminished production and availability of records, provided the technological advances which underlay the third great period of the phonograph—the long-playing revolution of 1948. The German development of magnetic tape recording, which can be heard to brilliant effect on the recently released BASF series of wartime broadcasts, dovetailed neatly with the availability of vinyl, a light unbreakable plastic capable of registering finer grooves with vastly lowered surface noise than the heavy shellac mixture which had constituted the material for records since the beginning of the century. With the resulting increased fidelity and longer playing time (itself a product not only of the increase in fineness of grooves but also of the reduction in playing speed from 78 rpm to 33⅓ rpm) today's phonograph recording was in large measure complete.

It was now possible efficiently, cheaply and attractively to record everything musical that had ever been written, and to transfer to LP everything of any interest at all that had ever been recorded by the old process. This the recording companies now proceeded to do with material good and bad, interesting and uninteresting, permanent and ephemeral. When American Columbia offered its development of the LP to the entire recording industry, RCA Victor hesitated—and shortly introduced a competing idea, the 45 rpm doughnut-shaped disc which, though smaller and lighter, played no longer per side than the old 78 rpm record. The RCA 45 rpm format soon became standard for single recordings of pop songs, and RCA finally joined the LP bandwagon in 1950, followed by EMI in 1952. In the interim, numerous small companies—perhaps over 2,000 of them—had entered the LP market, recording for the first time enormous amounts of baroque music, chamber music, and the latest productions of the avant-garde, all for an audience which had hardly been thought previously to exist. Nor was this all; every opera, for instance, in the international repertory—and many that never will be—became easily available in complete performances. And as might have been expected, the standard pieces were recorded in tens of versions, most destined to be available for only a few years and then to disappear, with the better ones finding reincarnation later on budget reissues.

In 1958 the whole process of technological obsolescence started again with the introduction of stereophonic reproduction. Recordings, by no longer coming from a single-point sound source but rather from two widely spaced speakers, gained a new transparency and apparent realism. Again vast amounts of repertory were newly recorded, and the process may still be repeated at least once more. For new developments in the past decade (none of which has as yet caught on) have increased from two to four the number of tracks capable of separate utilization in home sound reproduction, and suggested as well the possibility of the application of digital computer techniques to the entire process of sound recording. Whether these developments will represent a significant advance over stereophony, and indeed whether stereo itself represents such an improvement over monaural LP recording is as yet unclear; both the acoustic process and the 78 rpm retained the loyalty of a small but sophisticated body of opinion for years after they had in theory been relegated to the garbage heap of history.

But whatever the future of the phonograph may hold, it cannot be doubted that extraordinary riches in music and its performance have been preserved on records. Early in the electrical recording era, Maurice Maeterlinck paid a proper tribute to this treasure in a foreword to the program of the Columbia reception at the Théâtre des Champs-Elysées:

Les plus hauts chefs-d'oeuvre du génie de l'homme reposent désormais
à l'abri de la mort dans quelques disques, lourds de secrets spirituels,
qu'un enfant de trois ans peut tenir dans ses petites mains.*

It is thus paradoxical as well as troubling that these records are so
poorly documented, and that so little of genuine interest exists to
describe and explain recordings and their history. Such a gap certainly exists in the vital area of memoirs by central figures in the
recording world itself.

Of the five great record producers and executives whose
names come immediately to mind—Fred Gaisberg of HMV,
Charles O'Connell of Victor, Goddard Lieberson of American
Columbia, Walter Legge of EMI, and John Culshaw of English
Decca—only Gaisberg, the earliest of the lot, has received anything like adequate treatment. His memoirs as well as a recent
biography exist; of the others only John Culshaw has provided us
with a considered account of a major recording product, a fascinating description of his part in the first complete recording of
Wagner's *Ring*. Charles O'Connell, in *The Other Side of the
Record* (1947) did little more than gossip about such lovable characters as Grace Moore and Arturo Toscanini, while Walter Legge
has restricted himself to fascinating but alas fragmentary
glimpses of the enormous contribution made by those other than
musicians to the outcome of the recording process.

And the situation is equally bad with regard to the existence of
up-to-date catalogues listing all the LP records produced for sale
the world over since the coming of the LP in 1948. Current catalogues do, of course, exist, as do such valuable publications as the
English *Stereo Record Guide*. But current catalogues list only
currently available discs, and the *Stereo Record Guides* are selections of what the editors feel to be important recordings, rather
than listings assembled with an eye to completeness. Catalogues
of a broad range of acoustic discs have existed; and in the area of

---

*The greatest masterpieces of man's genius will repose from now on safe from
death in some recordings, full of spiritual secrets, which a three-year-old child can
hold in his little hands.

vocal records there are two pioneering efforts, John Steane's ad-
mirable if necessarily arbitrary treatment of the entire history of
singing on records (*The Grand Tradition,* 1974) and Rodolfo Cel-
letti's close to exhaustive listing and discussion of all the complete recordings of opera (*Il Teatro d'Opera in Disco,* 1976). 78
rpm electrical discs were reasonably well documented in the
three editions of the American *Gramophone Shop Encyclopedia*
(1936, 1942 and 1948); such records, along with the early LPs,
were definitively covered in Clough and Cuming's monumental
English *World's Encyclopedia of Recorded Music,* including its
third and most recent 1957 supplement. But Clough and Cuming
is hardly up to date, and it is unfortunately symptomatic of the
state of scholarship in this field that it is ignored by Gelatt.

What has been written here, however, has been written from
the standpoint of a putatively cultivated music lover whose interest by definition lies in the enduring masterpieces of a genteel
tradition. It is to Gelatt's credit that in spite of his obvious love
for that tradition he goes, in his new last chapter, a large part of
the way toward describing how small a role such musical gentility
plays in the life of Edison's invention. For no matter how touching we may find Maeterlinck's flattery of his audience and ourselves, in point of fact the chief function of the phonograph, in
the United States as increasingly in the rest of the world, has
been to spread popular culture quickly and cheaply. What began
with whistlers and comedy acts and continued with dance tunes
and Bing Crosby played on jukeboxes has reached its maturity
with the Rolling Stones and their many successful epigones.

Statistics provided by the Recording Industry Association of
America document the present condition; 61 percent of records
sold in the United States are "contemporary" (and may be loosely
grouped under the term "rock"), 12 percent are "country," 11
percent are "middle-of-the-road" (Sinatra, Como, Mathis, Welk,
etc.), 5 percent are "jazz," and 5 percent are "classical." Even
more impressive than these statistics by themselves is the infor-
mation contained in the recent memoirs (*Clive: Inside the Record
Business*) of Clive Davis, the deposed head of American Colum-

bia. His book is littered with success stories of the "rock" record world, but his chapter devoted to classical music—21 pages out of the book's 335—begins ominously: "Classical music caused me more than a few problems." But the basic problems he describes are only two: no interest, and no sales. When recordings by some of our most esteemed serious artists sell fewer than 10,000 copies—while the most popular "contemporary" discs sell as much as 9,000,000 copies—one can begin to understand not only why the recording of classical music is poorly documented but also, and vastly more important, why it is so unreal to see in the phonograph primarily a tool of high culture.

What can be learned from the history of the phonograph (if that history were to be written without treating classical music in the way we all, including Gelatt, would like to—as the phonograph's *raison d'être*) is not simply that the phonograph, no more and no less than any other technology, is neutral in human affairs; we may also learn just how limited and how tenuous is the grip serious music, and by extension all great culture, now has on our minds. That this lesson will come as an unpleasant shock to those whose livings are made by administration and socialization of the arts cannot be doubted; neither can it be doubted that what is unpleasant may often be corrective.

17

The Prodigy in Old Age

THE LATEST FLUTTER (1978) in the American piano-playing world concerns the emergence from obscurity of the seventy-five-year-old former child pianist Ervin Nyiregyházi.

Nyiregyházi's life story is depressing if not bizarre. He was born in Budapest in 1903, the son of a tenor father and an amateur pianist mother. He showed his musical abilities before he could talk, and by the age of five was already studying the piano and composing. He appeared in a command performance for Queen Mary at Buckingham Palace in 1911, but at first played little professionally. His gifts were, however, widely recognized; Géza Révész's *The Psychology of a Musical Prodigy* (1925) gives a good indication of how they were thought of at the time. If the comparisons with Mozart read strangely today, there can still be little doubt as to the young Nyiregyházi's precocity.

In 1920 he came to America to make his New York debut at Carnegie Hall. Though he did achieve some success, his career as an adult was nipped in the bud by conflicts with managers—a not-unknown experience for solo musicians—and, one suspects, an unwillingness on the part of an American audience in the process of acquiring cultural sophistication to take Nyiregyházi's particular brand of pianistic self-expression quite seriously.

Eventually Nyiregyházi moved to the West Coast, where he became submerged in the Hollywood swamp. He was barely able to support himself by playing jobs in the movie studios: for example, his were the hands which appeared on the screen as Chopin's in *A Song to Remember*—the face was Cornell Wilde's and the sound of José Iturbi's. Always in need of female companionship, he gained nine wives and lost six by divorce and three by death. He drank a lot, and lived the life of a near-vagrant. Though he continued to play, for forty years he did not even own a piano.

His move back into the limelight began with a concert in 1973 at the Old First Church in San Francisco. The pianist played a program of music which has always been particularly close to his heart, including examples of what are now to most music lovers among the lesser-known pieces of Franz Liszt. In the audience was a piano devotee armed with a cassette machine; the results of this amateur recordist's efforts came to the attention of Gregor Benko, a guiding spirit of the International Piano Archives, a New York organization devoted to the preservation and revival of the piano's good old days.

Benko was enraptured by Nyiregyházi, whom he found a true relic of the romantic nineteenth century. Largely as a result of Benko's interest, the 1973 recital tapes, along with some 1974 studio performances, appeared commercially on the Desmar label. This recording, although it came from a small company and contained mostly little-known works played by a forgotten performer, excited wide interest among those who take piano playing seriously.

Chief among them was Harold Schonberg, the music critic of the *New York Times*. On the evidence of the Desmar record, he called Nyiregyházi's playing "madness, but a divine madness." Financial backing for the penniless old man was also found, in the shape of stipends from the Ford Foundation—an unlikely sponsor for the resuscitation of the pianism of a century ago.

The market clearly existed for another recording, this time professionally made for a major label. The honor fell to Columbia, which in January of 1978 sent its producer Thomas Frost to San Francisco to collaborate with Benko on a new, two-disc album. The tapes were made despite various divagations on the part of the capricious pianist, and the normal prerelease ballyhoo was being cranked up when contractual disagreements between the Ford Foundation, the International Piano Archives, and Columbia threatened to delay or even annul the project. But everything was soon cleared up, the Columbia set was released to an expectant market, and 15,000 albums were sold in the first week.

So there are now more than two hours of Nyiregyházi's playing on disc, surely enough to judge his playing in pianistic and musical terms. There can be little doubt that his technical equipment is both natural and prodigious. Its naturalness is demonstrated by the fact that he doesn't need to practice a great deal before he plays, even at an age when most pianists find exacting mechanical tasks beyond their grasp. Its prodigality is demonstrated by the extremes of dynamic and tempo contrast at the pianist's easy command.

But these pianistic virtues come to seem primitive and even uncouth if one's concern as a listener is with the music rather than the playing. Unfortunately the works which Nyiregyházi has chosen to play are all too often pieces which show Liszt at his flashy and maudlin worst, and their circulation on these records can only cast a shadow on the composer's entire achievement. Liszt's strengths lay in his innovative compositional techniques, his gift for melody, and his ability to make the piano sound both lyrical and brilliant: his defects—overwhelmingly present in Nyiregyházi's favorite music—lay in a tendency to superficiality, spurious religiosity, and cloying sentimentality.

The pianist plays these works—which include the two *St. Francis Legends*, his own transcriptions of the symphonic poem *Hamlet* and the "March of the Three Holy Kings" from the oratorio *Christus*, and other, later pieces—in a wayward rhythmic style, striking huge clusters of notes at tremendous volume, and generally emphasizing the power of the piano to impress and even shock, rather than its ability to communicate and clarify large-scale musical structure. The general impression one gets from Nyiregyházi's playing is that he has found in the music only the improvisatory and theatrical aspects inherent in romantic harmonies and pianistic roulades. Taken all together and in one sitting, these six record sides mark a steady progression downhill from the mock-sublime to the really ridiculous.

The crass way Nyiregyházi is being merchandised as both musician and man adds a special kind of unpleasantness to the whole phenomenon. It may be thought harmless though curious that Columbia Records is selling T-shirts emblazoned with the pianist's name. Rather more disquieting was the way the television program produced by NBC and shown across the United States in the spring emphasized the pianist's drinking habits and his dissolute life-style; an advertisement for the program in the *New York Times* called him "the hobo pianist", and a title card in the program itself described him as "the skid-row pianist." One cannot know whether Nyiregyházi is pleased with his new reputation, but one may be permitted some doubt as to the value of a career paid for with personal indignities.

And beyond the tragedy of the pianist's life—a tragedy which only seems compounded by his present notoriety—a further question must be raised: what does it mean that an old man can be raised from the depths by the performance, no matter how astonishing and eccentric, of deservedly forgotten music? Perhaps the most plausible explanation for this twin resurrection is the present vacuum in musical composition, as demonstrated by the almost total failure of music written in the last generation to find a wide audience among music lovers or even practicing musicians. It is this vacuum which has furthered the exhaustion, through overperformance, of a standard nineteenth-century repertory, and prompted the frenzied search for the new among the old rather than the new among the new. It is the hope of Nyiregyházi's backers that jaded critical palates and apathetic audiences alike will respond commercially to this latest mining of the past. One hardly knows whether or not to wish them well in their quest.

18

The Dubious Art of Contests

CONTESTS are increasingly becoming the major new source for the supply of talent, especially pianists and violinists, entering the music business. Now, when discussing the problem of contests, it is important to distinguish between two kinds. Everyone takes for granted that kind of contest which is essentially nothing more than a competitive audition which chooses the best participant to receive a scholarship or perform in one particular concert. Such a process, though rarely pleasant, has the virtues of efficiency and directness, and is devoted to the accomplishment of a clearly stated, limited goal.

What I am concerned with here is that kind of contest which claims for itself the maximum significance in a context of maximum publicity. Such contests are presented as international; they aim to do nothing less than discover artists and launch them on major careers. These events have grown in number enormously since World War II. Every country in the Western world seems to have several, and indeed there are now so many taking place that it is difficult to tell either winners or prizes apart without a scorecard.

Why this great proliferation? It is easy to list the virtues of musical contests. The money, the future concerts, the experience, the encouragement, the contacts; all of these add up to one thing—a career—when all other roads seem blocked. And for some it has worked this way. Cliburn is of course the storybook case, the very stuff of which myth is made. But for every more recent winner of a major contest who has thus been launched on a career there are twenty winners who have disappeared into teaching, bitterness, or both.

The defects of contests are more difficult to talk about, for the understandable reason that every criticism of contests by those most directly involved—past contestants—seems either like ingratitude or sour grapes. It seems like ingratitude when a winner criticizes what has tried to help him; is it anything but sour grapes when a loser disparages what he has not won? To follow these restrictions, however, would be to place contests beyond criticism and therefore beyond discussion, for what must only be praised cannot be spoken of intelligently.

Surely it must be possible to point out that contests do not choose *concert* artists, but rather *contest* artists. Contests are after all at best only artificial concerts, attempts to make mock musical performances in situations where no one has come to hear the music. All the defects of contests—constriction of repertory, loss of artistic individuality, the emergence of a contest "type"—flow from this original sin of artificiality. For when the audience, judges and observers alike, come not to participate in the experience of art but rather to judge, art goes elsewhere. And its inevitable substitute becomes mere athleticism, the worship of skill, and the transformation of content into style.

And what of the contestants? These unlucky people work for years learning special pieces (often the *same* special pieces), cultivating a proper mental attitude, and in general pointing their lives toward a few moments in the sun of public exposure performing excerpts of works arbitrarily chosen and often but perfunctorily heard. And for what? To be told, if they succeed as only one in thousands can, that they do not sound like what they are.

It cannot have escaped a careful reader's attention that the highest compliment a critic of the *New York Times* can pay a contest winner is to say that he doesn't sound like a contest winner, but rather has the possibilities of being someday a real artist. This might seem only an ironically humorous comment, were it not for the hordes of young music students—the best and the brightest, by the way—out there molding themselves into proper contestants.

Though not often publicly remarked, all this is widely recognized. As the number of contests increases, the value to each winner decreases. In addition to the rapidly growing number of losers—with all that losing implies for the destruction of artistic self-confidence—there are now too many winners for winning itself to be in most cases of any commercial significance.

The real problem here is that a winner rapidly becomes a former winner, who after a short year is replaced (long before he has had a chance to prove himself) in the tenuous affections of his music business contacts by the new winner who is himself soon to be replaced. For the simple fact is that there are more winners than concerts for the winners to support themselves by playing. Contests are of course not the only factor causing the present oversupply of solo musicians but because of the public prominence of major contests, their responsibility for encouraging and then dashing the hopes of even those who succeed in them must be mentioned.

So I must ask the question again. Why, then, are there so many contests? Not, I submit, for musical reasons, and not for commercial reasons. Not, in other words, for the benefit either of art or of the contestants. Contests are staged, rather, for the benefit of the sponsors. No less than professional golf tournaments and automobile races, music contests exist to bring publicity and glory to those who put up the money.

Publicity comes to contest sponsors for one simple reason; until the winner is chosen, there is nothing for the publicity to fix on other than the contest itself. And once the winner is chosen the sponsor's publicity organization begins cranking out the puffs for the next contest.

What I am saying applies equally whether the sponsor is a government, a musical institution, a foundation, or an individual. Of course in some cases—notably those American contests founded by individuals before World War II—contests have been chosen as the preferred form of philanthropy because of the sponsor's very real love of music. But even here it is a general rule that the tendency is inevitably for the contest to be more important than the winners, for the winners to be interchangeable, and for the contest itself to become immortal.

Of course it is natural and understandable that sponsors should want to receive public recognition for their philanthropies; it is a reasonable return to them for all the good their money can do. But at the same time it is necessary to understand that it cannot be assumed an identity of goals exists between sponsors and the artists in whose hands the keeping of music must lie. Thus every effort must be made to ensure that the financial support music so badly needs is not spent in accordance with the publicity requirements the nonmusician sponsors have in mind, but rather to further the artistic goals chosen by the musicians who are themselves involved in producing the art. The function of philanthropy must, in so far as possible, be to support the arts financially—not to determine what is done.

Help for the present problems of music and musicians' careers does not at this time lie in the great numbers of contests we now have. Our efforts, and those of the philanthropists who want to help us, must be directed toward making an atmosphere in which musicians can work. One way to do this is to educate the audience through the presentation of more and better concerts. This means also the raising of the audience to the level of the highest art by making the most serious performances widely honored and easily available. And it means more money spent on the internal, behind-the-scenes conditions for music—more rehearsals, better preparation of contemporary pieces, and above all, freeing artists from the necessity to skew their art toward the big box-office. In a condition of increased musical activity, new artists will find their way more naturally than they do now in the hothouse world of contests; perhaps then young musicians will find it more possible to realize that their primary relationship must not be to commercial success but to music. For music must, in the final reckoning, be done for its own sake alone.

19

Summing Up:
A Tour d'Horizon

IT WILL COME as no surprise that when I talk of music, I mean what used to be called serious music. It is the fashion today to see a convergence of serious and popular music, and to cite such figures as Steve Reich and Philip Glass as evidence of that convergence. Such a wishful synthesis not only muddies the facts, but also serves to hide the motives of the prophets and seers who have been dealing in the vision of these two musics growing ever closer together. While it is clear—at least to this writer—that serious music still exists as a separate and definable genre, there can be little doubt that recent years have seen an enormous growth of popular musics of various kinds, and that this growth has made the largest possible inroads on an increasingly disorganized and doubt-ridden elite. The privileged young, as part of the goal of downward cultural mobility, seek to imitate the styles of assorted groups of underdogs, and the result is a pop culture based on musics at once vulgar, temporary, and corrosive.

As might be expected in a time of instant electronic communication, all of this is a worldwide phenomenon. In some way we do not understand, cultural developments transcend differing politics, economics, and ethics. They circulate quickly, they progress with steady uniformity, and they die simultaneously everywhere. That which one dislikes in one's own society spawns a thousand imitators across the best-policed borders; within the life-span of each new trend, contagion is complete and refuge is impossible.

But this problem, so naturally described in epidemiological terms, is a manifestation of the pop world; the central problem of serious music, as we have seen, is the opposite: the absence of new music. Technically, of course, new music does exist. It is written everywhere, and even widely performed. These performances are however largely extorted under various forms of subtle and less subtle economic and intellectual pressure, and no matter how expert the performances or how well programmed the audience, the end result is the same; the music is largely unloved and soon forgotten.

Every nation, every locality, every college and conservatory, pushes its own composers. The composers prosper financially, at least on the level of physical survival; never have so many composers lived so well and been socially so secure. But this proliferation of people putting notes on paper cannot be allowed to obscure the facts of the repertory. The canon of great music was closed at least forty years ago. Those composers who were included when the curtain came down—Strauss, Stravinsky, Bartók, Prokofiev, and Shostakovich—have been allowed to finish out their creative lives with pieces which, with rare exceptions, command little more than a respectful hearing. For the rest, the outcome, no matter how great the ballyhoo, no matter how great the simulation of interest, is decline; and, as is increasingly clear in the case of even such an unmodern figure as the late Benjamin Britten, devaluation and perhaps eventual desuetude.

In this connection, it is instructive to realize the remarkable metamorphosis we have witnessed in the use of the word "modern" as it applies to music. Fifty years ago modern music was the music then being written. Now a half century has passed, and the same music is still modern in the estimation of performers and audiences alike. And it is modern not only in the sense that it still sounds new; it is modern in the most brute sense of being as difficult to assimilate—to learn and to hear—as it was the day it was written. It must be said that young musicians who have specialized in contemporary music are indeed able to prepare this music

quickly and accurately; but for their traditionally oriented colleagues, as well as ordinary music lovers, modern music remains,
regardless of the success of modernism in the area of handsome
painting and provocative literature, stultified and ugly.

The effect of this problem on performers has been enormous.
The absence of greatly successful new music has given added impetus to a development which began in the nineteenth century—
the replacement of the music by the performer, of composition
by performance. But in the nineteenth century the greatest virtuosos like Beethoven and Liszt, and on a lower level Paganini,
were of course also composers; in the case of Beethoven and
Mozart before him, we remember only the composer and not the
performer. Even in the first quarter of our century, the greatest
pianists were composers as well—Rachmaninoff and Busoni
come immediately to mind. And Kreisler, though only known as
a composer for his light pieces, did enrich the violin repertory.

But now great performers hardly ever write music. In the
absence of the possibility of performing their own—or anyone
else's—new music, even the success of the performer is beginning
to seem autumnal, for the concentration on the playing of the
music of the past has subjected performance itself to an increasingly academic and dutiful scrutiny. Performers, aided by
records, now are more than ever concerned with what other
musicians are doing; critics and audiences indulge in an orgy of
comparison, searching for historical authenticity and exact re-
creation of an imagined past.

Recent years have seen the end of many historically important
careers. Though their records live on, Arturo Toscanini and Wilhelm Furtwängler, are dead, as are Pablo Casals and Gregor Pia-
tigorsky; Artur Rubinstein, in his nineties, no longer plays, and
Jascha Heifetz, fifteen years younger, is semiretired; Vladimir
Horowitz, also in his mid-seventies, continues to play a limited
number of concerts, but plainly one day soon he, too, will stop.
Great careers have succeeded these legends, but whether one
looks at such stars as Karajan, Rostropovich, or Gilels among the
older generation, or at Cliburn, Perlman, or Levine among the

younger, it is plain that such careers no longer have their former aura of universality and magic. In general, among the young, the ranks of concert and operatic artists are full of curiously interchangeable figures who seem long on stage personality and youthful charm—as well as the endurance necessary to withstand jet travel and the nerves necessary to get through underrehearsed performances. In the will and desire to affect the course of music, today's performers appear largely lacking.

For Americans, all of this has a special seriousness. Most of the names one associates with serious music are still European, and the reason is clear: not only is Europe the cradle and perhaps the eternal homeland of our Western high musical tradition, but it still possesses the largest sophisticated audience which supports that tradition.

The present conditions of the music world take a special form in our country. The American condition is the product, for good as well as bad, of history and economics, operating to shape more narrow musical factors. The history of this country is in its origin a story of early settlement by ethnic groups which were not to bulk large in the development of eighteenth- and nineteenth-century European music; added to the musical incapacities of the founding fathers was the unfortunate isolation hardly avoidable in an age of primitive transatlantic communication. And after the middle of the nineteenth century, when immigration from societies with a rich musical life—German, Italian, Slavic —began to take place, the initial and most creative flowering in the immigrants' homelands was mostly over, to be replaced by expansion and development.

Nonetheless, America, with its economic riches and relative ease of life for the many, did provide the opportunity for individual self-improvement and cultural growth. As can be seen from Howard Shanet's history of the New York Philharmonic, nineteenth-century musical life in New York, as elsewhere in the United States, both relied on immigrant musicians and faithfully followed European trends. As a result, in the orchestral field, American organizations early rivaled European groups, and by

World War I American orchestras were recognized as being at least the equal of any in the world. To some extent the same was true in opera; it is still generally unrecognized just how many American singers made important and even legendary careers at the Met in the 1920s and 1930s, and just how integral these native artists were to the Met's world position in the performance of the standard operatic repertory.

Sadly, creative contributions of Americans—composition—remained laggard. Having come late into the world of music, Americans could not boast of having great composers among their national forebears; as a result, instead of following in American footsteps, our composers, as in the case of MacDowell, took European models. Though Ives, at the price of eccentricity, did chart a specifically native course, the history of American composition was until the late 1930s and the work of Copland, Harris, and Thomson, a colonial history.

But despite the work of these three men, and the ambiguous influence of the ambivalent John Cage, the same dependence on Europe remains true for the years since World War II. The years immediately after the war saw the influence of Arnold Schoenberg succeeded by the school of Darmstadt and post-Webernian serialism. And as regards national origins, the best that can be said of electronic music is that technology knows no motherland.

Though America may now boast practical self-sufficiency in performers in the sense that our musical life could easily be carried on with recourse only to our own artists, Europe still remains the source for us of many of our most admired soloists and also the place where American artists must go to prove themselves. As a symbol of the power of Europe in our musical minds, it cannot be forgotten that Van Cliburn—surely the most publicly successful of all our performers—has made his great career on the basis of Soviet blessing in the Tchaikowsky Competition of 1958. On a perhaps musically more significant level, we find today few American conductors at the head of our major orchestras; indeed, of our most important orchestras, only Cleveland has an American-raised conductor, and that conductor made his career entirely in Europe prior to being chosen in Cleveland. It is true that the music director and principal conductor at the Metropolitan Opera is an American by both birth and training, but surely that job is at least as much administrative as performing. Among instrumentalists there are honorable exceptions to the rule of European primacy, but these exceptions (as in the case of a young American pianist whose signing by a major American record company was publicized as the first by that company in over a decade) gain visibility by the very fact of their rarity.

The one area where American artists have made world careers in sizable numbers is singing. Here American artists have excelled, and furthermore have been credited at home for their achievements. It is hardly a detraction from their success to remark that, on the highest level of artistic fame—that of becoming the spokesmen for the works they perform—they have been handicapped by the fact that their great roles have been in works written in European languages and coming out of a past European culture.

Still, despite certain handicaps, there is obviously a highly developed musical life in this country. We have an unprecedentedly large number of orchestras ranging from small, only semiprofessional community efforts to the five or six virtuoso groups of our largest and most important cities. At the professional level, the musicians involved are better paid, both in absolute and relative terms, than ever before. And in the best tradition of body counts, we are told that audiences are larger every year. Alas, if a high rate of activity were only all that were needed, an observer might perhaps be forgiven for questioning the spectral character of these famous audiences; for example, our newspapers and mail give palpable evidence of the extraordinary effort in advertising currently being made to attract customers and induce them to sit still long enough to be counted. That these efforts have sometimes, at great cost, succeeded—not only in the area of orchestra concerts but also in the growth of chamber music and regional opera—cannot obscure the enormous stress presently being placed on sheer numbers as a reason for the existence of musical activity.

But the solo recital, that backbone of music for the last century in its unrivaled ability to gain listeners for masterpieces through experiencing them under the impact of idiosyncratic performing personalities, seems to be in a morbid state. The two mainstays of solo careers—concert series in small and smaller cities and towns and college and university concert series—have increasingly been filled by group and pop attractions. Helped along no doubt by the widespread feeling that the number of performers seen to be capable of filling large halls has dwindled, this change has been spawned by the search for larger audiences in order to justify new halls and public financial support.

Academic music life itself presents a complex picture in many ways difficult to evaluate but in any case depressing. Hundreds—perhaps thousands—of college music departments across the country, staffed often by musically incompletely prepared graduate school products and the embittered products of our higher music schools, understand that the only thing it is widely possible to do with music professionally is to teach it. Music, no less than the other humanities, has in our schools become a kind of self-perpetuating educational pyramid scheme. But the price of all such schemes is sudden contraction. Recent years have seen just such a possibility, with the resulting almost total extinction of new jobs. Such jobs as there are seem reserved for the beneficiaries of affirmative action. Since what was said about Supreme Court justices applies almost as well to professors with tenure—few die and none resign—all too often, the few lucky candidates find themselves circulating from one low-level position to another, rather than entering the normal course of academic preferment.

Moreover the proliferation of contests—supposedly a democratic method of choice, although in fact its highest development has taken place in Eastern bloc countries—to allocate the available performance careers, has become little less than obscene. Not only do major contests often not do what they are supposed to do—that is, to deliver careers—but they have lent themselves to shameless exploitation by their sponsors as a cheap means of getting publicity at little more than the cost of press consultants, the printing of applications, and the travel expenses of a few cir-cuit-riding judges. Though the eventual winner does receive a cash prize, much of his real compensation is in the form of con-cert engagements which would otherwise have been commer-cially filled in any case by young and inexpensive artists. Above all, it cannot be overlooked that the real raw material of contests, indeed, the real underwriter of the whole process—the contes-tant—is free to the sponsor.

Nor does the recording business present an encouraging pic-ture. Not only is classical music responsible for no more than one out of twenty records sold in this country, but it has been sug-gested that this percentage is actually dropping. The inevitable result is that increasingly the American record market is the preserve of the great European giants, secure in their own do-mestic markets. These companies, among which are Decca (Lon-don in this country), Deutsche Grammophon, EMI (Angel here), and Philips, have in recent years begun to record American or-chestras, thus filling the vacuum left by the voluntary withdrawal of American firms—RCA and Columbia—from the classical mar-ket. Though Columbia at least has fought an honorable retreat, it is left now with an exclusive arrangement with only one Ameri-can group: the New York Philharmonic.

Also important, naturally, is the nature of the repertory and the choice of the artists large-scale projects by big American companies. Significantly, the pieces for the most part are either tame or trite; when they are not trivial, interesting items are usually recorded in Europe—sometimes with a smattering of American artists—and only released here. The one exception to this caution might have been Pierre Boulez's recordings of twentieth-century music with the New York Philharmonic for Columbia; but it is difficult not to feel that the lack of commercial prospects for such recordings was merely one more factor in Boulez's unsung departure from the New York and American scene.

Though high recording costs are usually cited as the chief rea-son for the dearth of American recordings of serious music, the root cause must be the lack of an American market for classical music in general, and for American recording products in particular. Though one can hardly say that this lack is anything new—it goes back at least to the very beginning of electrical recording in 1925, and probably to the start of phonograph recording of the classics almost eighty years ago—the fact that it is still present in the time of our supposed cultural maturity does raise serious questions about the future of the industry.

Then there is the problem seldom mentioned in serious discussion of the condition of music but of genuine influence, and that is the problem of the managers and agents. There is no space here for a full discussion of commercial management. Suffice it to say that like Gaul, it is divided roughly into three parts, consisting of one colossus, three celebrity booking services, and a largely ineffective group of small independent operators. As a whole, this group of operators seems doomed to continue forever in a frantic search for yesterday's successes. But whether their successes are yesterday's or tomorrow's, the result of this concentration of effective power in the hands of a few successful management firms is an increasing ability to promote careers by fiat—fiat determined as often as not by personal whim rather than musical merit or, surprisingly, audience success. For young and poorly paid artists, then, this mode of organizing the commercial field in which they must ply their art all too often has a devastating effect.

Beyond the plight of individual artists is that of today's concert- and opera-producing institutions. Here the efforts of musical organizations are not directed simply toward increasing the sizes of their audiences as an end in itself, but more importantly as a means of convincing patrons—whether private, quasi-public, or governmental—that the activity in question is worthy of support.

Now obviously patronage—and on a scale far exceeding the mere buying of a ticket or even the repeated subscription to a series of concerts or operas—has always been a necessary feature of the musical life. Aristocratic patronage, responsible for so much great art, was replaced in the nineteenth century, by the contributions of the emergent middle class, though as late as the 1870s Wagner was able to complete the *Ring* and get Bayreuth started only because of the lavish support of mad King Ludwig of Bavaria. In this century the beneficent effect of merchant money on American music may be seen in the relationship between such men as Otto Kahn and the Metropolitan Opera, Clarence Mackay and the New York Philharmonic, and Augustus Juilliard and the music school named for him. Or, to take another example, in the much more intimate environment of San Francisco an entire generation of Jewish philanthropists of German origin constituted Northern California musical life in its own image.

Now such philanthropy is dying, if not dead. The nexus between music and the merchant classes has been broken, at least in the particular case of the individual music patron. Not only does publicly manifested love of music no longer serve as an easy means of upward social mobility, but the rich are wary about courting public disfavor through conspicuous expenditure, even for culture. Nor can more strictly economic factors be ignored in the decline of private large-scale support; increases in taxation and the resulting difficulty of forming, keeping, and transferring huge fortunes have taken place at the same time as the costs of musical enterprises have risen dramatically. But whatever the reason, private support has been increasingly swamped by the rise of foundations and latterly by the appropriations of the government itself for culture.

The enormous increases in such support in recent years is so well known that it requires no documentation here. All that needs to be said is that government support—federal, state, or local—has become indispensable for the present organization of the arts. Evidence for this statement may be found in the regular and predictably demeaning appearances before those official bodies responsible for appropriating funds as take place when artists and administrators face down their patrons in the legislature. And beyond the evidence of such unlikely love feasts, there are all sorts of signs of the extent to which arts organizations must now devote their time to the devising of plausible grant requests and the preparation of the endless forms which constitute both the *modus operandi* and the *raison d'etre* of every self-respecting bureaucracy.

The immediate danger arising out of the relation between music and the government is not so much that it breeds the possibility of *direct* political control—though it must be admitted that the recent statement by the Vice-President's wife quoted in the *New York Times* is worrisome: "Politics in the arts? . . . That's human nature. Politics exists when human beings get together in an organized way." And the *Times* goes on to attribute the following thoughts to unnamed "White House aides":

. . . expenditure of Federal funds in a democracy must necessarily reflect political forces. These are the facts of life, they argue. They also say this is the way things should be: Those whose funds are used have a right to have some say in how they are spent.

Still, real and obvious political meddling in the arts would be both too risky and too inefficient. But what is more dangerous than that, because it already exists, is the tendency federal funding encourages—like patronage itself, nothing new—of cutting the artistic suit to fit the financial cloth. Always a factor affecting the artist's decisions about what to work on, it gains new immediacy given the centrality of the government's new funding role.

Evidence for this state of affairs is hard to come by if only because of people's normal reticence in these matters. But every aspiring musical organization—and every aspiring musician—is aware of the number of times government officials have made it clear in advance of any application that there happens to be or happens not to be grant money available for some project. Of course the project in question may be undertaken regardless of the possibility of a grant; conversely, the project may be one which would have died even if money had been forthcoming. But no musical organization can escape the recognition that as far as the struggle for survival is concerned, the existence of money for a particular kind of project becomes a tempting reason for that project to be undertaken. Not to mention the obverse, that unavailability of money for a particular kind of project becomes a compelling reason to look for something more to official taste. And even so much power of government funding is increased— almost geometrically, as it were, by the use of matching grants. Also, private donors are showing themselves increasingly unwilling to support activities which the government has not blessed.

What I have discussed above applies to the country as a whole. But it may be of special value to examine how the present condition of music is reflected in New York City, not only the capital of American music but also one of the major platforms of world music. How this great city is responding to the present pressures can serve at the same time as a case history and example—and, if necessary, a warning.

In addition to the city's being the commercial center of the music business, New York's musical institutions are made up of opera companies, orchestras, concert series, and schools. On all sides we are told that this is a golden age of culture in New York City. But in point of fact, wherever we look, the signs are ominous; disguised in the best-financed cases by tinsel, in others by mere hope, but overall betraying depression, pessimism, and even in some cases a touch of panic.

At the top of New York's musical ecology in glamour, publicity, size of both budget and audience, and perhaps even artistic achievement, stands the Metropolitan Opera. Presently under the management of three men—a music director, a production director, both in turn presided over by an executive director— the administration of the Met remains without public strain. Not only has this troika pushed the wolf away from the door in the past few years, it has, after a somewhat shaky interregnum following the retirement of Rudolf Bing, restored orderly procedures (most notably in casting). It has also succeeded in bringing the Met before the local and national public by means of a publicity effort unparalleled in the world of serious music.

Even if the Met has enjoyed major gains in the stability of its very existence, however, this undoubted achievement has gone hand in hand with a continuing shortage of artistic excitement.

On the level of repertory, the Met has substituted a recycling

of the romantic past for any pretensions to discovery of the future
or even some reflection of the musical present. While the singing
remains close to the highest international level, the conducting
lacks both the capacity to stir an audience in performance and the
kind of imagination in musical conception which renders individual efforts memorable. It is significant that the greatest interest
in conducting at the Met during recent seasons was occasioned
by the 1978 appearance of the then eighty-three-year-old Karl
Böhm in *Die Frau ohne Schatten* of Richard Strauss; but Böhm
was already a major conductor more than forty years ago, and his
successors—at least as far as the Met is concerned—are nowhere
in sight. Paralleling the routine nature of much of the conducting, productions, both in execution and conception, have played
it safe both intellectually and artistically, hewing largely to the
smartly traditional.

And over all lies the worry about long-term financial prospects.
Caught between the vastly increasing costs of singers, orchestral
musicians, nonmusical personnel, and administration on the one
hand and the increasing difficulty of securing support from the
largest individual givers, the Met has gone public in two senses:
the small giver and the government. It is difficult to believe that
small givers can, in the long run, do very much more than cover
the enormous cost of their solicitation, but this building of a wide
contributing public is of the greatest importance in enlisting government support, and is in today's political world a more per-
suasive argument for state and federal backing than any artistic
case which can be made. And however much trouble the Met is
having in raising money, it is clear that nowadays it is doing better than anyone else, a success produced by its reputation, the
solidity of its performances, and the quality of its board.

It is instructive, at the same time, to look at how its colleague
on the Plaza at Lincoln Center, the New York City Opera, is
doing. Here the situation is grim. Though the difficulties of the
New York City Opera present themselves at this moment as financial, it is clear that at the root of the City Opera's present condition is a crisis of artistic function. Performance levels of this
company continue much as they have in the past; splendor of ex-

ecution has never been the *raison d'être* of this company. Its function—and the reason for its secure place in operatic history—has in the past been its introduction of new operas by contemporary composers, and its American presentation of unfamiliar works of the past known to connoisseurs but ignored by the Metropolitan. Not only has the Met become more adventurous in its revival of older operas, but the supply of new works has ceased. Neither public nor even enlightened opinion has shown any interest in the expensive and difficult undertaking of performing contemporary opera.

Thrown back as a result upon the mounting of familiar works done better by the Met, the City Opera finds itself faced by the same economic problems which confront every other musical institution—but without the public image and inner confidence which can only result from artistic purpose. A recent ominous sign was the decision of Beverly Sills, its most famous singer and a product of the City Opera, to retire from her musical career and become co-director with Julius Rudel, the company's director since 1957. It was immediately speculated that the marriage would be uneasy and therefore short-lived. And as if in confirmation of these speculations, it was announced at the end of 1978 that there would be no co-directorship; Miss Sills was to become sole director as of June 30, 1979. It was plain that dissatisfaction with Mr. Rudel was the reason for his partial, and now for his total, replacement. It remains unclear what serious purpose, other than publicity and spectacular fund-raising, can be served by bringing in a famous diva without administrative or nonsinging musical experience to run as notoriously complex and tricky an organization as an opera company. Whatever happens will no doubt happen quickly, for it has already been speculated in the press—in a perhaps officially inspired article—that the only hope for the City Opera lies in the federal government.

While New York still has two resident operatic organizations, it has only one full-time orchestra. The Philharmonic is rich in history, musical capacity, and financial backing. Under its last music director save one, Leonard Bernstein, it was publicly successful in concert, on recordings, and on television in a way new to it. The Philharmonic's experience under Bernstein's successor, Pierre Boulez, has made it clear that as far as commercial prosperity is concerned, intellectual stimulation and a sense of discovery, no matter how much honored, are no substitute for show-business glamour in the performance of the familiar nineteenth-century repertory.

As an orchestra, the players now possess, as a result of their experience (chiefly under Boulez), an unrivaled ability to quickly prepare the most ambitious and outré new music. But not only is this music unattractive to any audience outside New York's many music students; concentration on this music's difficulties has in the past served both to coarsen the tone of the orchestra and deprive the group of the time necessary to rehearse the standard repertory by which it will inevitably be judged. To this not-dishonorable predicament must be added the discipline problems produced by the sheer number of conductors who are marched before the orchestra for short periods in order to fill its year-round season, and even more importantly the fact of playing in an acoustically imperfect hall. Notwithstanding the efforts of the Philharmonic's new music director, the glamorous Zubin Mehta, to woo the audience in ways never open to Boulez, the orchestra remains in trouble, exchanging some of its morale and performance problems for diminished intellectual prestige and loss of musical interest.

The closest New York has come to having a second orchestra has been the American Symphony, the successor in New York musical life, via the Symphony of the Air, to Toscanini's NBC Symphony. A self-governing organization composed of free-lance musicians, its major activity before the musical public has been an annual series of Sunday afternoon concerts in Carnegie Hall. Despite its pride in self-governance, the orchestra has long been hampered by indifferent conductorial leadership, stemming in part from its democratic structure and in part from its inability to pay either soloists or conductors. It has also, in an attempt to attract an audience, often chosen weak, overfamiliar, or actually meretricious repertory. Despite its recent appointment of the talented Sergiu Comissiona as music advisor, the combination of democracy and poverty, unless both can be overcome to some extent at least, is bound to leave a musical organization like the American Symphony something less than a true, full-time second orchestra.

Any discussion of the presentation of concerts in New York outside those of the New York Philharmonic involves consideration of the current status of local concert halls. There are, in principle, two kinds of concerts presented by New York auspices: full orchestra and large group attractions, and solo recitals and chamber music groups. It is also necessary to distinguish between rental attractions in which the hall management assumes no financial responsibility for the event, and those events which the auspices—usually but not always the hall management—itself produces for its own account; it is the latter with which I will be concerned here.

One major concert sponsor—The Hunter College Concert Bureau—is no longer in existence. For a decade, from the early 1960s to the early 1970s, it was the major presenter of celebrity solo recitals in New York City outside Carnegie Hall; in addition, it was becoming an important presenter of chamber music as well. It had been founded during World War II as a limited platform for a few star events catering to a sophisticated audience swelled by the influx of European refugees. Though it eventually became the home of many well-attended brilliant series for both traditional and moderately avant-garde tastes, the coming of the urban and student troubles in the late 1960s made Hunter College an inhospitable place for such outside culture; and college administrators were both unwilling and unable to support the concerts financially. By the mid-1970s, the operation had been drastically cut back and soon was entirely liquidated.

But another institution continues to sponsor concerts as it has for the last generation: the Metropolitan Museum, though limited by the small capacity of its Grace Rainey Rogers Auditorium and by a certain reserve in programming, presents valuable concerts to an audience very much its own. Part of the slack caused by the demise of the Hunter series has been taken up by a revival of music at the 92nd Street YM-YWHA, but here once again, a too-small hall restricts the size of the audience, and in addition exigent financial pressures seem to require both more celebrity events as well as more artist-sponsored and rental concerts than might seem desirable for the highest musical—as opposed to per-forming—interest.

It is clear that on the recital level, as everywhere else in New York music, the center of gravity has shifted to Lincoln Center. Mention has already been made of its three large performing musical institutions, the Metropolitan and New York City operas, and the New York Philharmonic. In addition, the past decade has seen an enormous expansion of Center-sponsored recitals and concerts by visiting orchestras at Fisher (formerly called Philharmonic) Hall, the home of the Philharmonic. And the smaller hall of the Lincoln Center complex, given by and named for Alice Tully, has quickly become the venue of choice for the largest number of concerts paid for by the artists them-selves. Tully Hall has also become the home of the Chamber Music Society of Lincoln Center, the most prestigious small resi-dent performing group in the United States; Tully Hall is also being integrated into the large and commercially successful Great Performers at Lincoln Center series, which is still based in the much bigger Fisher Hall.

It is clear that Lincoln Center now combines both the major at-tractions and the desirable halls of New York City musical life. As if to set a public seal on its triumph, the 1977–78 and 1978–79 concert seasons saw the emergence of Lincoln Center on pub-licly-sponsored television as the proud presenter of the Metro-politan, the Philharmonic, the City Opera, and such of today's superstar soloists as Luciano Pavarotti. Whatever the musical value of these programs—European television productions still seem both more elegantly conceived and better performed—there could be no denying either the massive publicity campaign which supported these productions or the large size of the audience which viewed them.

In New York City itself, Lincoln Center's rise in the last two decades has marked a revolution in the places New Yorkers go to hear music. Prior to this rise, the Met had performed in its old house near Times Square; the Philharmonic had been resident in Carnegie Hall since 1892; the City Opera was located in the old City Center on West 55th Street behind Carnegie; and the major hall for recitals and small groups was the acoustically extraordinary Town Hall, also near Times Square. Of these buildings, the Old Met has been torn down; the old City Center presents only dance; Town Hall's reprieve from the wrecker's ball, achieved through a planned shift to presumably more commercially viable theatrical attractions, remains in doubt; Carnegie Hall, having lost the New York Philharmonic and not having as yet found a real replacement, is in trouble over booking, finances, and administration—and all this despite recognition of its superior acoustics.

Indeed, the condition of Carnegie Hall, losing orchestras and soloists, audiences, and public relations prestige to the newly renovated Fisher Hall, is merely another sign of the centralization of musical life at Lincoln Center. Better financed, more intelligently run, Lincoln Center is able to coordinate its bookings and its massive publicity campaigns. Should Carnegie Hall, as now seems possible, become either a straight rental house putting on ever fewer of its own productions or even be closed altogether, New York City will in essence end up with one large concert hall, one opera house, one orchestra, one major opera company (in the case of the City Opera's either folding or becoming as now seems likely increasingly an all-American producer of pot boilers mixed in with novelties) and one small prestige recital hall—and all at Lincoln Center.

In this connection it is necessary to examine another of Lincoln Center's constituents, the Juilliard School. Though Juilliard also trains actors and dancers, it is music which undeniably remains the school's most important educational area. Founded in the 1920's as an elite graduate school, it became larger in the 1940s through merger with the Institute of Musical Art. Its closest competition was the Curtis Institute in Philadelphia, founded (also in the 1920s) by the Bok family, and long associated with Josef Hofmann. For many years, of the two schools, Curtis had a slightly superior reputation; but despite being led during recent years by Rudolf Serkin, Curtis entered upon a long and slow decline. Today, with Serkin gone, it seems badly weakened. Juilliard, on the other hand, at first under the presidency of William Schuman (later president of Lincoln Center for several years) and now under Peter Mennin, has gone publicly from strength to strength.

Now occupying securely the position of premier music school in the United States and perhaps in the world, Juilliard possesses magnificent physical facilities, a famous faculty of instrumental and vocal teachers, and its pick of the most talented and ambitious students. It has a brilliant record of turning out sparkling young musicians with relatively easy access to solo careers. At the present time, only its opera program has not shared in the general acclaim; these lavish productions have failed to find general favor in the critical press. But as far as instrumentalists are concerned, Juilliard has the field pretty much to itself.

And yet, lurking just behind this striking achievement, lies the question which today plagues schools everywhere, distinguished and undistinguished alike: Music education for what? Short of audience success, it would seem that Juilliard, for all of its excellence, has found no other answer than to replicate the Moscow or St. Petersburg conservatories in the heyday of Russian music around the turn of the century. This kind of education—perhaps best described as play or perish—emphasizes the star system, public favor, and the assiduous imitation of models selected from among the major successes of the past.

This concentration on emulation in performance is coupled with an ignoring of the world outside the teacher's studio and the concert stage. In line with what an old teacher of mine used to say—reading is bad for the hands—Juilliard education includes no more than the most perfunctory attempt to relate music to art, ideas, and life. This failure to develop the minds of the very bright students the school attracts may have been acceptable at a time when the future of music was secure in the hands of composers capable of writing viable new music; to thus handicap young people today, to send them into the world equipped only with curatorial skills, is to relegate music to the status of an object in a museum.

If Juilliard has the problem of finding a purpose to accompany its present success, the problems of New York's two other major music schools are more immediately dangerous. Both the Manhattan School of Music and the Mannes College of Music are widely said to be in grave financial trouble, lacking either the musical distinction or the remarkable access to philanthropy of Juilliard. Rumors and press reports of conflicts and difficulties have swirled about both schools; recently, the merger of the two schools was contemplated, but eventually abandoned. In any case, despite individual excellences at each school, neither has been able to become publicly visible or to attract the most highly qualified students; like other American music schools, but more embarassingly because they are geographically so close to their competition, they move very much in Juilliard's wake. Barring some unexpected turnaround, their future is bleak indeed.

The final element of New York's musical life is of course its critical press. Here the story is unfortunately a short one, for without doubt only one review now counts—that of the *New York Times*. There are other local reviews, chiefly those appearing in the *New York Post* and the *Village Voice*. As is also the case with the limited coverage of the weekly magazine *New York*, reviews outside the *Times*—regardless of their actual content— share in their papers' failure to find a consistent musical readership willing to act at the box office on the basis of the papers' recommendations.

In past years, the situation in New York was quite different, for there then were many newspapers, each with its devoted musical readers; among these was not only the *Herald-Tribune* with Virgil Thomson, but also the *World-Telegram* with Louis Biancolli and the *Journal-American* with Miles Kastendieck. But now, for all serious purposes, New York is a one-newspaper town. It is here—not in any specific objections to *Times* policy or personnel—that the problem lies.

The power this monopoly confers on the *Times* reviews is thus twofold. Musical events which are not covered in its pages all too often remain nonevents, and those that are covered are inevitably subject to the tastes and the specific competences of one person. To the *Times*'s credit, it has endeavored to provide a high standard of disinterested writing, and in this attempt it has succeeded far beyond the achievements of almost all other American newspapers. Yet there remain important differences between the individual writers the paper employs, and as a result the outcome of the coverage of any one concert often impresses a listener to that concert as the outcome of a lottery.

And beyond the reviewing function, one misses in the *Times* sustained, reflective, intellectually serious consideration of music both in the long run and in the wider world. This is a kind of critical work more difficult than the identification of trends or the expression of nostalgia for a vanished Romanticism. It is basically an attempt at understanding the permanent intellectual significance of musical events by placing them in a context of culture and society outside music. Though the *Times* makes this effort in art, and even to a limited extent in literature, in music the paper's staff seems more concerned with what a recent article called "the hottest ticket in town."

The purpose of this *tour d'horizon*—in the country in general and in New York in particular—has not been to denigrate music and musicians, or even the institutions which exist to support the art. It has been to describe in the cold light of day, rather than in the hot flush of professional optimism, a situation at once uneasy and confused. A further purpose has been to make clear that the problems of music are vastly more than financial, and that increased support, though desirable, cannot by itself cure the internal problems of an artistic enterprise. It is our besetting sin as a nation to think that money can solve all things—human exploitation, poverty, unhappiness, and even the shortage of new music. It is not so, and the punishment for believing in nostrums is no different in music than elsewhere: frustration, disappointment, bitterness, and anger.

Epilogue:
Music at Retreat

THIS BOOK, it seems to me, has been a double exploration. It has first been an attempt to examine several salient musical questions of the day. It is in addition an account of how my own thinking about music has proceeded under the requirement of an intellectual rather than a performing approach. In looking over what I have written, one conclusion has become clear to me: viewed from the awesome standpoint of the masterpiece, music is indeed in a bad way. For the lesson of a lifetime in music is that there are few new masterpieces, but countless old ones. As a result it is difficult not to feel that both music's present and its future are increasingly the property of its past. Only a hardy soul would prophesy a new golden age when nothing at all save the creative emptiness of today seems in sight.

But who can argue against the masterpiece? So we continue to live musically as if nothing has changed since the nineteenth century. Not only do we immerse ourselves in old music, rapturously discovering forgotten works by known composers. We simultaneously judge every fresh composer of our time by the standards of the hallowed past. Though all fail the test, we still cherish the fantasy that a new Beethoven—or anti-Beethoven— lurks in every contemporary sensation. Even those of us who have long given up the present confidently expect the future of music to continue in the same way as the past, strewing immortality across our path every time we go to a concert. To look forward with any less hope would be to betray our optimistic faith and put into doubt our own cultural credentials.

And while we wait, the gap between our hopes for tomorrow and any palpable evidence of their realization becomes ever greater. When one asks what has gone wrong, the culprits are as numerous as the accusers, for in such failures everyone is both plaintiff and defendant. Composers, performers, audiences, economic systems, society, technology—all are found guilty; only the fact that we cannot do without any of the culpable prevents their summary execution.

Perhaps we are asking too much from the present. Is our treating the history of music as if it were (or ought to be) a continuous succession of masterpieces not, in fact, defensible? It is widely recognized that artistic styles have lives and deaths; what if art forms themselves, like cultures and nations themselves, also have life cycles? What if music, as every other art, has its golden ages, its dark ages, and its many periods of contraction and even desuetude?

On this view, it seems possible that the flood of musical genius as our great-grandfathers knew it is for the time being over; it may further be that the late romantic period of the last years of the nineteenth century and the early years of the twentieth did not signal an extension of the basic Romantic achievements but rather, by a spirited testing of their outer limits, marked precisely their consolidation and codification. It is also plausible, notwithstanding the fact that many representatives of the nineteenth century continued to write music well into our own time, that no renewal of musical Romanticism is today possible, either in musical sound, technical procedure, aesthetic aim, or social ambition.

Does this mean the end of music as we know it? Hardly. No matter how humbling this diagnosis of musical retreat may be to our sense of cultural self, it ought to be really troubling only to those who, in their jaded taste, cannot live without daily sensation. For those of us who are less sated, due to the prodigious gift of the nineteenth century (and before) there is surely enough music of quality and contrast for everyone. And as far as the needs of the educated among us are concerned, the work of musicological, historical and intellectual classification of the huge Romantic corpus has only barely been begun. It thus does not seem too much to say that for those in the audience who wish it so, there is no urgent requirement for new music at all.

What about those who, though they love and respect the old, yet feel the need, both for the sake of music and for their own pleasure, of new sounds? Are these restless listeners and musicians fated to remain unsatisfied for the foreseeable future? Any answer to these questions must be in two parts, for the problems of performance and composition are quite different.

The urgent need of performance is to free the performer from the received ideas of how the masters should be played and how his predecessors played them. To free the performer from this struggle for pious emulation we need only realize that the masterpiece exists prior to the performance and will exist after it regardless of how it is played. Should we cease to see performance in terms of embodiment or perversion, of fidelity or betrayal, of humility or arrogance, performers might find relief from the conformity and resultant paralysis which today infect their minds and work. Rather than being curators, performers might once again become quasi-original creators, not serving simply as neutral mediums but rather as actors giving us their ideas about great works for their own (and our) pleasure and at their own risk.

It will come as no surprise that composition, functioning as it does at a vastly higher creative level than performance, presents a vastly more difficult problem today. The audience, which can give its immediate and warm-hearted approval to performers who play known and beloved music, can in no direct way influence composers; yet the long-run approval of the composer by the audience is vital for the composer's own self-regard. There is an important antinomy here: not only can the composer not be told what to do—surely the failure of Soviet musical policy proves this simple rule—but the audience cannot long be expected to support what it neither likes nor understands.

Though there can be little doubt that music as a whole stands only to benefit from the collapse of the post-war avant-garde, this collapse has resulted in a vacuum in contemporary composition. Attempts are being made to fill this vacuum by a highly touted return to the presumably eternal verities of melody and harmony. That this return seems more a regression than an advance accords ill with the high-powered publicity swirling around the new composers. Nevertheless, both the widespread nature of this new musical movement and the seriousness with which it is being taken by critical observers make it a development of real cultural significance.

Thus in composition the only counsel which can be proffered is one of watchful waiting. Whether and when there will be new musical masterpieces belongs to the presently unknown. But what in any case will remain will surely be a group of people—practitioners and listeners alike—who find music, whether new or old, beautiful. These sensitive creatures will doubtless support their pleasures and discriminate among them, as a few individuals have always done since men were first charmed, in the faraway dawn of prehistory, by the sweet sound of music.

Acknowledgments

FOR THIS BOOK I owe a debt of gratitude to many friends. Among them I want particularly to mention Diana Trilling, who first thought that I should write and then took steps to get me started; Neal Kozodoy, who edited several of these pieces in their original form and facilitated with wit and kindness the preparation of others; Midge Decter, my editor at Basic Books, whose idea this book was and whose insight identified the thread which runs through it; and Norman Podhoretz, who has taught me so much and stimulated me so greatly. And a special measure of gratitude I give with love to my wife Jeaneane, who first inspired and then encouraged it all.

Index

Index